MW00623688

Imagintelligence

Beyond Emotional Intelligence

William Marts

Jeremiah 3:17:
… neither shall they walk any
more after the imagination
of their evil heart.

Imagination
INSTITUTE

2000

© 2000 William Marts. All rights reserved.

Except for short quotations for scholarly, reporting, and reviewing purposes, as permitted under the Copyright Act of 1976, no part of this publication may be reproduced or distributed in any form or by any means, including recording, or stored in a data base or retrieval system, without prior written permission from the publisher. Exception: Chapter 1, The Parable of the Coin: Permission is hereby given to copy or reproduce this text in any way.

For information address:
The Imagination Institute
236 Bonnacroft Dr.
Hermitage TN, 37076

http://www.imagintelligence.com

ISBN 0-9679157-3-2

PRINTED IN THE UNITED STATES OF AMERICA

A note to the reader:
This book is designed to supplement regular care programs by physicians and doctors and is not intended to replace or substitute such care. This book is not designed to treat, diagnose, or prescribe. Neither the author nor the publisher shall be liable or responsible for any harm, damage, or illness arising from the use of information contained herein. Consult your physician or psychiatrist before practicing the information outlined in this book.

Editing by R.K. Edit
Cover and Interior Design by Lightbourne

Publisher's Cataloging-in-Publication
(Provided by Quality Books, Inc.)

Marts, William
        Imagintelligence : beyond emotional intelligence /
    by William Marts
    Marts -- 1st ed.
        p. cm.
        Includes bibliographical references and index.
        LCCN: 00-132372
        ISBN: 0-9679157-3-2

        1. Kingdom of God. 2. Christian Life.
    3. Imagination--Religious aspects--Christianity.
    4. Visualization--Religious aspects--Christianity.
    I. Title.

        BT94.M37 2000   231.72
                                    QBI00-431

I believe deeply that we must find, all of us together, a new spirituality. This new concept ought to be elaborated alongside the religions in such a way that all people of good will could adhere to it. We need a new concept, a lay spirituality. We ought to promote this concept with the help of scientists. It could lead us to set up what we are all looking for—a secular morality.

—The Dalai Lama

Contents

Introduction

The concept of emotional intelligence is gaining popularity with each passing day. The problem of controlling and overcoming negative emotions has been humanity's Achilles' heel since time immemorial. *Imagintelligence* (a term coined from *imaginational intelligence*) is beyond emotional intelligence for the simple reason that the faculty of imagination, where all that is created beyond mere awareness, is the level where a person can intervene between the stimulus of the environment and the suggested emotional response by the body.

I have attempted to provide a workable and simple path through this book to the insights needed to learn emotional intelligence, nirvana, enlightenment, total God realization, and open the mind to its hidden powers.

Learn Imagination Control Therapy and Imagery Management as a means to help you achieve a blissful state of mind, emotional control, and the insights of a philosopher. Become a healer. Gain optimum health. Learn the true power of the mind. Enter into The Kingdom of Heaven on Earth.

You can learn all these things through a more complete understanding of your imagination. Einstein said if we spark the imagination we can conquer the Universe and he believed the mystic experience to be an emotion that can be developed. *Imagintelligence* will give you insight to the true teachings of Jesus in a description so vivid that average person can easily grasp them. Have the secrets revealed to you that seekers of the truth have suffered for years to gain enlightenment. This new mental thought process will promote your success in anything you endeavor that is good. You will not only have your every desire fulfilled, but it will reveal to you how to refine your desires to a state of benevolence, acceptance, and appreciation.

You will experience the physiological changes that lead to the necessary developments of brain cell and body neurotransmitters that lead to higher levels of thought. This occurs as more and more of God's light fills the body as a result of your own imaginings. This path leads us to enlightenment and, if enough effort is put forth, I believe that transfiguration may be possible.

Imagintelligence is a result of a divine experience explained through my life studies within the knowledge acquired from the Bible, The Bhagavad Gita, Hinduism, Buddhism, Zen, Yoga, Self Realization Fellowship, Martial Arts, Eckankar, medicine, nutrition, physiology, psychology, the human emotional response, the philosophies of Aristotle, Plato, and Socrates, Scientology, New Thought, and metaphysics.

Imagintelligence contains everything of the old that was good and is tied together with a crystal clear explanation brought about by the revelations of a mind illuminating divine experience. The science evolves around a simple new thought process, which, when practiced, will give you the opportunity to discover enlightenment in an instant or a short time.

We begin to develop thought processes at a tender age. We then add to our thought processes as we age. Unfortunately, we develop thought processes that suppress our true potential. The power of negative thought is the undoer of everything we try.

Now, everything good comes together with the teachings of *Imagintelligence.* And as you study, you will immediately realize the teachings are true because you have learned bits and pieces of this puzzle all your life. It feels right. This just ties together all you have learned. The soul knows when it hears the truth.

You Can Help!

Humanity has avoided the fact that imagination is the first manifestation of the order of thought. Our elusion of imagination has placed religions and psychology at the great disadvantage of continually denying and suppressing the true nature of the mind.

With the new millennium approaching, scientists, psychologists, and the heads of religion must distinguish the imagination as the primary manifestation within the natural order of mental activity.

Scientists have advanced in this field known to them as visualization. Psychology has dabbled with visualization and has achieved good results, yet has failed to approach the amount of serious research that is desperately needed. Mystic religionists have somewhat recognized imagination as part of our mental ability, but not the primary source of thought itself. Independent research in the medical profession has yielded wonderful results in healing, yet the AMA does not officially sanction visualization as a must in medical practice.

It is my intention to incite serious research and development regarding the primary source of mental activity, the imagination. The evolution, health, and welfare of humanity are depending on this basic understanding of our minds. No greater step can be taken for the benefit of humanity than practicing imaginational intelligence. This is the key to the collective consciousness of mankind evolving as a whole. We have made a quantum leap in technology, yet have neglected to realize and control the primary manifestation of mental activity, imagination. This is our opportunity for our humanity to catch up to our technology.

I ask for your help. Though I have applied *Imagintelligence* to a Christian orientated spirituality, it may be applied by atheists, practitioners of any religion, scientists, biophysicists, psychologists, psychiatrists, spiritualists, and the layman in general. Participation from all walks of life is desperately needed to initiate research and development.

The root of world problems can be found within imaginations running haywire. As we begin to control the imagination in the collective consciousness of the human race, life on Earth will experience a renewal that is no less than remarkable. This change will be brought about through the control and development of the primary source of mental activity, the imagination.

—*William Marts*

1

The Parable of the Coin

Luke 17:20-21: *And when he was demanded of the Pharisees, when The Kingdom of God should come, he answered them and said, The Kingdom of God cometh not with observation: Neither shall they say, Lo here! or, lo there! for, behold, The Kingdom of God is within you.*

To all who may perceive, comes this gift of illumination

This story is yours, so tell it if you understand it—PLEASE! *Telling this story deepens its concept each time it is told.* I see such illumination of the mind in so many cases that I know those who don't hear the story the first time or even the tenth will hear it someday because it is a story that should be told for eternity. This story concept is the beginning of the resurrection of mankind's minds. Its effects are so powerful to those already partially illuminated that I predict The Parable of the Coin concept will make mankind's use of negative imagery and emotion not only outdated but also obsolete. Rebuking the use of the negative spectrum of imagination and emotion will become a common practice, not only concerning the religious values contained therein but also for practicing this exact science of the mind that frees the need to engage in the negative spectrum of thought. Negative emotions are unhealthy. They contain only the imaginings of a disturbed mind. The more time a being spends dwelling in negative imagery, the more disturbed the mind and body become. The Parable of the Coin concept is to free the mind of **negative imaginings**. These are the so-called demons of this world, manifesting their deeds of darkness onto the face of the Earth. Rebuking negative imaginations and emotions leaves the individual in a divine state of mind. It shall become the sophisticated way to conduct oneself. This is the composure of the resurrected mind.

The Parable of the Coin was revealed to me during an intense three-day divine experience. As I could feel the indwelling presence of the Christ swelling in my heart, a divine being related this analogy to me in a beautiful vision. I later learned his name to be Gabriel. All this I ask God to bless in the name of Jesus the Christ, Amen.

The Parable of the Coin

The beautiful angel of light was holding a coin in his hand. He began to slowly spin the coin in his fingers. I did not hear him speak, though the word concepts poured into my head as follows: "Liken the spinning coin to your walk through life. One side shows and then the other as the dramas of life dictate your emotions, for the mind is of a dual nature." He stopped the coin and held the side showing heads toward me. "Liken the side of heads to all positive human emotion." Flipping the coin to tails, he said, "Liken this side to all negative human emotion."

As he flipped the coin again to heads, he said, "This side contains your love, faith, trust, reverence, honor, patience, understanding, benevolence, kindness, sweetness, laughter, forgiveness, love of life, valiance, charity, your goodness, mercy, compassion, and wisdom. These are the imaginings of Spirit, your divine self. This is the gateway through which God manifests His good works upon the Earth through you. This is where God lives on Earth, in *the imaginations of the thoughts of your hearts.* It is through this gateway that the indwelling God moves His will through you, offering you the highest quality experience each and every moment."

He flipped the coin again to tails. "Liken this side of the coin to the gateway of the darkness within you. Through this gateway, darkness manifests its deeds upon the face of the Earth. Darkness is the result of negative imagination and emotion. These are urged by the desires of the lower nature caused by your fears and the feeling of separation from God. Many of you have these fears imbedded within your body's emotional system, known as the serpent, and these fears come as your first feelings or urges. Let not the serpent persuade you to eat of the fruit of the tree of the knowledge of good and evil, which is the delusion of judgment. This darkness manifests itself through your fear unfolding as hate, greed, lust, suspicion, anger, mistrust, worry, depression, false pride, envy, anxiety, dishonor, cowardice, jealously, foolishness, murder, violence, arrogance, conspiracies, plots, selfishness, sloth, revenge, covetous; your negative, dark or evil side, the lower or animal self.

"To be free of the lower nature, learn and strive to rebuke any creation of the negative spectrum of imagery. Learn to do this on a moment-to-moment basis. Negative thoughts will come, but you must light up the darkness from which they came. When you are moved to dwell in negative imagination and emotion, acknowledge the thought and then flip your coin over to the positive spectrum of imagination. The longer you permit your consciousness to dwell in negative imaginings and emotions the more power you give to them, permitting more darkness to flow through you.

"Each and every emotion is the direct result of an **imagination.** As a co-creator with God, a child of light wills only the imagery of the positive mind into the Universe. Create only positive images. Within this imagery is the secret to aligning your thoughts with the God-Mind to avoid the darkness of separation. When your imagery is aligned with God's offer of the highest quality of experience, you are then accepting God's offer of love. **Imagination is the key.** Emotion is the tangible or physical manifestation of the intangible imagination. Your imagery is the primary manifestation in the order of your mental activity. These images are many. The images you choose to associate yourself with, you then call thought. And these choices are what governs the quality of your experiences."

He then flipped the coin back to heads and continued, "Do not spend any time creating negative imagery. Positive imaginings are where your consciousness must dwell to have your minds and hearts parallel with the intention of God. The imagery creations of the positive self are the builders of life where the Lord will open all His doors and provide all your needs. This true self will also develop a more benevolent concept of your needs. You will experience an awakening as your body begins a re-chemicalization process as the chemicals born of negative imagery fade. Negative images produce harmful, toxic chemicals within the body. Positive images produce chemicals that contribute to higher levels of thought, health, and awaken power centers within the body that stay dormant until negative imagery ceases.

"Jesus said that The Kingdom of Heaven is within you, at hand, in the midst. The constant dwelling of your mind within the positive spectrum of imagery is your consciousness being in The Kingdom of Heaven as Jesus tried to teach you. Jesus told you to humble yourselves as little children to enter The Kingdom of Heaven. Within the little children's minds are the virtues of acceptance and the sweetest innocence containing wonderful imaginations. The Kingdom of Heaven is at hand, in the midst, within you, in the imaginations of your most innocent thoughts—the imaginations of your positive spectrum of self. Guilt stems from your negative spectrum of imagination. Keep your state of mind positive and if the world falls down around you, you will rebuild it and feel connected with the love of God."

As he flipped the coin back on tails, he then said, "Know that if you resort to creation within the negative spectrum of imagery in any fashion only further darkness can result. Negative imagery is the absence of light, a lessening of the true intentions of God, and the absence of the Christ consciousness through the illusion of separation from God.

"God has been concerned about your evil imaginations since Genesis 6:5-6, when He said that He was displeased with man because you walked in the imaginations of your evil heart continually. Jesus was resurrected to demonstrate the results of ceasing to create erroneous imagery through unity with the Father."

The angel then told me to read all verses in the Bible containing the word imagination. I discovered the word imagination was used mostly with negative implications, until the occasion when Mary was pregnant with Jesus and told Elisabeth that the Lord has showed a strong arm and has scattered the *proud in the imaginations of their hearts,* (Luke 1:51).

He continued, "Jesus said that He will dwell within you, (John 6:56). You will unite with the Christ within you through the practice of creating only positive and divine imaginations. Then, it becomes your responsibility to spread the good news of love and bring more people to the light. Heaven starts now, here on Earth, and you must become a giver of the light. This is the beginning of learning. When you accept God as your Father/Mother and create imagery only through your positive self, you are allowing God's light to move through you while He unveils His divine plan in your life. The path to perfection is found by interlacing the positive spectrum of imagination and emotion together with love until all are attributes of love. Jesus said to love each other as He has loved you. Know these things and serve mankind through brotherly love.

"Now, you have The Kingdom of Heaven on the head of a coin. Keep your mind and heart on the positive side of the coin and God's divine plan will unveil to you in a series of wonderful coincidences. ' . . . . Seek ye first The Kingdom of God, and his righteousness; and all these things shall be added unto you. Take therefore no thought for the morrow: for the morrow shall take thought for the things of itself. Sufficient unto the day is the evil thereof.'"

Seek first to be positive within your imagination and all will come. Think not of tomorrow, for tomorrow will take thought of itself. Sufficient today is the negative imagery thereof.

This is The Parable of the Coin. I pray that it may bless you as it has blessed so many others. Learn it and tell The Parable of the Coin to all you know. Each time you bring light to someone by telling this parable, you will feel more and more light coming through you. God bless you and may your mind be resurrected. Amen.

Imagination:
The Primary Manifestation
of Mental Activity

Luke 1:51: *He hath shewed strength with his arm; He hath scattered the proud in the imagination of their hearts.*

The image is the starting point and in some measure the immediate matter of all our intellectual operations.
—The Catholic Encyclopedia

Imagination defined: *n. 1. The action of imagining, or of forming mental images or concepts of what is not actually present to the senses. 2. The faculty of forming such images or concepts. 3. Psychol.; the power of reproducing images stored in the memory under the suggestion of associated images (reproductive imagination) or of recombining former experiences in the creation of new images directed at a specific goal of aiding in the solution of problems (creative imagination) 4. The faculty of producing ideal creations consistent with reality, as in literature, as distinct from the power of creating illustrative or decorative imagery. 5. The product of imagining; a conception of mental creation, often a baseless or fanciful one.*[1]

The first definition explains that the concepts or mental images formed are not actually present to the senses. In many cases, such as utilizing the creative imagination, this may be true, yet we do form an image of what *appears* to be present to our senses consistently—about every two-fifths of a second. In addition to this standard definition, it is necessary to consider that we think in images. And, as you see the terms *imagination, imaginings, and imagery* used throughout this text, familiarize yourself with the concept that this is the *faculty and method* by which our mind creates thought—through imagery, the substrate of our mental process. Even when we are engaged in internal dialogue, it is a mirror of our imagery. This is important to understand. Even if our attention is so encapsulated by our senses that we are neither aware of nor see our imagery, it is forming nonetheless. The mind files moment-by-moment mental image pictures as its memory. These images contain all the perceptions of the senses and also an emotional record.

Our senses are limited to the material world. Our five senses—sight, smell, touch, taste, and hearing—cannot contribute significantly to the intangible realm of spirituality or faith yet they act as the interpreters of reality to the mind and its faculty of imagination. Though we create images or concepts of what is not actually present to the senses, we usually base the images we create on what we *believe* is reality. Paradoxically, we many times rely on previous imaginations or memories of past internal dialogue that, a great part of the time, are made up of misconceptions, to evaluate our present reality. The mind creates images—mental image pictures. These images contain the perceptions and memories from our senses and the images that we form out of our creative imagination and creative intelligence. Our core belief systems and our filtering systems (what we highlight as important to us as distinct from what appears to be insignificant) greatly influence our perception, creative imagination, and creative intelligence (creative imagination with intelligence).

We Are Co-creators

The imagination is the faculty that we use to co-create the Universe with God. For us, everything begins in the imagination.

It is much, much more than a fantasy faculty. The imagination is our creation faculty. And we have a great responsibility to use our ability to create in a positive way, a way that is in unison and aligned with the ideas and intentions of God.

In this dimension of matter, energy, space, and time, the imagination is the first manifestation of the formless pure ideas into this world. It is the first something from nothing. And just like a kid behind the wheel of a car for the first time, God has provided us with an imagination to begin our learning process of becoming powerful, spiritual, divine co-creators. We just have a time lag in our manifestation time—except for emotion. Emotion is pretty much instantaneous. The reason we feel so uncomfortable when we become negative emotionally is to deter us from creating negative imaginations. Once you become aware of this, it helps you stop.

The Domino Effect

As in dominos, the image is the first cause of manifestation. Between the worlds of consciousness and matter, The Formless and form, the image is the lead domino—the cause of the effect of our awareness of the physical and spiritual worlds. We create, or are suggested an image by the body's emotional system, which in turn causes or supports a feeling or an emotion. As a child of God, you have the option of ignoring your body's image suggestion and can subsequently align your imaginings with the God-Mind. Emotion, in the long term, brings about moods and states of mind which in turn affect our reality and our spirituality through perspective and manifestation.

Emotions are an indication of our imaginings in this material world. Emotion is the tangible of the intangible imagination. It is the direct chemical result of our image creations. This physical manifestation is immediate. Although moods and states of mind may not have an immediate affect as do emotions, they are the result of imagery that is re-experienced, re-enacted, held for lengths of time, or running as a response loop at subconscious levels. Our reality and spirituality are also the affects of long-term imagery.

Fear and Pain

Nothing affects the negative imagination like fear and pain. Fear and pain spark the imagination in ways that can last a lifetime. Think about it. Have you ever been afraid or hurt in a way that you could not get it out of your mind? Do you have fear or pain from your past that is baggage you carry with you always? All of us do to a greater or lesser degree—at least until we become illuminated.

Take a brief moment to think of some of the imaginations you've had after being afraid or hurt. Murder, wrath, vengeance, plots, and violence are common imaginings. Take a moment to try to perceive all of the negative imaginations of all the people in the world happening at the same time. You can then begin to realize that the appearance of an evil force, such as a devil, is created by the sum total of the negative imaginings of humanity itself in response to our own illusion of being separate from God. Proportionately, the more people imagine themselves as individuals separate from the Whole, the more they fail to consider or even care about the suffering of most other people. By focusing on the self, people carry the illusion that they are controlling or relieving their own suffering. Yet, by doing so, the world becomes a place that induces the greatest amount of suffering to the greatest amount of people. The very thing that motivates selfish concern ends up as our major source of pain. Selfishness is merely an inability to see the big, big picture.

New Thought metaphysics teaches us that there is but one force in the Universe—love. The absence of God's love is comparable to the absence of light. Darkness is not a force within itself; yet, it is darkness nonetheless. And darkness does *appear* to have a force. Our negative imagery is the absence of God's light. This is an essential concept to develop if you desire to become a co-creator in the Universe. People who busy their minds hunting for a devil or demons always find one. But try to perceive the destructive force you may be participating in by believing that the world is going to Hell while only a few elect (and those who believe this usually think they are one of the elect) are blessed to attain entry into Heaven. When thousands of people believe that they see Satan at work in millions of (other) people, that's a mighty force. It's where the Inquisition came from. It's why people kill in the name of religion. It is time to wake up to the disturbing reality that erroneous and evil thoughts are born of negative imaginings manifested into erroneous, negative actions. There is no evil entity willing evil. There is only humanity over-looking such an abundance of information that choices and decisions are made that are erroneous and appear evil. When people were killing and burning people in the name of Jesus, you don't think they thought they were doing something evil, do you? Realizing that there is no evil force out to get you relieves an abundance of fear and pain. The mind may begin to calm to where it can accept more and more love. And if there is no evil entity out there, you must start to take responsibility for the lower self within you that justifies creating negative imagery. You don't want to appear to be a part of the evil force you have pre-viously feared, do you?

We actually act out few of our negative imaginations, but they are there influencing our viewpoint and distorting reality. Though most of us act out few severe negative imaginings, inter-nalizing them renders us vulnerable to the influence and encouragement of the negativity of others. That is how negativ-ity spreads as an infectious disease. Other people creating negative imaginings ally with our negativity like a demonic force. Darkness breeds darkness.

When we create negative images, we constantly sift reality to find signs to reinforce them. After all, if we have no validity for creating negative images we most likely wouldn't create them. When you do this, you are only seeing what you believe.

We have complexes that are negative imaginings about our-selves that are grouped together. We constantly sift reality for signs, symbols or patterns to reinforce these beliefs. Normal everyday occurrences become symbols to validate our negative imaginations in the form of complexes, unfulfilled desires, disappointments, heartbreak and other emotional pain, as well as fear of physical pain. This gives the illusion that your belief system is valid.

Pain and fear of pain influences every aspect of our negative imagination. From our pretenses, dreams, goals, and ideals to our heroes, role models, and traits, *pain causes us to create imaginations that give us the illusion of coping with the hurt and of protecting us from future hurt, and it is all based on fear.*

A farmer I once knew had a huge bull in a field with an old single-wire electric fence around it. This fence had no electric power to it for years. The bull would not go near this single strand of wire because it had been trained as a calf not to touch it. This training consisted of leading the animal two or three times into the fence for a shock. The bull avoided the wire the rest of his life because it had been hurt (severely shocked). He simply formed a subconscious program to not touch this wire again.

Our groups of negative images are like this electric fence containing the bull. Each group of similar negative images has a common cause like that of the animal kingdom—kill, dominate, repel, and avoid—based on The Fight or Flight Response initiated by fear. These groups form by similar states of mind caused by our previous fear or pain or witnessed experiences. They are encompassed by our mind's quest to keep us from similar future pain by focusing on the negative aspects of our environment and by anticipating, through creative imagination, more possible fear or pain. This causes you to look for everything that may be a threat, which is everything negative. This is what is known as a mental filter. All positive information is filtered out while all negative information is acknowledged, classified, categorized, and identified with the experiences of the past. This encapsulates our attention to the point that we overlook an abundance of positive attributes in the present that life is offering us.

In his book, *Christian Healing,* Charles Fillmore states, "Each thought of mind is an identity that has a central ego. By this we mean that every thought has a center around which all its elements revolve and to which it is obedient when no higher power is in evidence. Thoughts are capable of expressing themselves—they think."

In our congested world where many of us have little space, we may try to avoid and repel others, but too many times we just don't have the space. We all can't dominate, and we certainly can't kill, so, many times, we become irrational with negative imaginings due to our running imaginary skits in our minds, over and over. These have been called, by Dr. Frank Young, negative emotional response loops. Subconsciously we may be trying to gain relief from the urge to kill, dominate, repel, or avoid by instead creating a mind movie of ourselves acting out these desires. As the star of this movie, in our mind we temporarily set things the way they "should be." Yet the only thing we accomplish by this is upsetting ourselves and initiating The Fight or Flight Response.

The only hope of escaping our past fear and pain and gaining control of our experiences is to consistently stop the negative spectrum of thought at its first manifestation—the imagination. At this level, you have a *struggle-free choice* in your response to your environment. Your entire realm of past fear and pain influence will have no conscious effect on you when you do. Through *consistently choosing the imagery that will create good feelings,* we can then conquer the negative subconscious mind. This is not suppression! It is the consistent creation of positive imagery. And this is the path to a growing alignment of thought with the intention of God. This is renewing the mind with the constant business of co-creation with God—willing and manifesting positive, loving things into the Universe. Suppression is when you have created the negative images, hold them and attempt to bury them or not act on them.

The thought processes evolved within the negative spectrum are illogical. Even when they seem logical, in the long-term they will manifest illogic. Fear and pain are the keys that unlock the door to justifying the use of our negative spectrum of imagination, thought, and emotion.

We hate because we have been hurt or made afraid. We lust sexually to bring relief from the fear or pain or the loneliness of longing for intimacy. We worry in anticipation of fear or pain. We lust after riches in the form of wealth and become greedy to bring relief from our fear, pain, or misery. We become angry when fear or pain threatens us. We become anxious, wanting the fear or pain to stop, and depressed when it does not. Other than the fear of death, our fear of pain is probably our greatest fear. Conquering your lesser fears will inevitably lead to conquering the fear of death and to conquering your fears of the many painful ways of dying as your spirituality grows.

The majority of us experience a great deal of fear and pain. Some suffer atrocities. Few escape fear and pain altogether. So now you must realize beyond the shadow of a doubt that *we develop a dual personality based on fear and pain, or love.* In our imaginations we appear to be Doctor Jekyll and Mister Hyde— positive and negative, good and evil, loving and afraid—in proportion to our fear or love response, in proportion to the positive and negative imaginations we create.

This duality is a reflection of our inability to see God in each situation. Although this may be difficult at times, the illuminated mind can and does consistently find the God expression in all, for there is good to be found in every situation. There is indeed a silver lining in every cloud. It is simply necessary to train and develop the mind to see it. You can still see the cloud; just focus your attention on the silver lining. The good to be found may not be in the situation itself. But the situation may lead to the good. So be patient. While you are being patient, create a powerful, spiritual, divine imagination of the situation as it could be if God's good were there. Visualize it. Images manifest that are held by a powerful, spiritual, divine mind.

The Fight or Flight Response

The illogical, inhibited, unable to reason rationally, negative mind relies on the body's Fight or Flight Response mechanism. This is a highly primitive response that we modern humans rationalize into what we believe is careful thought. Our fear or our perception of fear that initiates this response causes us to give up the ability to consider the whole of reality and spirituality within our reasoning—rendering us highly delusional. Positive aspects of the environment become insignificant and are filtered out by the mind. Most of our focus is on the negative aspects of the environment and there are always lots of things *wrong* to be found. The negative creative imagination runs amuck sifting reality for potential harm or danger as it so diligently endeavors to protect us. The *attacks* or *threats* that initiate The Fight or Flight Response may be as subtle as someone telling us they don't like our shoes or thinking we have received a look we do not prefer from someone as opposed to legitimate life threatening situations.

The Fight or Flight Response is usually responsible for the negative mind becoming dominant in our creative imaginings, which in turn initiates delusions since the whole of reality is considered or perceived less and less. This is a pattern of delusions caused by fear proportionately causing a failure to consider more and more information. The more you fear, the less information you consider. The more you fear, the less you consider the Whole. The less you consider the Whole, the more delusional you are in your imagery creation. Until you gain control of your imagination, ninety-nine percent of the time The Fight or Flight Response will be initiated unnecessarily. So don't imagine you are being threatened if you don't physically see yourself about to be harmed. Even when people overtly threaten you, the greatest percentage of these threats is merely hot air. I have seen people in a constant state of fear over getting slapped by a bully, or something of this sort, when the slap could never hurt as much as the long-term intimidation. Create a powerful, spiritual, divine imagination. But most importantly, grow to understand the physical process of The Fight or Flight Response. That's not *you* experiencing that unnecessary fear or intimidation;

it's your body. Just busy your mind with positive co-creation with God. This too shall come to pass.

The Time We Spend in Our Faculty of Imagination

We spend more time in our imaginations than most people have ever realized. No matter what self-help book you read, most of the techniques involved rely on manipulating the imagination; but the approach is mostly indirect because few have perceived that imagination is the sole key to self-improvement and spirituality. It's almost as though no one wants to admit that we spend as much time in our imaginations as we really do. When we understand this basic principle, we unlock the secrets of the mind. People are consistently creating either negative or positive imagery, scanning through or recalling past imagery creations, or recalling internal dialogue that is based on past imagery. We always have our mind movie running, even in times of narration. This narration is our internal dialogue.

The average person spends a great deal of time reviewing or creating positive imaginations such as planning, hoping, dreaming, receiving impressions, perceiving, and using our creative intelligence. And people spend a great deal of time in negative imaginations misinterpreting, assuming, jumping to conclusions, plotting, forming and using complexes, fretting over unfulfilled desires, misjudging others, judging themselves harshly, and cultivating resentment. It can be safely concluded that *the majority of your thoughts are a product of the imagination. Once you realize this, the next step is to become conscious of your imaginations—your mind movie.* Reality sets the stage, but the imagination creates what we believe is the plot behind the scene and assigns motives and intentions to people. The amount of images we create and store in our memory banks with the creative imagination well outweighs those created by sensual input. A powerful charge is given to the images when they are fear or pain oriented. We then rely on these memories just as we do for images created by sensual input and we usually give them the same or even more validity.

The mind is in constant creation. The creative imagination and creative intelligence (another facet of the creative imagination) are constantly creating our reality, our existence, our perceptions, our paradigms, and our schemata. The imagination is also extremely fast in its ability to scan previously created images. If someone pulls out in front of us on the parkway, the imagination will most likely, consciously or subconsciously, scan over every other time such an occurrence happened in our life and remind us through association of how we felt in the past. As The Fight or Flight Response focuses our attention on the negative aspects of our environment, we become the creators of a negative reality.

The Level of Struggle-Free Choice

By focusing your attention on your imagination, you can take charge of your life and life itself as the result of your choices in the imagery you create. *When you do not focus your attention on your imagery, you are then focusing your attention on the physical world through your senses.* This permits the physical world to influence your imagery as a return feedback loop rather than your imagery influencing your emotional and physical world as a direct intention and determination of your centered spiritual self.

At the level of imagery, control is a result of your choices. You simply choose what images you create. As you make the correct God-aligned choices through creating positive and divine imagery, your self-control is inherently found within your choices. As you control your imagination through correct choices, you gain control over your thoughts and emotions. Control your thoughts and you control your emotions; control your emotions and you clear your mind for higher levels of thought. You gain insights. You mature in your emotional response. You change in your heart. You are transformed by the renewing of your imaginings.

There is no greater counter-productive force than the imaginings the mind creates during periods of negativity. *Negative imaginings blind us to many productive options that are available.* Our reality is what we think it is; what we imagine it is. We cannot escape being a product of our own thought. Albert Einstein said, "You can fill a man with knowledge and all you will have is a man filled with knowledge, but spark his imagination and he can conquer the Universe."

Creative Imagination and Intelligence

We are more than aware. Being only aware means the mind has no conclusions or creations to accompany information. We all constantly create more information out of the information we have and receive. Our creative imaginations are not limited to arts, crafts, and design. We create internal dialogue, skits in our minds, assumptions, daydreams, impressions, and an array of other creations within the mind. Our intelligence collects information and makes more information out of this data. And, we all add our unique twist to our imaginings that may or may not be founded in reality. Anything more than just being aware is affected by our ability to create with the faculty of the imagination.

Pretending

When we are children we use our imaginations to pretend. Children pretend they are any place or with anyone they desire. As we mature, we are taught that we should stop living in our imaginations because this world is not reality. Yet we never stop using our imaginations. We believe that we stop pretending, but we do not. We merely progress to new realms of imaginations such as daydreaming, or the images we create attempting to figure the plot behind the scenes of the play, presuming the motives and intentions behind the actions or appearances of people. To justify pretending we succumb to the notion that we may daydream, but we are not willfully pretending; this is merely a lack of concentration or a pleasant thought to take a break from reality.

It is natural to have pretenses of attaining our goals, wants, needs, expectations, and ideals. We feel our pretenses are more mature thoughts when they come in these fashions. We do this thoughtlessly, inadvertently, with no regard to pretension. We are taught to control our emotions, but we assume the imagination is well under control because we are not willfully and knowingly *pretending* in the same style as we did in our earlier years of life. As a child, we pretended naturally and had no awareness that we were using our imagination. We enter school and are taught the left-brain logic of reading, writing, and arithmetic. We evolve as a left-brain being ceasing to consciously, willfully and intelligently utilize our right-brain skills. Neglecting to give attention to the right brain, we leave it to run amuck, undisciplined and unguided. That is why we lose our natural imagination skills as we mature. We deny that we are using the faculty of imagination and we are told not to pretend. We don't want to wind up living in a pretend world. So, we create an alternative pretend world— a dream world of the awake mind that is based on a feedback loop of the appearances of the physical world rather than on the Formless Ideas of God.

Positive imaginations from pretending are healthy as long as their preoccupation does not interfere with life's obligations. Daydreamers usually are reprimanded if daydreams interfere with obligations. A tremendous amount of good has been manifested in this world from the positive images we may have created early in our youth. I cannot emphasize enough that all positive emotions are the result of positive imaginations or images within the mind. On the other hand, the images while pretending or daydreaming in the negative spectrum are very unhealthy. They are counter-productive and expand into mental and physical disturbances. If you want to stay in touch with your negative life experiences, creating and dwelling in negative imagery will do just that. All present negative imagery is stacked upon previous negative imagery. Primal Therapy and

Holotropic Breathwork™ are technologies that relate our negative experiences back to birth and the prenatal experience. We can tie the influence of our entire negative life experience in a chain of events back this far. Through dwelling in and creating negative imagery, you keep in touch with your negative life experience and constantly bring its influence forward. If you want to break free from this chain, stop creating negative imagery and the past will lose its negative influence.

All disturbed minds (excluding the physiologically handicapped mind) originate from these negative imaginations. These are the seeds for future expansion. Pain and the fear of pain, whether from abuse or unfortunate life experiences, are major contributors to this thought process. The degree of imagination vividity and intensity seems to vary greatly among people and, when the mind is negative, can also be a major contributor to mental disturbance. The world of evil or darkness begins in the imaginations of the negative spectrum of thought founded in our undesirable life experiences early in our childhood.

Whether we know it or not, we pretend. Thus we need to devote our attention to the creation of positive imagery in order to direct our experiences toward God-Mind alignment.

Fantasy

The '60s brought an awareness of fantasies. People began to justify much of their pretend world by attributing these thoughts to fantasies. We were informed that everyone has them and that they are harmless and meaningless unless acted out when they are not accepted as socially normal or responsible. These imaginations are much more willful than daydreaming. Adult fantasies became a psychologically OK'd new toy. We were told—if we were responsible enough to realize that these thoughts were mere fantasy, and, of course, didn't carry them out—that it is OK to imagine choking our boss or even plotting murder. We suffer the illusion that negative fantasies of lust, greed, vengeance, violence, and the like are harmless if not acted out. Some psychologists believe this may vent undesirable bottled-up emotion and could be beneficial for blowing off mental steam. Sexual fantasies were given the OK and people engaged wholeheartedly. We simply return to reality and the fantasies are gone.

But there is a problem with our so-called return to reality. We become lost in our imaginations to the extent that reality is greatly affected, distorted, biased, prejudiced, twisted, garbled, and misinterpreted—with many factors erased, ignored, or unconsidered. *The imaginations we dwell in set the stage for our viewpoint.* This greatly affects the paradigm in which we interpret the plot behind the scene. All imagery in the memory is subject to recall and may be assigned a high validity. Paradigms are identified patterns of imagery. It stands to reason that fantasies factor into our reference patterns. For example, if a man consistently fantasizes about having extramarital sex, he will be more likely to condone an extramarital affair by another man. If you have fantasies of choking the boss and someone chokes the boss, the act is more likely to be condoned or sympathized with.

Positive fantasies are healthy while negative fantasies are not. This is spiritual principle. We need to cleanse our mind of all negative fantasies in order to ascend spiritually. A negative fantasy is a disalignment from the God-Mind. This includes lust. I am sure any twenty-one year old reading this will scoff, but preoccupation with sexual fantasies can only lead to frustration, to say the least. The same thoughts at the highest extreme can lead to murderous rape. It is true that hormonal influences are present, endeavoring to perpetuate life through the sexual act, causing a preoccupation of a multitude of sexual desires. But discretion is of the utmost importance. Spirituality is rising above the urges of nature.

I once read a study where a goat was given a single female to sire in the period of one day. After the initial sexual response, the male was no longer interested in that particular female. The next day this same goat was given a new female immediately after each copulation until the total reached seventeen. The study was done to illustrate the inborn desire of a male mammal to reproduce with as many females as possible. The hormonal urge in a human male is strong but need not prevail. When we consider that one of the purposes of spirituality is to overcome the desires of the flesh, these sexual fantasies can be rebuked for the sake of spiritual ascension. It's a matter of priority.

I am not implying there is anything wrong with sex, but unscrutinized it is a major distraction to spiritual ascension. Lust diminishes the character and creeps into our relationships with others and becomes counter-productive and disruptive. For the male, it is probably one of the hardest negative thought patterns to conquer because it is genetically encoded in the male's physical makeup. Loving someone because we have sex with them is much different than having sex with them because we love them. When we are young, our hormones would have us just love sex. Ironically, the more we permit our attention to dwell in sexual imagery, the more our hormones secrete, and the more we are urged to create sexual imaginations. Due to the chemical response in the body and the forming of mental habits, an act of spontaneous indiscriminate sex is probably far less inhibiting to our spirituality than consistently dwelling in lust and never actually having sex.

Negative fantasies engage the emotions a great deal. They can add greatly to stress. If spiritual ascension is your goal, they are taboo and should be avoided. It is entirely possible to experience an attraction for another without creating a sexual scene within our mind movie and dwelling in it. And it is much more profitable to create a positive mind movie about our boss or others that may be bugging us or abusing us. Imagery urges behavior. The potential for serious consequences is in the embryo stage with negative fantasy.

Dreams

Our dreams, and I am referring to our aspirations, start to form in our positive imaginations at an early age. As children we have simple dreams. We dream of being given an ice cream cone or going to Grandma's. As we mature we have more sophisticated dreams. We start to speculate about our profession or career and the kind of life we ideally wish to live, commonly referred to, here in the United States, as "The Great American Dream." We see ourselves in a nice home, with a nice car, with a desirable husband or wife, a good job and the likes. We form imaginations of what we would like our personality to be like based on our heroes, those we admire, and with the idea of pursuing what interests us. We also desire to live the lifestyles of these people. We have perceptions of these role models. Everything is fine and healthy as long as these imaginations are positive.

As we experience the pains and fears of life, whether they are physical or emotional, our negative imaginations are born from the negativities instilled in us though fear. Aside from accidental injury, emotional pain, having our feelings hurt with ridicule, disappointment, angry or hateful criticisms—fears and anxieties creep into our lives through the negativity of others causing our negative imagination thought processes to form. The vividness of imagination and sensitivity to pain and fear are major contributing factors to the viewpoints and paradigms these imaginations form.

Good positive dreams are the foundation of the world in which we live. While on the other hand, the world is abased with the dreams of negative imaginings. People acting out their animal urges dreaming of power, money, unethical sexual fulfillment, greed, and the likes will attempt to realize these dreams at the expense of almost anyone in the way. People having negative dreams have little conscience regarding their fellow human beings. A conscience is developed by the positive spectrum of imagery. Since our lower self or animalistic nature creates the negative spectrum of imagination, it is not bound by ethical considerations.

When an individual focuses on his or her individuality regarding decisions and choices, the consideration of the Whole is overlooked. This is the *I win and too bad if you lose* mentality when interacting with others. Delusion always grows in proportion to the lack of consideration of the Whole picture.

As the indwelling God attempts to manifest through us, we are urged by His desires to enter into the arts, professions, vocations, and services that are the dreams of our heart. Staying true to the dreams of our heart is staying true to God. Yet we get drawn in by the veil of ignorance born of the illusion of limitation that originates in our negative mind. As we deny the dreams of our heart, we do so at the cost of our zeal for life. Be true to yourself and God by following the dreams of your heart.

Goals

Goals are the more analytical imaginations we create that are the results of intentions or a purpose. They are more calculating and sound. Goals are the shorter-term stepping-stones to our dreams. We can have moment-to-moment goals, daily goals, weekly goals, monthly goals, and yearly goals. As we create the images of our goals time after time, these images sink into the subconscious mind where programs are developed to manifest consistent images into reality.

As our goals and aspirations are imprinted on the subconscious mind, we begin to make the new decisions and choices aligned with our transforming belief system. We notice by association. When we set a goal, we begin to notice information in regard to the goal—that is, if we are not blocking the information with negative imagery.

Good sound positive goals are sound and productive imaginings manifesting into the physical world. This is God manifesting through us. Negative goals have the qualities of demonic plots.

Ideals

Ideals are hope of the ultimate realization of our goals and dreams. We are usually willing to accept less than our ideals, but hope to attain them. In this compromise, be not led astray from the dreams of your heart by being untrue to yourself.

Special care needs to be taken in choosing ideals. We base our dreams on our ideals in the same respect as our goals are based on our dreams. Consider the Whole and be true to yourself.

Again, there is as much good in our positive ideals as error in our negative ideals. There are no true negative ideals. There is only the illusion of such a thing. As in negative dreams and goals, this illusion overlooks the laws of spirituality and karma. Born of the illusion of a separation from God, these images are created in darkness and are anything but what God intends for us.

Heroes

Our choice of heroes is critical to the kind of ideals, dreams, and goals we create in our imagination. Through television, movies, books, people we meet, and family members we form concepts of heroes. Positive heroes are good role models to pursue, but negative heroes are disastrous. Our pain and fear influences us to hold the dark hero in esteem; this is owing to the appearance of power they seem to possess that we may hope will protect us and care for us. This illusion of power stems from a negative self-image where one has self-imposed limitations he or she is trying to overcome. Nothing could be further from the truth. Positive people inspire us into positive growth. The real heroes are the positive attributes within each of us. For everyone is a hero in his or her own virtue.

Role Models

A role model may be a hero or someone we admire. They may be someone who is a major influence in our lives, positive or negative. When someone is admired or a major influence, we tend to desire to acquire the traits we admire in that individual. We desire to emulate what we admire so that we imagine ourselves as being like this person. Desiring traits to become like our role models is healthy to the extent that these traits are positive in nature. Admiring the negative traits of role models gives us a false sense of power, false security, false acceptance, and a potentially dark sense of authority. These tendencies are very counter-productive. Pain and fear are also major contributors for these negative tendencies. Environmental negative influences also contribute heavily to these negative imaginations.

By choosing role models with the virtues found in Jesus, Mother Teresa, great saints, and great men and women we open the door to modeling ourselves after the finest personalities on Earth.

Traits

Although some of our traits appear inborn, the majority can be said to be the physical manifestations of groups of imaginations that form our different viewpoints and paradigms that ally with those of our role models. These traits, patterns of behavior and thought, are symbolic of the imagination patterns a person is experiencing under a wide range of circumstances. They are the distinguishing qualities or characteristics of our personal nature—our personality. Analyzing our traits can tell us a great deal about our imaginations.

When traits are positive they are healthy and are counter-productive only in accordance with our lack of knowledge. When negative, they are forming patterns that will lead to counter-productive behavior and poor character. One serious consequence is that the possibility of severe mental disturbance is flowering and can grow to any degree.

A great part of self-awareness is the knowledge of our traits. Traits range from negative characteristics to positive competencies. As we transform ourselves, our traits become competencies or virtues. Generally speaking, our negative traits are representations of our illusion of separation from God while our positive traits represent God manifesting through us. In learning about ourselves, feedback from friends, family, and fellow employees can give us the perspective we need to step back and examine ourselves—providing those offering the critique do not have other agendas influencing their opinions. Even so, we can get a general forecast that can be very helpful in our self-awareness.

Happiness

When you cease the creation of negative imagery, you are rendered happy. Our unhappiness results from the dwelling in or creation of negative imagery. If you desire to feel happy, it is necessary to dwell in and create happy imagery.

Most people believe that they are happy as a result of their environment or possessions. But this is not happiness—it is *pleasure response*, which is much different. Happiness originates from within you, since the first manifestation in the order of mental activity is the image. Pleasure response is a result of sensual input that is being used as a feedback loop from the environment.

Happiness is a matter of attention. When we give our attention to what is good, positive, clean, pure, and honest we feel good, positive, clean, pure, and honest. Thus, we are happy. When we give our attention to negative qualities, we soon initiate The Fight or Flight Response if we devote more attention than required to acknowledge the situation. Acknowledge the negative and then quickly move to positive imagery. In this way, we can be aware of negative aspects without The Fight or Flight Response interfering in our mental processes. Thus, we are happy when we take responsibility in our co-creatorship in the Universe with God.

Education

Our formal education starts when we go to school for a formal learning process. Education through schooling is somewhat more solid compared with the verbal tutoring we receive from family, friends, and the life learning experience. This solid knowledge is extremely beneficial to the imagery we rely upon to carry us through life. It penetrates the mind in general, giving us an abundance of knowledge that is not open to interpretation when blended with the imagination. But like every other aspect of imagination, the negative spectrum of thought can find ways of perverting education by becoming more calculating in negative notions or selecting bits and pieces of the realities of facts to validate preconceived notions. We literally calculate, within our imaginations, whether we will apply our education positively or negatively. Many street cons and criminals demonstrate genius. If they had channeled their genius into the positive spectrum they undoubtedly would have experienced prosperity to a higher degree than they achieved or probably even expected through their activities of darkness.

Our education is truly an asset for the indwelling God to be expressed through us. As we surrender to Him and become a vehicle for His expression, we apply our education within the Divine Idea.

Verbal Information

A great part of the knowledge we acquire stems from verbal information. Parents attempt to teach us, we learn from our friends, we hear things on television, at movies, and hear things on radio. All of these life experiences appear to teach us how to live and conduct ourselves in our worlds. Yet a great deal of verbal information we receive is misleading, untrue, and superstitious. We pick and choose to believe whatever we may from this vast source of data.

This area is wide open to our vulnerabilities. Anyone desiring to manipulate you will, in general, look for the weaknesses you have that are born of misinformation, superstition, naiveté, and limitations that we impose on ourselves through the imaginations of fear and painful experiences. Of course, there is the area of weakness of character that is a blend of misinformation, ignorance, and non-confront due to imaginations causing shyness, complexes, a need to be liked, and foolishness; in general, these things attempt to cover up our fear.

Verifying verbal information with educational material is advised. The vulnerabilities to negativities are extensive in this area; especially in the form of superstition, which is negative imagination in its most seemingly logical state.

Impressions

We receive impressions of people, places, events, and things in general. In other words we have imaginations of certain types regarding these things framed by the total of our past experiences, whether positive or negative. From that time forward, the realities of our interactions are influenced by this initial imagination. Of course, if sufficient time passes and enough other imaginations are formed through further impressions, the initial impression will dissipate. Impressions become a preconceived notion in the form of an assumption that we view reality through and from which we search for signs of validation. Impressions are a strong effect produced by the intellect. If we consider that the intellect is limited to appearances, we find that the impression is a very limited consideration. We bring our impressions into God's light when we look past appearances by utilizing our spectrum of positive imagery as our impressing foundation.

Assumptions

We have created the images of ideals, dreams, goals, heroes, role models, and acquired traits. We fill our memory banks with knowledge in the form of schooling or verbal data. We also form many assumptions. Assumptions are based on groups or patterns of imagery, positive or negative, that we use to hypothesize or conclude within our belief system. When positive, an assumption can be a wonderful form of creative intelligence or co-creation; but when negative, an assumption is usually harmful. This is not to say that we cannot foresee negative occurrences or realize inevitable negative results. Yet what we assume to be true urges the manifestation of our assumption. How often do people engage in negative assumptions based on little or no data but rather on a mere impression or a pessimistic guess?

Negative assumptions are manifested in the personality and mainly influence our ability to process information about ourselves, others, and circumstances with consideration to the whole of reality.

The play on words, "When you assume, you make an [ass] of [u] and [me]," epitomizes what our negative assumptions are capable of. In the same way, positive assumption is a creative imagery process where we project love, knowledge, wisdom, and uplifting imagery, and teach ourselves and urge uplifting behaviors and situations. Negative assumptions reassign the intentions of others or God and interfere in many subtle ways with our interaction with life. These are conclusions drawn based on a lack of consideration of the Whole of reality—conclusions made with little or no love as the catalyst.

The positive analytical part of our mind will calculate from a wide consideration of facts stored in the memory banks. The negative analytical mind will not make this consideration but will, instead, permit groups of imaginations to search and sift the facts of reality for validations of the preconceived notion that formed the groups initially. From this perspective, we can perceive that negative imaginings create parasite-like formations of images in the mind. This is why the ability to reason, when in a negative state of mind, is greatly inhibited. We literally have a new paradigm to go with the emotions our imagery stimulates.

Neville has defined what he termed The Law of Assumption in his book, *The Power of Awareness*. The Law of Assumption can be a powerful tool for transforming the mind. He states, "By desiring to be other than what you are, you can create an ideal of the person you want to be and *assume that you are already that person*. If this assumption is persisted in until it becomes your dominant feeling, the attainment of your ideal is inevitable." This may be applied to others as well. What we assume another to be will urge that kind of behavior in that person.

Positive assumptions cause positive manifestations. To

assume that everything will go wrong urges just that. On the other hand, assuming things are going to go well urges positive occurrences in the future.

I am particularly stricken by another application by Neville of The Law of Assumption. He claimed that the willingness to bear witness to the flaws of others is not an indication of superior insight but rather an ignorance of The Law of Assumption.

Assuming can also interfere with our ability to communicate. We can just assume things rather than ask questions or clarify our views. This usually leads to a negative chain of events that result from the original assumption.

Perception and Conception

There is considerable debate about the image being the substrate of thought. Arguments state that the image is not capable of reason, of perception, or conception. This is based on a notion that imagery is sort of one-dimensional. A classic argument states that we can visualize a man on an incline. Is the man going up or down? However, this argument intellectualizes imagery down to a one-frame event. We understand, conceive, and perceive by forming an image of a pattern identification. So when we continue the frames of the man on the incline, we can identify whether or not the man is going up or down.

Others have argued that we can form an image of the president, but not the office of the president with the concept of its duties. Yet this is also an identification of an image pattern. Nature uses patterns all throughout its creation. The pattern is at the very heart of all design from the atom up. It stands to reason that the brain would utilize pattern identification for its perception and conception processes.

Every "ah-hah" you experience is an identification of a pattern. It can be math, behavioral, or spiritual. It doesn't matter; there is a pattern to identify. Patterns are images. The neuron network within the brain fires in patterns as each image is created or recalled. This is basic neuron mechanics. This becomes quite clear once you bring your mind movie out of your peripheral attention into your main focus.

Expectation

When we expect something, it is a reflection of what we believe. We're not going to expect something if we don't believe it. As we develop our spirituality, we naturally begin to expect more. When you are connected to God and permit His intentions to flow through you as a vehicle of His will, you expect more. We tend to get what we expect since this parallels with what we believe. Expectation is a good way to witness your beliefs if you're not sure what they are. When you expect something, you are solidifying your beliefs about the situation. Generally, you'll get what you expect.

Viewpoint, Paradigm, and Schema

The negative imaginations within a person's mind form the paradigms, schemata, and perceptions related directly to fears, superstitions, traditions, pain, hurt, preconceived notions, and assumptions. Influenced by other varying negativities, these set the stage for our negative viewpoint. Paradigms are patterns of imagery, thought, emotion, behavior, or occurrences that we rationalize. Although these seemingly identified patterns seem to stem from legitimate insights, they are seldom more than assumptions until we study psychology, philosophy or meta-physics. And even then the patterns we think we identify are usually incomplete. We just don't have the mental capacity to consider the Whole of All.

When born of a negative mind, paradigms are based on information with much of the positive attributes removed owing to the mind's filtration system during The Fight or Flight Response.

Schemata attempt to form concepts from past experiences and knowledge for a frame of reference on which we can base our paradigms and viewpoints; thus we have a form of reference and identify patterns forming our viewpoints.

Viewpoint is usually related to a certain attitude of mind or circumstance that contributes to the attitude. Our positive viewpoint is the sum of images created by our positive experiences, analytical conclusions of the full scope of reality, and creative wisdom and faith influenced by varying other positive attributes—less that margin of error, ignorance of the facts.

Ultimately, our viewpoint is formed from a blend of positive viewpoint handicapped by negative viewpoint. It is rendered to the position we take regarding our life experiences. Tradition and superstition may handicap our viewpoint. A highly educated professor may feel superstitious about picking up a coin on tails. It seems no amount of education, other than spiritual education, can eliminate many of our negative thoughts. Our world's most intelligent minds still suffer from negative mind movie scripts.

Negative imagery in the previously mentioned viewpoints opens the possibility of reality being viewed from any perspective of a 360-degree circle of viewpoint. An enlightened viewpoint of reality, by contrast, attempts to encompass an awareness of the entire 360-degree circle of possible viewpoints and, at the same time, takes no strong point of view. That's why it's called a point of view, because it is viewing from a particular point while not viewing from other points. A 360-degree awareness is attained by lovingly giving an equal consideration to all of the facts; at least to the extent that is humanly possible without influence from the negative mind while softening the degree of seriousness to everything.

The influence from the negative mind causes many deletions of facts, rendering our reality a conclusion that is greatly or partially incomplete owing to this lack of considerations. One can see the same thing as always, but our viewpoint changes as our paradigms and schemata change. Older people look old until we become older—then older does not look so old. Everyone looks at life a little differently, in a unique way, according to their personality, wisdom, perceptions, state of mind, faith, conditioning, negativity, and countless other factors such as such as preconceived notions. When we look back ten or twenty years, we see the viewpoint of that era in terms of what was fashionable and modern; yet, today these older fashions and concepts are outdated.

In his bestseller, *Unlimited Power,* Anthony Robins describes the way we "see" situations as framing. The way we frame something is the relative viewpoint we take regarding a particular event, circumstance, person, place, or thing. So our viewpoints have relativity to what we saw last, what we think we already know, what we expect, and what we imagine. Yet we can choose to frame our situations relative to other than what may be common or popular. We can utilize our imagination to create a frame of divinity and spirituality that promotes love and peace.

Shankaracharya, a guru I see in Nashville and author of *God Alone Is,* explains this as "the color of the glasses we wear." If you wear red glasses everything looks red; green glasses make everything look green. If we move our viewpoint to find the silver lining in the cloud, we are re-framing or changing our glasses. Is the cup half full or half empty?

Preconceived notions greatly influence our viewpoint. A waitress may see many coffee cups left half empty, but fill them halfway with gold dust and they suddenly become half full.

Psychology defines schema as our cognitive framework consisting of a number of organized ideas—a frame of reference for recording events or information.

To ascend spiritually it is necessary to make a great change in viewpoint toward spirituality. I like to imagine that every one of us is one of God's angels or divine beings put on Earth to learn lessons or remember who we really are by having the human experience. When we overcome the flesh we will begin to "earn our wings." Now, when I look at the world, I see angels and divine beings everywhere. I imagine that although most people do not know it yet or remember who they are—and commit many errors in their imaginings and deeds—they are still divine. I imagine everyone experiencing the growth and enlightenment that will create Heaven on Earth. It's a good viewpoint. It works for me. It creates endless possibilities of understanding, compassion, and mercy. I am not saying we all should believe this, but something in this ballpark would not hurt. Rather than thinking we are a humans endeavoring for a divine experience, the thought that we are divine beings having a human experience is the desirable paradigm. The point is that, as I see it, my world is a world of angels and divine beings. And I am trying to help people remember who they are. Sometimes I feel like an angel when Spirit is moving me and I am really helping someone. Our positive attributes are angelic. I am not trying to be self-exalting, but it is a great way to feel and things are in perspective when our motivation is to serve.

We can test our viewpoint to see if it needs improving by merely looking back at the fruits of our viewpoint. What has it brought into this world? What love or fear has it brought into our life? And the more spiritual-minded you become, the more spiritual your viewpoint will become because you are cleansing your mind and heart of negative imaginings.

Disassociated Paradigms

Most of us have heard of disassociated personalities. The concept of the disassociated paradigm is much the same. We have a mental filtration system that specifically highlights the importance of facts or information, or deems it insignificant as we enter into different emotions. We have all said things like, "Catch me when I'm in a better mood and I'll probably do it." If a beggar asks you for some change and you are joyous, you probably will respond generously; if you are stressed, you may respond snappily.

Visualize a parking lot with hundreds of holes big enough for a person to squat down in and hide. Each person represents a piece of information. Some of the people stand up into view and yell out their information while most of the others stay hidden. This is how our mental filters highlight some information while failing to consider other information. This creates a pattern from the information we have highlighted and neglected each time we have entered into particular emotions.

When we consider that an emotion is the direct result of an imagination, we then see that the negative mind movie scripts result from facts and information being highlighted and neglected in our imaginations. This is how The Fight or Flight Response unfolds into the wide variety of negative emotions we may experience. The facts and information considered changes. But more importantly, you change. As you create negative imagery, your paradigm changes as the imagination changes the importance of facts and information. You become a different self with every negative line of the script in your mind movie.

The awareness of how we change our paradigms as we create negative imagery can be the single most powerful deterrent to justifying negative thought. Who wants to throw away all the self-improvement they have worked for so that they can become an older self that is possibly a representation of our worst self? This may happen only for a few moments, but it is experiencing a poor representation of the renewed self we have developed into. Our most productive positive self goes out the window when we begin the creation of negative imagery. Our most positive paradigms fade and are replaced by a self that represents the fear, anger, and separation from God that we have experienced in the past.

As we study, practice mental disciplines, work, and pray to develop and grow spiritually, we reach new paradigms of love and unity with God. This is the part of ourselves we refer to when we use the word "I." We don't consider the flaws of "I," we think of the best parts of "I." A great part of our development is put on hold when we enter into the creation of negative imagery. We become another self, another personality because we're in another personality, another pre-established mode of thought.

The next time you begin the creation of negative imagery or feel yourself becoming negative in emotion, introduce yourself as this new personality. Warn the others around you. That is, if you refuse to stop being negative and immediately begin the creation of positive imagery.

Attention

Within our consciousness is our attention. We focus on specifics within the wide range of what we are aware of by devoting attention to these considerations. This can entail the mind moving from area to area of specifics much like the steel ball in a pinball game. We can literally become lost in the long list of areas that need our attention. The more attention we give one thing, the less we give others. Our attention is a key factor in highlighting the importance of facts and information and neglecting other data. It's like shining a flashlight around in the dark. What is getting lit up is receiving our attention. Our entire existence can be summarized according to what gets our attention and what doesn't. And this boils down to our routines.

Each time we experience a negative emotion—the result of negative imagery—we record the paradigms of the data involved and the emotional charge that the data was relative to. In this physical way of recording our memories, we record our physical state of mind. The chemical response that the body was engaged in when the memory was recorded is imbedded in the image that the mind uses for its recording method. Past negative imagery has emotions imbedded in it and the emotions have data highlighted and neglected. This is the result of how we apply our attention in situations and of what we permit to encapsulate our attention. This is why giving regular attention to God is so important; otherwise you wind up acting like an android with a bad program. We can become very predictable when our emotions, moods, and states of mind are observed. Even as children we knew when and when not to ask our parents for certain things or privileges. We looked for the state of mind holding the most likely paradigm in which they would understand what we wanted. We try to approach people, from our boss to our friends, with this same caution when we are looking for a specific response. We all seem to have an intuition that everyone changes paradigms as one's mood changes. But it is more than just a mood; it is a transformation of the self.

Most of us find it necessary to be responsible for a vast array of details. To keep up to so many details, we develop a routine that leads our attention through association. One detail leads to devoting attention to another detail. This way we can keep things within our scope of awareness. If we don't bring our attention around to something for a long time, it begins to slip away from our awareness. Some things are harmless to neglect; others cost us time and or money. Devoting attention to the right things relative to our desires can greatly enhance our success in fulfilling them. But there is more to tending our desires than just being willing. Our self-image, our core belief system, our ideas of who and what we are in relation to our life experience—as well as a summation of all our realms of imagery—all work together to create programs that direct our attention. Our conscious and subconscious programs make the difference between being distracted from or fulfilling our desires.

The I AM controls our attention programs. Our choices and decisions are based on our assumptions about who and what we believe we are, relative to what we are trying to accomplish or become. This is why our attention is so vulnerable to negative imagery. When we feel a limitation, our attention dwells on the limitation while we compare it to the possible solution that seems out of reach. Any time we spend focusing our attention on the negative is less time that we have to spend on the positive. Our fear initiates a negative focus. Only that which is a threat is worthy of our attention when we experience fear or threat, whether it is real or imagined. This is the basis of The Fight or Flight Response's filtration system where positive aspects of our environment are given less consideration. It's a shift of attention from positive to negative. Fear, whether in the subtle form of doubt or being scared stiff, is the greatest distraction of our attention. The limitations we impose on ourselves can steal the greatest part of our attention away from exactly what we are trying to accomplish. Dispersed, divided, undisciplined attention severely affects our awareness level. When we are not aware of opportunities, we miss them.

Jon von Neumann mathematically calculated that the human brain is capable of storing up to 280 quintillion (280,000,000,000,000,000,000) bits of memory. The brain may be operating at speeds faster than our fastest supercomputer. Becoming aware of all the information that we may be capable of would most likely lead to madness if only from inundation by mundane meaningless trivia. We need a filtration system to sort out information because our attention can focus in only one area at a time.

In his book, *The Einstein Factor*, Win Wenger, Ph.D., states that calculations of researchers reveal most brains can pay attention to only about 126 bits of information per second. Directing our attention to hearing someone speak uses up about 40 bits of attention. This leaves only 86 bits to watch facial expressions and body language, and to think about what we may say as a reply. It's like having a PC with a huge hard drive and a tiny RAM that needs to omit a lot of data to keep from crashing. Our minds are literally flooded by hundreds of times more information bits than we can pay attention to. But we try—when we aren't busy creating imagery.

We seem to develop a subconscious radar program that directs our attention toward imperative concerns. For example, among many distractions, a mother will check on her baby regularly. We get feelings about things that need our attention. Many times, our minds scan through countless images in relation to what we are experiencing now. Rather than bother our attention with all this information, the sum total of this information comes to us as a feeling. Thus, feelings of this nature contribute to our intuition.

Though our many responsibilities may distract our attention away from our imagination, we need to discipline ourselves in order to focus our attention on our mind movie to know ourselves and develop our spirituality. Developing a routine where we periodically return a portion of our attention to God renews our unity and connectedness with the God-Mind. This also develops our partnership with God. What we devote attention to we get more of.

It appears that psychology has unquestionably accepted the century-old conclusion of William James where he states that "attention cannot be continuously sustained." Inasmuch as psychology holds this belief, James also stated that "the faculty of voluntarily bringing back a wandering attention over and over again is the very root of judgment, character, and will." The very principle of meditation training is to gain control over attention by consistently bringing it back from its nature to wonder within imaginings.

At the heart of visualization exercises that develop our compassion, understanding, patience, and empathy is the giving of our attention to these different considerations so they may become a part of the data we are aware of in our decision-making. Basically, this is extending the attention far beyond the self. As we become aware of the states of consciousness of others and more data to consider, we base our decisions on a greater part of the Whole.

Archetypes

The archetypes have been known throughout history. Carl Jung developed his concept of archetypes when he noticed the recurring symbols and themes in his patients' dreams and as he realized that those same symbols and themes have appeared in both ancient and modern art, mythology (particularly in the assortment of Greek gods and goddesses), fairy tales, legends, and religion (including Buddhism's *Tibetan Book of the Dead* where the archetypes are encountered in "the Bardo"). Plato has described archetypes as "ideal forms." Europe's rationalistic philosophers described them as our innate tendency to perceive and understand in a particular manner. Practitioners of various types of divination, such as numerology, runes, I Ching, and astrology have described archetypes within the signs of the zodiac.

Jung identified what appeared to be archetypal patterns

within the collective unconsciousness of humanity. These include particular personality concepts, deity prowess, and even animals such as the dragon. They are concept patterns common to the collective unconsciousness. It's almost like they are encoded in our DNA.

Often we jump to conclusions by attempting to fit things and people into archetype paradigms. An old man with a white beard says the right thing and suddenly he becomes the wise old man archetype in our imagination. Many times after a war was won, it was thought, "Our god is more powerful than your god. That is why we won." Dragons have been identified in worldwide cultures. Our minds seem to slip easily into the archetype paradigm. It's almost as if we all have a preset storehouse of these patterns of imagination that surface universally. Being aware of archetypes, we can refrain from unwanted slips into such paradigms that may inhibit our judgment. Fitting appropriate patterns into archetypes is fine, but we need to beware of jumping to conclusions.

Visualization

Doctors and psychologists have researched what is termed visualization therapy. The theory is based on the faculty of imagination. Create an image in the mind of the healing that is needed. This can be done literally or by imagining a cartoon. If you break a bone you can imagine the blood cells carrying the needed repair materials to the break and depositing them quickly. Or, if you know little about physiology, you can imagine tiny bricklayers carrying cement to the break and repairing it. The point is to give conscious attention and effort to the desired outcome and to create an image of the desired outcome. This works so well that experiments of visualizations created by people other than the afflicted have an affect in much the same way that prayer for others affects the one being prayed for. If you are not using visualization therapy—start.

Mental disturbances can be resolved by visualizing that they no longer exist. For example, someone with a low self-esteem can resolve this issue by creating visualizations of his or her self as confident, good, and worthy. By creating these positive images of the self and refusing to visualize the self within the old complex, the new self-image takes dominion. We can reinforce this positive self-image by also speaking to the self while engaged in internal dialogue as though we are a confident, good and worthy person. Our internal dialogue mirrors our imagination.

Visualization can also be used to manifest things into the physical plane. Create an image in your mind about a goal, for instance, and you enhance your likelihood of attaining it. Create an image of an improved self, a more spiritual self, a thinner self; this will enhance the probabilities of attaining these goals.

During meditation, visualizing Jesus, angels, divine beings, or deities will create the feeling of being in divine presence. A powerful technique I especially like is to visualize an angel meditating directly in front of me, facing me. When I feel the divine presence of this angel, I then visualize a frame around the angel and imagine that I am actually looking in a mirror seeing this angel. It is surprising how your mind immediately feels an extreme sense of responsibility when you see yourself as being an angel. I feel my mind aligning its thoughts in accordance with this responsibility. It is truly a wonderful experience. The body cannot distinguish between sensual input and imagination.

One of the most outstanding visualization programs I have found is the audio program, *The Power of Visualization*, by Lee Pulos, Ph.D. Dr. Pulos vividly describes countless visualization exercises and routines that range from ancient imagery practices to the most modern visualization concepts offered today.

The Nonlocal Mind & Era III Medicine

Dr. Larry Dossey first introduced the term *nonlocal mind* as applying to the consciousness of humanity in his book, *Recovering the Soul*. The term has recently become more popularized in Dossey's latest book, *Reinventing Medicine*.

Nonlocal mind appears to be a more scientific term for

Christ consciousness, Buddha mind, or the Universal Mind. It has become the focus and heart of Era III medicine. Era I medicine is surgery and antibiotics. Era II is mind/body medicine. Scientists and doctors could no longer ignore the profound effects the mind has on healing the body. Era III incorporates Era I medicine, Era II practices, and the nonlocal mind—the power of the imagination of others at a distance. In *Reinventing Medicine*, Dr. Dossey cites study after study by major universities and by independent research that demonstrate the power of the nonlocal mind.

Dr. Dossey also cites Mercy Medical Center as a model of Era III medicine practices. Mercy, says Dr. Dossey, has issued Era III bracelets to identify Era III patients entering the emergency facility. Equipped with an Era III trauma room, Mercy treats participating patients with doctors and nurses who are trained in visualization, prayer, and other forms of Era III techniques. The patients' names are entered into a computer and sent to worldwide participating prayer groups to initiate healing prayers or visualizations. Statistics show considerable affects on healing improvement.

As nonlocal mind, the imagination affects not only you, but also others at a distance. As more and more people participate in consistent uplifting imaginings throughout the world, health and abundant living will become more and more established within humanity.

Internal Dialogue

In her lectures and self-help recordings, Rayma Ditson-Sommer, Ph.D., states that we speak about 45,000 words per day to ourselves internally. It must be noted that the mind does not screen this internal dialogue for positive talk. Ultimately, all internal dialogue is stored in the subconscious for later recall. "Little negatives" form a foundation for more powerful negative images. Observe what you are saying to yourself. It will show you what script you are writing in your mind movie.

As mentioned, some image theories note that we create a mental image picture about every two-fifths of a second. We are awake about 16 hours per day. This calculates to 57,600 seconds and 144,000 mental images. If we consider our 45,000 words of internal dialogue per day, saying only positive things to ourselves creates an estimated 108,000 positive images out of the 144,000 images or about 75 percent. If we consider that the remaining 25 percent of our images are created as we involve ourselves in our external speech and deeds and that our internal dialogue heavily influences these images, we can see the great importance of positive internal speech. Just as the video runs hand-in-hand with the audio in a movie, our internal dialogue coincides with our imagery.

The subconscious mind takes things literally. If every time we forget something we say, "I always forget that," we will always forget that. By refusing to judge by appearances, we can say, "I always remember that," even though we have forgotten it. After several times, the subconscious initiates the new image, "I always remember that."

Anything we say to ourselves again and again becomes the subconscious program. Thus the greatest part of the limitations we experience are the result of the limitations we talk ourselves into. Again, this is the I AM principle. Focus on what you say to yourself and say only what you desire to manifest.

Spiritual Ascension

When we ascend spiritually, enlightenment is achieved when we overcome the creation of negative imaginations to the extent that the consciousness spends very little time dwelling in the negative spectrum of imagery. Notice I said very little time. This is because negative images will always come into the mind. However, we must control the body's blueprinted response to them by rebuking the negative imagery. In order to ascend spiritually it is necessary to be able to analyze our negative imaginings and be aware of the percentage of negativity within our essence.

This may be quite difficult to do alone. Ask your friends and family to tell you about your negative self. They all know and probably are negative enough themselves to already have engaged in gossip about your negativities.

We all have judged someone as not being in reality. The truth is that we create our own realities within our imaginations to the point that what reality may be begins to lose its relevance. The intentions and motives we assign and assume others have—in regard to their actions, our judgments of others, our conclusions of the seriousness of situations, and our lack of consideration for the whole of reality—cause the real scope of the big picture to become lost. Sometimes we are accurate; sometimes we could not be further from the truth. Therefore, a great part of reality becomes an assumption. The assumption is based on our belief system. We believe our imaginings by sifting reality for validations. We are deluded by the validations we believe we've found that appear to logically justify our negative imaginings. It can even seem logical to be illogical, but as long as it justifies our imagery and emotional urges we go with the thoughts.

To ascend spiritually, it is necessary to habitually think spiritually. We must create spiritual imaginations. Testimonials from countless people's spiritual experiences are not delusions. It is not enough to merely know about spirituality. We must furrow neurological pathways by continual and persistent spiritual imaginations. *Spiritual experiences are built on a thirst and hunger for spirituality that is manifested in our physiology through our imaginations.*

To the enlightened, everything is OK. Nothing is so serious as to pull them from their center. No matter what situations develop, the point of our experience is not *what is happening* but *who we become* moment-by-moment as our life experience unfolds and we observe through loving eyes and hearts. Our experiences can be of the highest possible quality when we respond as though we are powerful, spiritual, divine beings taking responsibility for our co-creatorship with God.

In their book, *New Thought: A Practical American*

Spirituality, C. Alan Anderson and Deborah Whitehouse explain how every moment, God offers us the highest quality experience possible.

Negative Is "Anti"

It has been my observation that all imaginings of the negative spectrum of thought are pure trickery. They are anti-life, anti-productive, the anti-you, anti-logic, anti-spiritual, anti-love, anti-faith, and anti-hope—the world in general of a conceivable self-imposed hell.

Imagine looking into a mirror. The world in the mirror is the opposite image from the real world where you are. The anti-world of negative imaginations is comparable to the mirror image. The logic in the negative world is the opposite of positive imaginations. We can apply this to any imagery or emotion. The logic of love is certainly the opposite of the logic of hate. Although hate is counter-productive to life, many people find it perfectly logical to hate. Through this logic of hate a person can destroy one's life, yet the logic somehow seems appropriate to this individual. The logic of forgiveness is always productive, yet some find it perfectly logical to lust for revenge or hold a grudge. This revenge logic can destroy the person, yet the destruction somehow appears logical and necessary. The point is that negative imaginations and the negative emotions they manifest cause an illogical response, to a greater or lesser degree, in every case and are counter-productive.

Oriental schools of thought teach of conquering the ego. To me, the ego is nothing more than the negative mind—a mind void of considerations of God—a mind that thinks it is separate from God. Tibetan Buddhism speaks of Samsara, a world of delusion that we become lost within. This is the world of the negative mind.

When we no longer dwell in or create negative imaginations, we are freed from our mirror image in the opposite anti-world. We can devote the rest of our life to trying to fix the negative mind in an attempt to gain relief from psychological problems; yet unplugging from it is the solution that offers the speediest path to bliss. The emotional charge of our past fear and pain can be likened to a fire we must tend in order to keep it alive. Each moment we dwell in past memories of fear and pain or each time we create new negative imagery, we stoke this fire. We are giving attention to our fear and pain. Let the fire go out. This fire is the anti-world.

Imagine yourself as a writer for a television show that has a wholesome, happy, spiritual format. Each show is to have no characters yelling at each other, no characters with complexes or limitations, and no disrespect. Characters are to be productive, spiritual, dignified, and ethical—all following the dreams of their heart. The purpose of the show is to uplift all who see it, to leave them with a desire to be like the characters, to be uplifted. Now, suppose you are the star of this show. Will you be tempted to write the terrible things that happened to you in the past? Will your personal past affect your ability to create a script free of negativity? As a writer and star of a TV show, probably not. But as the writer, director, producer, and star of your own mind movie, we are tempted to integrate our past negative experiences into our script. Of course, somehow it seems logical to do so—in the world of anti.

The Great Gulf

The area between positive and negative imaginations can be likened to The Great Gulf. This is illustrated in Luke 16:26 with the story told by Jesus of the rich man and the beggar Lazarus where Abraham says to the rich man: ". . . between us and you there is a great gulf fixed: so that they which would pass from hence to you cannot; neither can they pass to us, that would come from thence."

We know that in Luke 17:21, Jesus said that "The Kingdom of God is within you." In John 14:2, He says: "In my Father's house are many mansions: if it were not so I would have told you." I perceive the first mansion to be The Kingdom of Heaven found here on

Earth in the spectrum of positive imagination and emotion. We cannot pass through the Great Gulf from negative to positive without changing our beliefs. Without renewing the mind, it cannot perceive the renewal. And a renewed mind cannot pass into the negative old belief system without changing back to the old way of believing—even if it is only momentarily. "And he said unto them, I beheld Satan as lightning fall from Heaven." (Luke 10:18)

Paul wrote in II Corinthians 12:2: "I knew a man in Christ above fourteen years ago, (whether in the body, I cannot tell; or whether out of the body, I cannot tell: God knoweth;) Such an one caught up to *the third Heaven.*" If there is a third Heaven, where is the first Heaven? Can it not be as said in Luke 17:21, *within you,* considering that The Kingdom of God and The Kingdom of Heaven were used interchangeably?

The Great Gulf in this first mansion is the distance between the two worlds of positive and negative imaginations and the belief systems that perpetuate them. This analogy of the rich man and Lazarus can well be applied to our heavenly realm on Earth. There is a great gulf between these worlds. A person stuck in the negative world cannot see through positive eyes. Once a person is illuminated in the positive world The Great Gulf is easily seen, but we must be transformed to cross over.

We See What We Are, And We Are What We See

We have all heard the saying, "I wouldn't have believed it if I didn't see it." The inversion of this is also equally true. "I wouldn't have seen it if I didn't believe it." The *eyes* of our paradigms can be directly related to imagination and emotion. Emotion is likened to *eyeglasses* of an array of different colors. When we put on red glasses, everything looks red. Wear blue glasses and everything seems blue. So it is when we look through the eyes of hate we find validations to hate. Look through the eyes of a poor self-image and we see many things in reality to give validity to those imaginations. If the feeling of paranoia creeps upon us we cannot escape the feeling it brings to every aspect of our life. The thought that in all probability something is going to harm us is so evident and can be seen with such clarity that it is almost like a revelation. Yet it is merely an illusion brought about by our consciousness dwelling in this area of our imagination.

The point is not to be tricked into trusting everything you perceive while in a negative state of mind. When we wear the glasses of love, faith, hope, patience, forgiveness, reverence, and charity, we see life in an *undistorted* way. One may begin to reason that I am suggesting we live in a pretend world where we are not facing reality, but this could not be further from the truth. Fasting the mind from negative imagery will not produce a fool who lives in a pretend world. Foolish thought is the product of the world of negative imagery. You can spend a lifetime kidding yourself in the world of negative imaginations. It is the world of illusion, and mankind has been falling for it since time immemorial.

We cannot escape *seeing reality as we are* and cannot escape *being the way we see* reality. Until the negative mind is unplugged, we will *see* through the *eyes* of our past fear and pain, misjudging by assigning too much importance to some information and too little significance to other information. When we unplug from the negative mind, we can see the reality that is needed in order to find the viewpoint where we can realistically create positive imaginations in our thoughts and hearts as a child of God. This viewpoint on a feather, blowing in the wind of a hunger for divine experience, will guide us through our trials and tribulations and give us the perspective on life that will permit us to experience life's interactions without the illogic of the negative anti-world.

Are We Just Thinking?

Imagination is limitless, boundless, misunderstood, and most of all, it has had little research. I was reading a psychology book that had a footnote after a mention of imagination. The notation stated that more research is needed on imagination. We are entering the 21st century, a new millennium, and know little about imagination—the area where people spend the majority of their time; an area that carries more influence with us in every facet of our existence than anything else.

I cannot emphasize enough that we spend more time creating, reviewing, and using our faculty of imagination than any other area of mental utility. We are planning, setting goals or dreaming, reminiscing, plotting, loving, hating, enjoying, sorrowing—what we have termed thinking, which engulfs all mental activity. We think, but what we think about is within the broad scope of our imaginings. So we are deluded into conceiving we are merely thinking when we are really engulfed in imagination. We do not merely think. *We are creating or scanning multiple realms of imaginations that become our thoughts as we associate ourself with them. We are either creating new images through the creative imagination or creative intelligence, or we are scanning the previously created images. We call this thinking.*

Negative Imaginations Sift Reality for Validation

Each group of like images sifts reality for validation to satisfy their very birth into existence. It is our nature to justify our imaginings. The only way we can truly have dominion over our imaginings is through faith. We must do this with a faith that is a blind faith; a faith blind to our own justifiers, our own reasoning, our own sensual input. I say this because a major part of our so-called reasoning is born of a negative state of mind. When we are hurt or experience fear, we conclude and develop a thought process to assure ourselves that this pain will not come into our lives in the future. The problem with the mind's capacity to reason in a negative state of mind is evident when we examine our own *case* makeup. All irrational imaginings in response to our environment can be traced to fear and pain. These thought processes born of fear and pain simply do not work. They are conceived while the mind is in a negative state and can only lead to irrational imaginings. The justifiers that we use to rationalize our negative imaginings and acts are delusions caused by not considering the Whole Picture.

Within irrational thought, irrational imaginings are found trying desperately to justify their existence with anything they can sift from reality. I use the term sifting reality because this is exactly the case. These negative imaginations break down reality into many facets such as time, space, people, places, things, words, phrases, gestures, facial expressions, events, intentions, motives, smells, tastes, feelings, and comparisons to earlier similar situations, past memories, and preconceived notions. This opens the door to the possibility of selecting bits and pieces of reality to reinforce or validate these imaginations because we cannot spread out our attention evenly over this amount of data while our attention is encapsulated. Thus we highlight and neglect information while our validations serve us by supplying the "proof" that justifies our viewpoint. When a person creates and dwells within positive imaginings, their tendency is to attempt to consider the Whole of reality. This can be difficult to do without a mind trained as well as Sherlock Holmes, but at least a rational positive person will try. This demonstrates the difference between acting out of ignorance as opposed to acting out of our irrationalities influenced by the negative mind.

For example, a child may tell her parents that she knows that they hate her because they will not let her play with John now. The conclusion is reached from the illogical, negative mind during an emotional episode, and overlooks all other considerations. On a much more grand adult scale, we can observe the same type of overlooked considerations. For example, John forgets to get his wife a birthday present. She says that she knows that he does not love her and this proves it. *But* John has been working two jobs because his wife's car was wrecked and he was so fatigued that he forgot. The hard work and loyalty were not considered. Reality was sifted for a sign of validation to justify an otherwise unjustifiable imagination that becomes manifested as an inappropriate emotion based on insecurity.

The basis to all delusions is the failure to consider the Whole of reality. The negative imaginings that we harbor can cause the mind to fail to give the appropriate considerations of the Whole of reality to the extent that they become like a demonic possession. Negative states of mind cause a selected memory loss regarding certain data; this is because the importance of a validation that is found is *highlighted to a highly memorable state* where other considerations do not have such an importance and are forgotten as well as overlooked. When we realize the amount of information that we filter out in our bombardment of data, we begin to realize the vulnerability we have for misconstruing the facts. We may simply eliminate many of them. Since I have been practicing Imagination Control Therapy, I have been in situations where it appeared that negative things were happening to me. It has appeared that things were being stolen from me or that people appeared to be lying to me. On several occasions, it turned out that I was completely wrong about the situation. Each time I was very thankful that I hadn't made a big deal of anything. I didn't allow these appearances to pull me off center. It's a good feeling to know that you didn't react negatively when all indications practically mandated negative behavior and, presto, you find out it is only an illusion anyway. It's a feeling of balance and it reinforces your gratitude for God.

The Struggle for Reality

Our personalities are born out of our imaginings. We hold ideals, heroes, our goals, and our dreams in our imaginations until they wholly or partially manifest into reality. The thought processes that we develop in a negative state of mind will delude us into choosing the wrong ideals, the wrong heroes, the wrong goals, and the wrong dreams. Blend this with inappropriate emotion and we struggle not only through reality, but also *for* reality. Lace this with enslavement to superstition and tradition and we have a concept of mankind's general state of mind. And it is all in the imagination.

Metaphysics teaches us that the flow of God's love is inhibited or perpetuated through us. If we consider our positive imagery as the vehicle for this flow of love, we can see how our negative imagery can stop the flow. Yet, we continue to manifest our imaginings into the physical world whether or not we are an expression of God's love. Your struggle dissolves when you are a continuous avenue for God's love to flow through you.

The Mind's Dual Nature

A beautiful book that I would wholeheartedly recommend for anyone to read is *A Stranger by the River*, by Paul Twitchell. The book's character, a master, Rebbazar Tarzs, states: "Now know this. God is All. You cannot believe that God is All. In your imagination, you have and create ideals and idols, and then believe that is God. There are only the attributes of God; for once you transcend time and space, beyond all creation, you meet perfection and find in the end that perfection is all, and all is perfection. This is God."[2]

He further adds, "Let me tell you this. Mind is of a dual nature, for it can change from the good to the negative, from the negative to the good, within the minute fraction of a second."[3]

The dual nature of the mind is critical to understand if you are interested in spiritual ascension. I see this occurring in love-hate relationships frequently. The more emotional a person is by nature (I should say lower nature), the higher a level of this change from positive to negative, negative to positive can operate. The imaginations experienced during these change episodes are fantastic. Lovers can imagine a life of happiness and harmony long overdue, and then, as the emotion changes to negative, they will imagine a life of despair and long-suffering.

We create an image in our mind as the foundation of every thought. Within our imagination we create our ideals, role models, heroes, love concepts, perceptions on how to live and survive in life, plans, goals, ideas of pleasure, ideas of fun, concepts of pain, insult, and offense, etc. In other words, we form our personalities and life concepts around and in our imagination.

Our ability to create results from the faculty of imagination. Whatever you imagine reality to be, it is for you. Life is exactly whatever we imagine that it is—what we imagine it into. By becoming aware of your mind movie, your imagination, you take the first step in eliminating the duality of the mind. Elimination of the creation of negative imagery is the cessation of the dual nature of the mind.

Physical Changes in the Body

The Kingdom of God is within you in the imaginations of your positive spectrum of thought. Our emotions are merely the way we can experience our imaginations physically in this world of matter, energy, space, and time. Once you conceive this and love according to the brotherhood of humankind—with the realization of God being our Father/Mother and we His sons and daughters—you have Heaven on Earth. Within the imagination, the mind can be in Heaven while the body is on Earth. It may sound quite eccentric to proclaim Heaven to be in our imaginations, but the real insanity is the hell we create with the erroneous, negative imaginings that have been the ball and chain of humanity since time immemorial. Once the mind is set to believe in the power and divinity of the positive spectrum of imagination, God's divine plan is activated unhindered in your life. God then starts to run our lives, instead of our ego running it. We give up trying to control things and succumb to the intention of God. We become vessels for the manifestation of God through us, which can be identified in this material world by our emotions, speech, and deeds.

This state of mind has been well known by masters of the East for centuries. Once the mind stays positive for a period of time it affects the pineal, pituitary, and hypothalamus glands which regulate and control the body functions. Neurotransmitters function at higher levels causing thought to be expanded in a similar fashion as LSD and other mind-expanding drugs. Only this is natural, safe, non-harmful, and a truly divine level of thought that is not artificial as in the case of a-drug induced state that eventually wears off.

The Power Centers

Divine imaginings cause absolutely fascinating changes in the body. The body's ganglionic nerve centers, described in the East as chakras, begin to awaken as well as other power centers. Charles Fillmore theorizes in his book, *The Twelve Powers of Man*, that we have twelve major ganglionic power centers. These centers are the faculties of the I AM (Christ). They are:

- Imagination
- Zeal
- Wisdom
- Will
- Power
- Order
- Understanding
- Love
- Elimination
- Faith
- Strength
- Life

Fillmore's perception of *imagination* is more correctly termed *creative* imagination. Since the image is the substrate of all thought, I teach that the imagination is the developer of and the key to the other eleven faculties, and more. The faculty of imagination is the key to the development of the I AM, the Christed faculty of the mind. Through the consistent creation of positive imagery based on the ethics and values of the other eleven faculties, the development of the entirety of all faculties culminates as the development of the Christ within us. *These are the realms of imagination that need the bulk of our attention.* **Study them. Talk about them. Think about them. Incorporate them into your daily routine imagery.**

Healing Chemicals

Divine positive imagery also releases healing chemicals that promote miracle healings of ailments from cancer to psychosomatics. The key is to consistently create or dwell in positive and divine imaginings. The ability to promote healing is greatly enhanced when we create the image that we are whole, that we are healed. Medical theories now abound that the greatest part of illness is caused by our own thoughts. By holding the image of our wholeness, the body will create the chemicals to make it so.

We cannot enjoy the changes of neurotransmitter and ganglionic power center enhancement if we start imagining how much we would like to choke our boss or if we dwell in past pain and activate The Fight or Flight Response. The images transmitted throughout the body must remain positive for the changes to come into affect. This is when true illumination starts.

Heaven and Imagination

Jesus tells us in Matthew 19:14: "Suffer little children and forbid them not to come unto me for such is The Kingdom of Heaven." When we read what Jesus says in Matthew 18:3: ". . . Except ye be converted, and become as little children, ye shall not enter into The Kingdom of Heaven," we find another comparison of The Kingdom of Heaven to children.

The most obvious attribute of little children is their innocence. And within that innocence are the most wonderful, incredible imaginations conceivable. Howie Mandel's children's cartoon, *Bobby's World,* is a perfect depiction of a child's imagination.

Acceptance is another attribute of a child. Our ability to accept must also improve greatly if we are to ascend spiritually. Innocence and acceptance are virtues that are left when we cleanse our consciousness from dwelling in and creating negative imagery. Negative imagery contains, exclusively, all of our guilt. There is no guilt is our positive imagery unless, of course, one is experiencing artificial positive emotions over something negative such as a robbery gone well. I am referring to pure positive imagery with ethics and values—imagery aligned with the God-Mind.

With acceptance we can allow God to run the Universe while our ego fades. Our need to control things is in direct proportion to our lack of faith and trust in God's ability to provide for us. Stress is a product of needing to control. When we need to have control we become angry, anxious, and stressful when things do not go as we think they should. Acceptance is the soother of life. Acceptance is a fundamental for staying positive in thought.

Jesus then said in Matthew 13:11-17: ". . . it is given unto you to know the mysteries of The Kingdom of Heaven, but to them it is not given. For whosoever hath, to him shall be given, and he shall have more abundance: but whosoever hath not, from him shall be taken away even that he hath. Therefore speak I to them in parables: because they seeing see not; and hearing they hear not, neither do they understand. And in them is fulfilled the prophecy of Esaias, which saith, BY HEARING YE SHALL HEAR, AND SHALL NOT UNDERSTAND; AND SEEING YE SHALL SEE, AND SHALL NOT PERCEIVE: FOR THIS PEOPLE'S HEART IS WAXED GROSS, AND THEIR EARS ARE DULL OF HEARING, AND THEIR EYES THEY HAVE CLOSED; LEST AT ANY TIME THEY SHOULD SEE WITH THEIR EYES, AND HEAR WITH THEIR EARS, AND SHOULD UNDERSTAND WITH THEIR HEART, AND SHOULD BE CONVERTED, AND I SHOULD HEAL THEM. But blessed are your eyes, for they see: and your ears, for they hear for verily I say unto you, that many prophets and righteous men have desired to see those things which ye see, and have not seen them; and to hear those things which ye hear, and have not heard them."

Jesus referred to the prophecy that stated that they might see and not perceive and hearing they may not hear and understand. And to the twelve apostles who were with him and understood he said, ". . . unto you it is given to know the mystery of The Kingdom of God." What did the twelve apostles have that the average person doesn't have? Divine, positive imagery, acceptance and surrender to God through faith, an understanding of the brotherhood of mankind, and a concept of being the sons of the Father, which ultimately means unity with the indwelling Christ. Filling the mind with the preoccupation of God flowing through you, healing people, loving people, working with people, and bringing people to the Light of God has a profound effect on the body and heart. What a mind movie the apostles had! And you can have a comparable mind movie if you let it happen.

If ever there was an identifiable vehicle for God to express through human beings, the spectrum of positive imagery is this gateway. Through our imaginings, we can identify with a united humanity and experience our unity with God.

Jesus was never quoted as using the word imagination. He gave us Matthew 18:3 and 19:14. These scriptures tell us to become as children to regain the power of using our divine innocent imaginations with acceptance to enter The Kingdom of Heaven.

Although the word imagination does not appear to be used by Jesus, the Bible illustrates God's concern for man's imagination as early as Genesis 6:5. From this point the word imagination is mostly used with negative implications or in a way that does not actually distinguish positive imaginings. When Mary becomes pregnant with Jesus, the word imagination is, for the first time, used in a way that distinguishes positive imagery in Luke 1:51.

What The Bible Says About Imagination

The following concordance search of *imagination* gives a fascinating insight of the negative imaginings of humanity.

- Genesis 6:5: "And God saw that the wickedness of man was great in the Earth, and that every imagination of the thoughts of his heart was only evil continually."
- Genesis 8:21: "And the Lord smelled a sweet savour; and the Lord said in his heart, I will not again curse the ground anymore for man's sake; for the imagination of man's heart is evil from his youth; neither will I again smite anymore every thing living, as I have done."
- Deuteronomy 29:19: "And it come to pass, when he heareth the words of this curse, that he bless himself in his heart, saying, I shall have peace, though I walk in the imagination of mine heart, and to add drunkenness to thirst."

Notice the implication in the above verse that it is taken for granted that the imaginations of the heart were negative.

- Deuteronomy 31:21: "And it shall come to pass, when many evils and troubles are befallen them, that this song shall testify against them as a witness; for it shall not be forgotten out of the mouths of their seed: for I know their imagination which they go about, even now, before I have brought them into the land which I sware.
- 1 Chronicles 28:9: "And thou, Solomon my son, Know thou the God of thy father, and serve him with a perfect heart and with a willing mind: for the LORD searcheth all hearts, and understandeth all the imaginations of the thoughts: if thou seek him, he will be found of thee; but if thou forsake him, he will cast thee off for ever."
- 1 Chronicles 29:18: "O Lord God of Abraham, Isaac, and of Israel, our fathers, keep this for ever **in the imagination of the thoughts of the heart** of thy people, and prepare their heart unto thee."

Although the above verse of scripture is one of a few references of *imagination* in the Old Testament without a negative implication, there is no positive reference either. The imagination of the thoughts of the heart is presented here as the potential for negative or positive. It refers to a prayer to keep the wonderful feelings, described in earlier scriptures, in the hearts of the people. I marvel at the consistent sequence of the scriptures where *imagination* is mentioned, then thoughts, and then the heart. It is indeed through *the imaginations of the thoughts of the heart* that we find the key to The Kingdom of Heaven. Yet, this key is found by eliminating the spectrum of negative imagery—known in these scriptures as the imaginations of thoughts of the evil heart.

- Jeremiah 3:17: "At that time they shall call Jerusalem the throne of the LORD; and all the nations shall be gathered unto it, to the name of the LORD, to Jerusalem: neither shall they walk any more after the imagination of their evil heart."

I predict that this prophecy is about to be fulfilled in the oncoming millennium. The goal of this book is to be part of this wonderful era. The time is approaching when we will walk no more in the imaginations of our evil hearts, and Imagination Control Therapy can provide a workable format to encourage God's love and intentions into the *imaginations of the thoughts of the heart of the people.* Jerusalem is known in metaphysics as the habitation of peace. As we each find peace within ourselves, we will walk no more in the imaginations of our evil heart.

• Jeremiah 7:24: "But they hearkened not, nor inclined their ear, but walked in the counsels and in the imagination of their evil heart, and went backward and not forward."

I especially love the way the above verse very vividly describes evil imaginations causing people to go backward and not forward. This is exactly what occurs with the creation of negative imagery. The mind is misaligned with the Mind of God in this condition and therefore suffering the illusion of separation from God. We then have no direction to go but backward.

• Jeremiah 9:13-14: "Because they have forsaken my law which I set before them, and have not obeyed my voice, neither walked therein; But have walked after the imagination of their own heart, and after Baalim, which their fathers taught them."

Walking in the imagination of our own heart is referring to the negative imagery born of our illusion of separation from God. Separated, we are deluded to think of ourselves as individualized, eliminating considerations as one of The Whole.

• Jeremiah 11:8: "Yet they obeyed not, nor inclined their ear, but walked every one in the imagination of their evil heart: therefore I will bring upon them all the words of this covenant, which I commanded them to do; but they did them not."
• Jeremiah 13:10: "This evil people, which refuse to hear my words, which walk in the imagination of their heart, and walk

after their gods, to serve them, and to worship them, shall even be as this girdle, which is good for nothing."

Metaphysically, we can consider the imagination of our own heart to be those imaginations not of the Heart of God. This represents our individual status where we feel as though we are not a part of The Whole and are separate from each other and from God. In this state of mind, we are prone to worship false gods, that is, passionately devote our attention to spiritually meaningless desires and activities that are basically mere distractions.

- Jeremiah 16:12: "And ye have done worse than your fathers; for, behold, ye walk every one after the imagination of his evil heart, that they may not hearken unto me."
- Jeremiah 18:12: "And they said, There is no hope: but we will walk after our own devices, and we will every one do the imagination of his evil heart."
- Jeremiah 23:16-17: "Thus saith the Lord of hosts, Hearken not unto the words of the prophets that prophesy unto you: they make you vain: they speak a vision of their own heart, and not out of the mouth of the Lord. They say still unto them that despise me, The LORD hath said, Ye shall have peace; and they say unto every one that walketh after the imagination of his own heart, No evil shall come upon you."
- Proverbs 6:16-19: "These six things doth the LORD hate: yea, seven are an abomination unto him: A proud look, a lying tongue, and hands that shed innocent blood, an heart that deviseth wicked imaginations, feet that be swift in running to mischief, a false witness that speaketh lies, and he that soweth discord among brethren."
- Lamentations 3:60-61: "Thou hast seen all their vengeance and all their imaginations against me. Thou hast heard their reproach, O LORD, and all their imaginations against me."

The word imagination is used in a purely positive way when Mary is pregnant with Jesus and is speaking to Elisabeth, the

mother of John the Baptist, and says:
- Luke 1:51: "He (God) hath shewed strength with his arm; He hath scattered the **proud in the imagination of their hearts.**"

The dictionary defines the word proud as, *adj., 1. Thinking well of oneself. 2. Feeling or showing satisfaction. 3. Having a becoming sense of what is due oneself, one's position, or character: 5. Highly honorable, creditable, or gratifying: 7. Majestic: magnificent.*[4]

Creating highly honorable, creditable, majestic, and magnificent imagery aligns our minds with the God-Mind.

- Romans 1:21: "Because that, when they knew God, they glorified him not as God, neither were thankful; but became vain in their imaginations and their foolish heart was darkened."
- II Corinthians 10:3-5: "For though we walk in the flesh, we do not war after the flesh: (For the weapons of our warfare are not carnal, but mighty through God to the pulling down of strongholds;) **Casting down imaginations, and every high thing that exalteth itself against the knowledge of God, and bringing into captivity every thought to the obedience of Christ.**"

We see the word imagination used in a purely positive way, free of any negative implications, only with the conception of Jesus. " . . . He hath scattered the proud in the imagination of their hearts." Jesus' mission was to guide our consciousness into our inherent divinity, that ultimate divine potential within each of us, steering our consciousness away from a persistence to create the *imaginations of the thoughts of our evil hearts.* He is the resurrection, which includes resurrecting the mind—the imagination. Jesus was instructing us to use that divine spectrum of our thoughts, our positive and divine imagination.

What Other Scriptures Say

The fact that Jesus never says the word imagination yet implies it through analogies reveals to us the power of our imagination even by the spell of dumbfoundedness that was left upon the imaginations of those *without the knowledge of the mysteries of The Kingdom of Heaven.*

"Suffer little children; . . . such is The Kingdom of Heaven. Verily, I say unto you, Whosoever shall not receive The Kingdom of God as a little child, he shall not enter therein." Thus it is through our creation of positive imagery that we enter the Kingdom of Heaven on Earth. Ceasing the dwelling in and creation of negative imagery is how we retain The Kingdom of Heaven within our consciousness. Through faith, create imaginings based on the principles of serving mankind through brotherly love and accepting God as the Father and Mother through the indwelling Christ consciousness. Become a vehicle for the intention of God to flow through you by keeping imaginings positive and the mind is in Heaven though the body is on Earth.

Jesus starts His conclusion of chapter 6 of Matthew in verse 33 after explaining how God will provide our wants and needs. "But seek ye first The Kingdom Of God, and His righteousness; and all these things shall be added unto you." This is the revelation of God's divine plan. Put your faith and trust in God. Seek first the imaginations of the thoughts of the heart within the positive spectrum. Make it a top priority to create only positive imaginations *and all these things shall be added unto you.*

Matthew 6:34 says: "Take therefore no thought for the morrow; for the morrow shall take thought for the things of itself. Sufficient unto the day is the evil thereof." When we realize that when we become negative in emotion we are creating erroneous or evil, negative imaginations this verse becomes a dynamo of guidance to spiritual ascension.

Sufficient unto the day is the evil thereof is more than truth; it is a profound principle. It takes no in-depth study, no deep soul searching, no deep philosophical or metaphysical insights to practice this principle. Yet, practicing placing our focus and attention on the erroneous imaginings of each moment of the day inevitably results in deep study, deep soul searching, and deep metaphysical or philosophical insights.

This principle clarifies that an average mind can ascend spiritually equally as well as a highly trained, well-organized, efficient, highly scholastic, sophisticated mind that appears to develop a "well earned" spirituality. *Sufficient unto the day is the evil thereof* principle may be fulfilled easily by any mind that is not physiologically handicapped. *By taking thought, we cannot add one cubit to the stature of God.*

This reminds me of a statement Jimmy Stewart once said in a movie. "If a man wants to be successful and he is not real smart, he had better be real, real pleasant." A mind that focuses attention on the creation of positive imagery, thus the elimination of the evil of today, is applying a principle of consistently allowing God to manifest through this mind. This may not be a powerful flow of a saintly nature, yet it is a consistent flow nonetheless. How many times have we heard that it is not the mountain we climb that fatigues us, but the grain of sand in our shoe? The little negative imaginings that we consistently permit to enter into our consciousness are the grains of sand in our shoe.

Shall God manifest more abundance, more love, a more wonderful life experience into the life of a brilliant, metaphysical scholar than an uneducated person of low IQ who is consistently kind, understanding, and faithful? The key here in the answer is, as Charles Fillmore has elaborated, total thought alignment with the God-Mind. The brilliant metaphysical scholar may have moments of intense mystical inner knowing and insights, yet many moments of anger or "misaligned thoughts" from the God-Mind, thus violating the *Sufficient unto the day is the evil thereof* principle. If the humble uneducated person of low IQ is consistently nice, pleasant, kind, and understanding in all situations, he or she has fulfilled the requisite of the *Sufficient unto the day is the evil thereof* principle.

The point is that we do not have to be smart, mentally disciplined within a particular school of thought, well educated, or clever to seek first The Kingdom of God or Heaven and focus our attention away from our urge to create negative imagery.

When we examine the idea behind this concept, we find that

evil can be considered erroneous imagery—imaginations based on the illusion of separation from God. Sufficient unto the day are the errors in imagery. Our negative imagery is the beginning of our negative thought processes and indeed is erroneous, causing a misalignment with the God-Mind. We can also see in the preceding scriptures that Jesus is suggesting *we take no thought* for our needs and for tomorrow. I understand this as Jesus telling us to keep completely positive in thought, that is, keep our thoughts consistently aligned with the God-Mind, yet we should let go of the illusion that certain mental strategies born of anxiousness will improve God's ability to provide for us. If we do this, tomorrow will take care of itself and our desires will be added to us.

Although it may be true that brilliance of mind, education, and schools of thought such as metaphysics and philosophies may bring more success in material considerations than a lesser mind may achieve, the real success in life is found in our spiritual ascension. And this usually manifests as much if not more good into mankind. Success is a *feeling, a state of mind,* and the ability to love and serve, not the accumulation of material wealth.

Jesus tells us in Matthew 5:28 that we commit adultery in our heart when we look upon a woman with lust. He was referring to our imagery being lustful. Jesus knew the chain of events that follow our imagery affect our heart. As we think, so we are in our heart.

Comprehending the principle behind *Sufficient unto the day is the evil thereof* opens the door to an extremely stable foundation in which we can establish our metaphysical, philosophical, and spiritual understandings. Truth becomes much less complicated, even simple.

All that we need is provided for us. In order for us to receive what God has provided us, all we need to do is focus our attention on our mind movie and create a script with no negative scenes. This is total thought alignment with the Mind of God. Doing this on a moment-to-moment basis is the fulfillment of *Sufficient unto the day is the evil thereof.*

By consistently rebuking erroneous thought, each and every time as it comes to the mind, we sustain a level of consciousness that uncovers God's good and we discover the blessings intended for us, and we remain clear minded enough to receive them. This is truly claiming our good today and not being concerned about the future.

When we rebuke erroneous thought, we are, in effect, seeking first The Kingdom of God, which is found within us in the spectrum of positive imagery, thought, and emotion. Seeking The Kingdom of God first and sufficiently removing erroneous imaginings work hand in hand to reveal the glory of God and the Christ potential in our lives. To me, *these scriptures represent the heart of truth.*

Jesus said in John 10:9: "I am the door; by me if any man enter in, he shall be saved, and shall go in and out, and find pasture. He again speaks of The kingdom Of God in Luke 17:20-21, And when he was demanded of the Pharisees, when The Kingdom of God should come, he answered them and said, **The Kingdom of God cometh not with observation: Neither shall they say, Lo here! or, lo there! for, behold, The Kingdom of God is within you.**"

When Jesus said in the explanation of the parable of the sower, Matthew 13:19: "When any one heareth the word of the kingdom, and understandeth it not, then cometh the wicked one, and catcheth away that which was sown in his heart," He was referring to the average Christian who can believe in His teachings with all his or her heart, but never attains illumination because the wicked one, our negative self, steals away the Word. Our negative self has us create negative imaginings of us as separate from God resulting in the flow of the Holy Spirit through us being restricted by the errors of our negative mind. "And when he sowed, some seeds fell by the way side, and the fowls came and devoured them up," (Matthew 13:4). . . . "This is he which received seed by the way side" (Matthew 13:19). Because so many Christians do not attain enlightenment, many have become superstitious and fearful about the thoughts of it. Many consider it a form of the occult, a heresy, the work of the devil. When we *receive* instruction in ceasing the creation of negative imaginings, we are not seeds that have fallen by the wayside.

I have heard preachers' sermons that were totally filled with the word of God and positive thought, but there was just enough superstition, suspicion, fear tactics, and holier than thou attitude that all their divine thought was being undermined with these negative images. The negativism must stop for the change to take place. If a church uses suspicion and fear tactics to frighten people into repentance it may control the people's behavior, but spiritual advancement is greatly inhibited because, however suppressed in the name of goodness, a great deal of their imaginings are still negative.

The physical change in neurotransmitters happens with many devout Christians. They just do not think of it as enlightenment. They feel gifted or filled with the Holy Spirit and others see them this way. Many succumb to the notions that they cannot attain such spiritual levels; those high levels of spirituality are out of reach unless you are "gifted." This cannot be further from the truth.

When we clean out all negativity from our imaginings, we then will naturally become righteous as our divinity manifests, filling us with light. This opens the door to the possibility that the human body could evolve to the point that it could live a thousand years or more. This sounds fantastic, I know, but we know thought can kill us quickly. Black magic works by the victim's negative imaginations becoming so engulfed in fear that the result is death. Why should positive, divine thought not give us longevity? I have begun to wonder if the stories of beings centuries old living in the Himalayan Mountains are more than legend. Humanity may evolve to this point when generation after generation persists in positive divine thought and this becomes encoded in our DNA.

In Matthew, chapter 6, Jesus really tries to tell us how things work. I have always been intrigued by this chapter and have marveled at the clarity of His words. Let us examine The Lords Prayer in Matthew 6:9-13: ". . . Our Father who art in Heaven, Hallowed be thy name, Thy kingdom come. Thy will be done in Earth as it is in Heaven. Give us this day our daily bread, and forgive us our debts, as we forgive our debtors. And lead us not into temptation, but deliver us from evil: for Thine is the kingdom, and the power, and the glory, for ever, Amen."

Only when we use our positive imagination can we picture things being done on Earth as they are in Heaven. But this is what the Lord wants of us—for things to be on Earth as they are in Heaven. It is not as difficult as it may sound to manifest this concept here, on Earth. When our minds dwell in the imagery of our positive spectrum and manifest positive emotion, and we realize this is the beginning of The Kingdom of God, we can then do on Earth as it is in Heaven. For as we become aware that God's divine ideas manifest through the positive imaginations of the thoughts of our hearts, we not only strike up a partnership with God, we begin to dwell in our minds and hearts with God. And God then becomes apparent in our minds, our hearts, our deeds, our motives, our intentions, our love, our love of life and our very essence of existence. And He can unveil His divine plan to us unhindered by our negativity. Life begins to have an interaction in the way God intended it to be.

Charles Fillmore interpreted *lead us not into temptation* in verse 13 in chapter 6 of Matthew as *leave us not in temptation*. This removes the idea that God actually leads us into temptation. Dr. George M. Lamsa, in his translation of the New Testament, *The Modern New Testament From the Aramaic*, writes verse 13 as, "And do not let us enter into temptation, but deliver us from error." Lamsa speaks the native tongue of Aramaic and claims to have a great knowledge of the linguistic intent and idioms of two thousand years ago. He also concludes that Jesus did not depict God as a leader into temptation.

The following scriptures conceptualize the indwelling Christ and God within all of us. As we grow to understand this concept, we can surrender to the manifesting process of God expressing through us.

- John 6:56: "He that eateth my flesh, and drinketh my blood, dwelleth in me, and I in him."
- John 14:17: "Even the Spirit of truth; whom the world cannot receive, because it seeth him not, neither knoweth him: but ye know him; for he dwelleth with you, and shall be in you."
- Romans 8:11: "But if the Spirit of him that raised up Jesus from the dead dwell in you, he that raised up Christ from the dead shall also quicken your mortal bodies by his Spirit that dwelleth in you."
- 1 Corinthians 3:16: "Know ye not that ye are the temple of God, and that the Spirit of God dwelleth in you?"
- II Timothy 1:14: "That good thing which was committed unto thee keep by the Holy Ghost which dwelleth in us."
- 1 John 3:24: "And he that keepeth his commandments dwelleth in him, and he in him. And hereby we know that he abideth in us, by the Spirit which he hath given us."
- 1 John 4:12: "No man hath seen God at any time. If we love one another, God dwelleth in us, and his love is perfected in us.
- 1 John 4:15: Whosoever shall confess that Jesus is the Son of God, God dwelleth in him, and he in God."
- 1 John 4:16: "And we have known and believed the love that God hath to us. God is love; and he that dwelleth in love dwelleth in God, and God in him."

If it can be established that God dwells within us, we can also eliminate everywhere He may not be within us. God does not dwell within us in a secret place that we do not know about. God dwells within us as the very force of life within us. And He expresses through us within our positive spectrum *of the imaginations of the thoughts of our hearts.* By consistently remaining in touch with the expression of God through us in *the imaginations of the thoughts of our hearts,* we can see Him on the screen of our mind and feel Him through our nervous system. He becomes a part of us, a part of our thought processes; and here we can unify with Him.

When we express our positive imagery, we can feel God's

presence. When we are kind or charitable, we feel the unity of our thoughts with God as God's will is expressing itself through us. God expresses through us in the highest quality experiences within the positive *imaginations of the thoughts of the heart of the people,* in our divine imaginations, in our divine thoughts, in our divine heart, and in the creation of positive divine imaginings based on love.

Mat. 6:22 says: "The light of the body is the eye: if therefore thine eye be single, thy whole body shall be full of light." The metaphysical idea behind this statement is focusing on the Good that can be found in everything. This single way of seeing is refusing to permit the focus of our attention to dwell in the limitations of life. We need to focus on only the Good in life, the Good in all situations. It's a difficult concept, yet we need not create more images of limitation and add to the negative images that created the appearance of limitation in the first place. Or, in situations out of our control, such as natural disaster, we can focus on the spiritual opportunities that are presented rather than focusing on the disaster itself. This is not to say that we do not acknowledge negative situations. We focus on the Good after we intelligently and spiritually appraise a situation and acknowledge its negative qualities. We then proceed to focusing our attention on what Good there is to find while being aware of negative perspectives. Through this awareness, we can be compassionate to others.

As we consistently focus our attention only on the positive in life, we develop an ability to urge positive things into manifestation where they may not physically exist.

The Greek word *haplous,* translated as *single,* may imply *clear* in its figurative sense. In order to see things clearly, universal laws or principles cannot be in violation. We see things clearly when our consciousness is not suffering the illusion that it is separated from God. This separation occurs as negative imagery.

Our whole body becomes filled with light, that is, illumination, when we continuously create positive imagery. This is truly co-creation with God.

Mat. 6:23-24 goes on to say: "But if thine eye be evil, thy whole body shall be full of darkness. If therefore the light that is in thee be darkness, how great is that darkness! No man can serve two masters; for either will he hate the one, and love the other; or else he will hold to the one, and despise the other. Ye cannot serve God and mammon."

Mammon is symbolic of the desires of the flesh. Through riches, we may attain all carnal desires. To *serve* mammon would have no other purpose than this implies. Serving mammon symbolizes our illusion of separation from each other and God. It is only through this separation that we begin to lust after the material things that appear to fulfill our individual concerns. By becoming a part of the whole, we cultivate the desire to serve humanity.

Luke 2:29-31 states: "And seek not ye what ye shall eat, or what ye shall drink, neither be of doubtful mind, for all these things do the nations of the world seek after; and your Father knoweth that ye have need of these things, but rather seek ye the Kingdom of God; and all these things shall be added unto you."

In Him our needs will be fulfilled. He will provide and life will interact in His divine way as He intended it. His goodness will come our way without us seeking. Just use your imagination!

- "He who has imagination without learning has wings and no feet." —Joubert
- "Imagination rules the world." —Napoleon
- "The soul without imagination is what an observatory would be without a telescope." —H. W. Beecher
- "Imagination is the eye of the soul." —Joubert
- "The poet's eye, in a fine frenzy rolling, doth glance from Heaven to Earth, from Earth to Heaven; and as imagination bodies forth the forms of things unknown, the poet's pen turns them to shape, and gives to airy nothing a local habitation and a name; such tricks hath strong imagination." —Shakespeare

• "The imagination of man can act not only on his own body but even on others and very distant bodies. It can fascinate and modify them; make them ill, or restore them to health."
—Avicenna

[1] *The Random House Dictionary of the English Language,* The Unabridged Edition. New York, Random House.

[2] Reprinted from *Stranger by the River* by Paul Twitchell by permission of the copyrightholder, ECKANKAR, P.O. Box 27300, Minneapolis, MN 55427, www.eckankar.org.

[3] *Ibid;* page 150.

[4] *Thorndike Barnhart Comprehensive Desk Dictionary,* New York, Doubleday.

Emotion

2 Corinthians 10:3-5: *For though we walk in the flesh, we do not war after the flesh: (For the weapons of our warfare are not carnal, but mighty through God to the pulling down of strong holds;) Casting down imaginations, and every high thing that exalteth itself against the knowledge of God, and bringing into captivity every thought to the obedience of Christ.*

Emotion is defined in the dictionary as: *n. 1. An affective state of consciousness in which joy, sorrow, fear, hate, or the like, is experienced, as distinguished from cognitive and volitional states of consciousness. 2. Any of the feelings of joy, sorrow, fear, hate, love, etc. 3. Any strong agitation of the feelings actuated by experiencing love, hate, fear, etc., and usually accompanied by certain physiological changes, as increased heartbeat, respiration, or the like, and often overt manifestation, as crying, shaking, etc. 4. An instance of this. 5. That which causes or affects such a reaction.*[1]

Emotion is the tangible way we experience and feel our imagery within the wonders of God's creation. Emotion is the physical manifestation of imagination. Emotion literally shows us the affects of our imaginations—past and present. Unlike other animals, humans are thought to be unique in possessing the faculty of imagination. As God expresses Himself in the animal kingdom, we can say that animal emotion is a manifestation of God's imagination in the form of instinct. The emotions of animals are entirely determinative. What is going on in their environment determines their reaction. We, as humans, have the ability to rise above our animal nature by controlling our response to our environment through focusing our attention on our substrative mental process of imagery, creating positive imaginings regardless of the appearance of our environment.

We have all heard many times that mind and body are one. Emotion and imagination are one in the same way body and mind are one. Think of emotion and imagination as parallel Universes in different dimensions. Yet, emotion is only the tip of the iceberg within the physical dimension. Emotions set off a domino effect of further chemical reactions within the body that virtually register our initial imagery within our every cell.

It has been long believed by many that we are, in many ways, helpless to our emotions. Yet you know that you are not helpless as to what you imagine. Emotional control, educating intelligence into our emotions, is a highly esteemed virtue. By focusing your attention on what you imagine and run through your mind, you can master emotional control and emotional intelligence.

The Science

Researchers are consistently uncovering an immense amount of information regarding the chemistry of the brain and body. The electro-chemical nature of the body is coming more and more to light. It is now estimated that the body is experiencing literally thousands of chemical reactions per second to run itself and give us the ability to think.

Imagery, the substrate of all thought, is now known to be a perfect example of telekinesis, the mind moving matter. Each image creates intricate electric and chemical patterns designed to conduct thought in the physical body. Imagery moves specific atoms and molecules to create neurotransmitters and neuropeptides within the body to carry specific messages. These specific chemical molecules, causing the sensation of emotions or feelings within the body as well as performing other functions, also govern the emotional center of the brain. As we feel our thoughts, this combination of imagery and emotion gives the appearance of substantiating our reality.

The king of our emotional center is the amygdala gland. There is a vast neuron highway between it and the prefrontal lobes in the brain. The prefrontal lobes are the emotional executive center, attempting to implement good judgment and understanding. Acting as the brain's alarm, the amygdala can override the prefrontal lobes to deal with the "emergency" it thinks it is handling. On the other hand, the prefrontal lobes have a hard time overriding the actions of the amygdala under intense emotional potency.

Imagery patterns are stored in our memories as neuron firing patterns. Neuron brain cells fire in patterns using millions and billions of cells, creating intricate and immense pattern networks for a single image. Each time a particular image is created these same neurons fire. In the 1940s, psychologist Donald Hebb discovered that neuron cells involved in these patterns experience neurological changes that make it easier for them to communicate in relation to firing patterns. Thus, neurons enhance their connections directly related to the pattern they are involved in as opposed to patterns they are not involved in. These have been termed Hebbian connections and are long lasting. Neurons develop enhanced firing habits through these Hebbian connections.

People who demonstrate control emotionally have developed Hebbian connections that make it easier to assume control over the amygdala through the executive faculty of the prefrontal lobes. Those of us with a more active amygdala need more practice to develop their neurological furrowing toward the executive prefrontal lobe override ability.

It is the amygdala that is our aggression center as well as emotional memory. Its stimulation can cause hostile, angry emotions. Its removal, in cases of severe epilepsy, has resulted in a sort of emotional amnesia. The amygdala helps stimulate the hypothalamus into initiating The Fight or Flight Response by causing a flood of hormones and catecholamines such as epinephrine, norepinephrine, cortisol, and corticosteroids (stress hormones) to be released within the body. These chemicals stay in the body for hours and a build up sets the stage for the amygdala to have a hair trigger and they poison the system.

The amygdala also stores emotional potency of both negative and positive experiences. Emotional potency returns as the subconscious very quickly (and very sloppily) associates the present factors in a situation with past similar factors. For example, if you are involved in a car wreck and a loved one is severely hurt, there are many possible factors. Let's say there is the sound of the ambulance, the smell of gasoline on the road, the smell of first aid supplies, blood, a train going by blowing its horn, and you are very hurt and upset with a high degree of emotional potency. In the future, you may feel upset because you hear a train go by blowing its horn. If more than one factor is involved, such as the train horn and the smell of gasoline, more emotional potency is factored into the present. This may all occur at a greater or lesser degree, but these associations are made and calculated into emotional potency by the amygdala.

Perhaps the greatest associations made by the subconscious mind are regarding the physiology factors of emotional or mind states. Studies have established that facial expressions, body language, vocal tones, and general physiology are universal within humanity. When you desire a change in feeling, you not only need to change your imaginings; it is necessary to reinforce positive imaginings with the physiology naturally associated with desired emotional and mind states. Mind and body are one and must harmonize to halt conflicting urges, influences, and internal messages.

Just as imaginings directly affect emotions, moods, states of mind, and the way we carry our body, the inversions are equally true. The way you carry your body sends internal messages of association to the imagination regarding states of mind, moods, and emotions. You can get a tremendous lift by standing up, reaching up at the sky, and smiling. Do this as you create a wonderful, enthusiastic scene in your mind movie and you feel great.

Probably our greatest problem with the amygdala is that we don't seem to register the emotional potency in the positive spectrum to as high a degree as in the negative spectrum. Rarely do loving, kind emotions contain the level of potency that fear and anger have. You could find a million dollar treasure and not produce the emotional juice that comes with being backed up against a wall by two angry Dobermans ready to tear your head off. Thus, we begin to subconsciously associate more emotional potency with fear and anger than with love. Of course, the whole system did not evolve to protect us from love. The emotional system evolved to protect us from harm, and emotion evolved to relieve us of the chore of lengthy contemplation.

Emotion is what you have (or thought you have) had to do in the past distilled into a feeling or urge to facilitate speed of action. Feelings and emotions are designed to save you the trouble of contemplation, of decision-making, of thinking. It is comparable to having an artificial intelligence program running within us that bases our response to our environment on past responses. All imaginings are stored and imbedded within the body to be utilized as future response urges through feelings and emotions. This can be compared to an artificial intelligence putting forth a virtual reality. The suggested imaginings and feelings seem very real.

Although the human body suffers severe punishment through the affects of negative imagery, it is virtually a perfect organism for exhibiting and developing higher levels of consciousness. There is nothing left out of the program. We can choose to experience feelings of a wide spectrum of imaginings—from love to hate—or anywhere within the spectrum of emotion from loneliness to a divine experience. All are available through our choices in imagery. It is all in the body's chemical program to be activated with the governing image patterns and associated physiology. We are chemically rewarded emotionally with comfortable, joyous feelings that result in optimal health when we engage in positive imagery, and smile. We suffer negative chemical consequences in the form of uncomfortable emotions that result in ill health when we engage in negative imagery and permit our physical posture to deteriorate.

There is now speculation that the mind and body are so

closely related that it is almost as though the entire body is actually a brain with our brain acting as the body/brain center. Research now reveals that neuropeptides and neurotransmitters created in the brain are also produced in organs and other areas of the body as well as in the immune system. There is speculation that the immune system may act as thousands of pituitary glands throughout the body. Is it possible that our organs help the body to think? We know that negative thought shows up as illness in the organs. We get gut feelings. Our heart can ache. We feel things in the pit of our stomach. Fear and stress suppress the immune system.

I viewed a documentary where a single cell was removed from a woman and placed in an electrolyte with a meter hooked up to it. The cell donor's emotion could actually be recorded on this meter hooked to this single cell. The donor was taken twelve miles away from the cell, yet the cell was aware of her emotions proving that the body and mind have a subtle telepathy with each and every cell. Our images are communicated throughout the body to the cellular level by electric signals, chemical messengers, and telepathy.

In another experiment with plant life, a grove of oak trees was infested with a strain of bagworms to observe the affect on the trees. The oak trees systematically raised the tannin levels in two out of three of the trees' leaves to make the leaf harder for the bagworms to digest. It is speculated that the tannins in the third leaf are not raised so the bagworms will seek these leaves, causing more movement, attracting birds. Amazing as it may seem, another grove of oak trees across the same meadow and not infested with these bagworms also raised the tannin levels in two out of each three leaves. How? These oak trees definitely exhibited evidence of a subtle telepathy connecting them.

Experiments in quantum physics now reveal that even matter has this subtle telepathy. Many physicists now believe that the entire Universe conducts itself like a huge mind. Electron experiments prove that the mind of the observer affects what the experiment reveals. Some physicists speculate that there may be stored information within the structures of atoms, possibly within the electromagnetic force fields.

Molecules of living tissue seem to contain information concerning the organism that synthesized molecules do not have. A neurotransmitter that is synthesized will not cause the same effect on the body as an identical molecule that was created by the body.

James Lovelock, creator of The Gaia Theory, has provided strong evidence that the presence of life and the way it interacts, manipulating its environment as well as adapting to it, suggests that the Earth conducts itself like a living breathing organism—regulating itself. After releasing his findings, he discovered that two out of three letters of response to his theory were of a spiritual nature. There was a great response from American Indians, who have told us all along that the Earth is alive.

Physics and biophysics are proving that our minds, bodies, the Earth, and the Universe are connected. They are demonstrating that spirituality is consistent with nature and the Universe. Our bodies are literally blueprinted for spiritual development, and quantum physics now parallels in many ways with the Eastern philosophies of spirituality.

So now that we have this information available to us, why do we not teach it in our schools and churches? Perhaps we are accumulating information so quickly in this computer age that it is hard to keep up with all of it. Becoming aware that this information exists by reading a book like this is a start. I challenge anyone to research the validity of this information. If you do, you will find that it is true and published by credible physicists, biologists, and researchers. The more you research, the more you will discover this truth.

Haven't we all known for years that a nature experience revives us? Trees, flowers, and chirping birds have been a reviving breath of fresh air since time immemorial. Nature, in all its wonder, is soothing and rejuvenating.

The Organic Artificial Intelligence Program

If we realize that feelings and emotions are organic artificial intelligence programs designed to save us the trouble of contemplation, we can gain an insight into how this program works within the mind/body connection.

The body's emotional system usually has the first word in our response. As the brain receives sensual input, it scans for previous similarities within our life experience and suggests a response in the form of a feeling (emotional urge) and imaginings. It is extremely important to note that this first impulse toward what we imagine and how we should behave is dominant within the mind/body connection for a second or two. During this period, we experience a virtual reality put forth by the artificial intelligence program. Only after this delay can the prefrontal lobes execute willful thought over the first impulse. Because the virtual reality seems so real, it is quite easy to surrender to its suggestions. Yet, until a high level of emotional potency comes about, we have the options of a prefrontal lobe override.

For example, we may have words with a co-worker and our first impulse is to yell or even hit. We subsequently have the ability to exert conscious willful thought to override the impulse. "I may be fired if I argue or fight at work."

The organic artificial intelligence is much more complicated than the above example. It contains our evolutionary responses in the form of instincts, reflex responses, and basic nature. It also contains our habitual behavior and conditioned responses as well as a complete record of how we have responded in past situations. So, your first impulse and first imaginings may be quite off target once you have decided that you desire to change the way you respond to life.

When we are trying to cultivate more loving and kind responses in our interactions, it is necessary to ignore an impulse of negative imaginings and negative behavior. It is the supporting thoughts in regard to the first impulse that results in surrender to negativity. Supporting thoughts validate the virtual reality. At the start of an impulse, the Christ potential within you is found within the prefrontal lobes and it is on a second or two delay. Once you have successfully developed your override ability for a time, you begin to install a total love response program into your body's artificial intelligence—the emotional system.

Emotional Intelligence

In his books *Emotional Intelligence* and *Working With Emotional Intelligence,* Daniel Goleman dissects emotion and the brain/body system into one of the most remarkable works on understanding our emotions that has probably ever been produced. To me, the most remarkable aspect of Goleman's work is his formula for the success of star players in the business world: one third is expertise and IQ and the other two thirds are emotional intelligence.

I first read *Working With Emotional Intelligence.* Halfway through the book it dawned on me that emotional intelligence is a more scientific, non-spiritual way of defining the basics of spirituality—developing empathy, caring, courtesy, being nice, thinking before you act, and basing our thinking on ethics, values, and character. Five hundred corporations studied their star players to conclude this formula. Even in the military, the ideal environment for the "hardball" attitude, the star players were the ones with emotional intelligence as their governing influence. Corporate America is discovering that the "corporate lion" attitude is less cost-efficient in the long run. A tight economy is mandating that people learn to work together as a team and forget the "me first" attitude.

Emotional Intelligence cites study after study on emotion from infancy to adulthood, putting forth explanations on how emotions are formed and developed over childhood and a lifetime. Basically, we develop emotions to save us time from lengthy contemplations and considerations. Instead, the past is compared, past emotions are compared, and we get a feeling, an urge—emotion—the influence to act. In other words, emotions are your experiences of the past thinking for you, saving you time.

The problem comes about when suddenly you find that your emotions, your responses are less than appropriate, less than intelligent, less than desirable by you or others around you. Then it's time to start thinking again and it is not easy to argue with chemical urges the body puts forth.

Inadvertently, the heart of the studies on emotional intelligence boils down to imaginational intelligence—thus, the term *Imagintelligence*. The imagination is the first manifestation in the mind/body connection within our thought processes. Intervening at this level halts the full physiological process of emotional urge and influence within the imagination. In other words, if you don't willfully run positive imaginings in your mind, your emotional storehouse has a few suggestions. And, as emotions become more potent these suggestions become commands.

Through persistence, repetition, and developing potency within the positive emotional recordings, you can educate your emotions with positive God-aligned imaginings.

The associations your mind, emotions, moods, and mind states make with your physiology provide you with a wonderful edge to reinforce any desired state you create with your imagination. The importance of harmony between mind and body cannot be emphasized enough. The imagination is the beginning of your personal world; your physiological appearance is the end of your personal world. Aligning the beginning and the end, mind and body, results in the way you feel, in the middle—feeling great—feeling anyway you care to choose.

Nature has seemed to provide us with a revision program within our physiology. Although feelings and emotions attempt to dictate our responses to environmental stimulation that build through similar circumstances and associations, there is a natural update program that runs physiologically. As thousands of our brain cell neurons naturally die each day, dendrite growth establishes new connections between the surviving cells. The new dendrite growth is in response to our environmental responses and perspectives that we internalize. As we change, these changes are reflected within the new dendrite growth and become part of our neural programming. The importance of holding positive imagery in the mind cannot be stressed enough since our renewed mind states are consistently becoming a part of our new neural network. In this way, the mind/body connection copes with the past and present by basing its response on our past life experiences while our renewed neural connections are based on our present responses that include the prefrontal lobe override.

Emotions Are Contagious

Have you ever watched a flock of birds or a herd of deer all move together in unison after being spooked? All it takes is one animal to become afraid and the rest immediately assume the same emotion. Evolution instilled this into life in order to enhance survival through the herd or flock moving as a single unit. As humans, we are also vulnerable to emotional contagion. When a few people smile in a group, the rest of the group is urged to smile also. When a few people become negative in a group, the rest of the group is vulnerable to also becoming negative.

We have built-in programs to detect the subtle cues of others that promote the same emotions to engage within us. Sudden movements, facial expressions, body language, and vocal tones of others urge the same response in us. When we resolve to create positive imagery in spite of appearances, we override this primitive urge to contract emotion.

Studies show that emotional awkwardness is a result of an inability to empathize with subtle cues from the physiology of others. Within a group, to fit in it is important to have the ability to return the appropriate physiological responses. An inability to respond with appropriate physiological cues leaves those around you feeling uncomfortable.

Re-chemicalization

Our imagery creates chemicals that create emotions that create the way we feel (our mental state), and contribute to our experience—all of which contributes to our state of health. So by choosing to create the appropriate imagery, we can feel any way that we desire. We are in control. Practicing and developing thought patterns through Imagination Control Therapy causes the body to "furrow in" neurological pathways by further developing Hebbian connections. *The more you practice, the easier it becomes to create the desired feeling, and the more intense you can make the desired effect.* The ability to create the feeling of total love, to feel God's love, to feel His divine presence is at your command through imagination control. It is not hard to get hooked on the wonderful feeling of God's love and His divine presence. It is so much better than our animal-like negative emotions. You can get to the point where, in order to get angry or experience hurt feelings, you literally feel as though the Holy Spirit is racing from your body to permit you to experience these base emotions. This is because in order for a change in feelings to take place, such as feeling joy and then becoming angry, the chemicals necessary to create the sensation of joy must change to the chemicals necessary to create the feeling of anger. This re-chemicalization of the body is very noticeable and uncomfortable. Imagery that is parallel with the intentions of the Holy Spirit must race from your mind to make room for the new angry imagery; the chemicals follow that create the feelings.

Feeling the Holy Spirit within you is not a different process than the other feelings our images create through our emotions in the body. We are a physical body. God has blueprinted a program within our bodies to feel his presence in the same way we feel everything else. The Holy Spirit enters first into our mind through our imagery; then the feeling is created throughout the body by the electro-chemical process of our physiology. Positive imagery has the potential of awakening more of our consciousness through the life enhancing chemicals produced by the body when we are engaged in divine positive imagery as opposed to negative thought that inhibits us while producing toxic chemicals.

The Mystic Emotion

Einstein said that he believed the mystic experience to be an emotion. That's quite a different twist on the conventional concept of mysticism. Yet, when you research the chemicalization process of emotion, the idea that mysticism may be developed in the same way as emotion is intriguing. By creating the images of a mystical experience we can develop the emotion of mysticism. We do this by visualizing being one with all of humanity and the Universe, swelling the greatest love we can muster bigger and bigger and visualizing it as encapsulating all life and the Universe, and visualizing ourself as powerful, spiritual, divine beings.

Re-chemicalization of the body occurs when the negative chemical content that is most regular (representing the sum total of your regular imagery) changes to mostly positive chemicals based on loving images. The chemical change is pretty much of a mystical experience in itself. When a mind is consistently creating or dwelling in negative imagery and suddenly shifts the regularly created imagery to positive, the change in chemicals is profound. Developing and expanding on the ability of your body to create the chemicals based on love expands your ability to become an expression of love resulting in a more unified feeling with God. Each time you take a step toward further unity with God, you have a mystical experience. Training the mind to return to this experience can be accomplished by reenacting the imagery within the mind. As you practice swelling your heart with love, your body develops its ability to produce love chemicals. Thus, love can intensify to higher and higher levels.

Emotion and Spirituality

Jesus said, *The Kingdom of God is within you.* The Kingdom of God, here on Earth, can be found within the wide spectrum of positive imagination and emotion. Actually, the positive emotion of all God's creatures is in this spectrum. Heaven can be found in the chirp of the bird, in the joy of the lion cubs at play, in the kindness of the dolphin, in the croak of the frog, in the soar of the eagle, in the purr of the kitten. The lowliest of beasts have positive and negative emotion, but instinct rather than imagination key in these emotions.

In the world of the beast, all things interact in nature's way, God's way, for God created nature. The beast cannot err in thought if it eats another beast. The beasts were not put here to become righteous and ascend spiritually. But we were put here to become more than beasts. Our spectrum of negative emotion is the beast within us, our consciousness on the animal plane.

And God created our emotions. How else could we *feel and experience* love if we had not the emotion? How else could we feel faith, trust, happiness, love of life, kindness, generosity, respect, adoration, freedom, pride, valiance, bravery, sweetness, honor, integrity, patience, understanding, benevolence, forgiveness, grace, and reverence? These emotions are the road signs to the gateway of The Kingdom of God, to the Holy Spirit dwelling within us, and are God's gateway to us. Our emotions tell us what type of images we are creating in our minds.

God created the flesh. God created flesh and the negative emotions dictated by the flesh came as a result of the needs and desires of the flesh and the illusion of separation from God. This is described in the Bible as the result of eating the fruit of the knowledge of good and evil. We can perceive this Bible concept as literal truth or as allegory, but the fact remains that our flesh is that of the mammal class and we have the same animal traits as our mammal family. And the flesh did conceive fear, hate, greed, lust, worry, false pride, anxieties, disgrace, foolishness, meanness, worldly attachments, disrespect, suspicion, and mistrust. These emotions are the gateway to the beast and are the beast's gateway to us. They simply are the primitive emotions of an animal. If we are to become Godlike in our spiritual ascension, it is necessary to rebuke using these emotions caused by our imaginings. We *feel and experience* these negative emotions as we dwell within the illusion of our being separated from God.

If we observe nature, we can see that it is common within the pack to struggle for dominance. Animals are prejudiced toward other packs and species. Animals can be very mean. They have wrath, vengeance, greed, and the likes of many of our negative emotions.

We are taught, as we develop, to place limitations on our emotions to stabilize our composure. We are also taught to place limitations upon our imaginations. But, our emotions and imaginations are persistent and somewhere in the apparent balance of control and persistence we find our composure, our disposition, our personality, our individuality, our essence.

The Bible describes good and evil to us as the different states of mind of which we may choose. The concept of good and evil is more conceivably described today as positive and negative when applied to emotion and imagination.

The terms positive and negative emotion were not popular language expressions to the individuals who authored the Bible. It is interesting to note that the word *emotion* is not used in the Bible at all. In searching for a mention of the word *feelings,* it appears twice, and the word *feel* appears six times in the King James Version. These more modern concepts of emotion and feelings are paralleled by the Biblical concepts, *the imagination of man's evil heart* and *proud in the imagination of the heart,* and also stated as *good* and *evil.*

When it is understood that the negative spectrum of human emotion and imagination is erroneous and taboo, and under no circumstances should the consciousness be permitted to enter into the creation of or dwelling within this dimension, you will be well on the road to enlightenment. There is no logical reason to resort to the use of the negative spectrum of imagination and emotion. The only thing it can offer is illogic, inconceivability, mental erasures, and an entire realm of irrational thought and action. Insanity, madness, frustration, pain, sins, and error are the products of the negative spectrum. When psychiatrists conceive that the imaginations of negative emotion are the root of many mental illnesses they will gain a deeper understanding of the mind.

For much too long, it has been considered healthy, for example, to "get that anger out of you" by using negative emotion as therapy for someone who has an immense amount of anger accumulated inside, buried away. Inasmuch as it may feel really good to express anger, research shows that expressing it does little for solving the problem. This is short-term relief only. Expressing anger helps a person build Hebbian connections in the neuron brain cells that make it easier to get angry. And, it is not good to suppress anger for the sake of being good. When we suppress emotion to behave well, we are only suppressing the emotion when we continue the imaginations connected with the emotion. Control the imagination and there is no emotion to suppress.

To express anger to rid one's self of it is certainly the long way to attaining the goal of healing the mind. The anger should merely be acknowledged and confronted. Forgiveness is the cure. If anger is so buried that it is denied or suppressed deep into the subconscious mind to the extent that the individual cannot remember because of erasures, then, perhaps, conventional psychiatric therapy is in order. But, therapy without a foundation of spirituality is slow. Spiritual therapy in accordance with the laws of the Universe will do far more good than conventional psychiatric therapy. Spiritual ascension is the healthiest path a mind can take. Imagination Control Therapy teaches us to practice changing our imaginations; thus changing our emotions and states of mind. If we continually practice the creation of positive imaginations resulting in positive emotions, the emotional charge buried deep within negative emotional memories will soon loose their influence or affect on us. By not concerning ourselves with the negative, it loses its power over us. By not granting attention to past pain and fear, the emotional charge within memories dissipates. Emotional charge within memories must have its fire tended by refueling it with present time emotional charge.

When unbearable memories are acknowledged and confronted, they are no longer buried and suppressed, waiting to influence us in the future. Yet, the purpose of confronting these memories is not to deal with them as much as it is to deal with why we so often return to them or use them for a frame of reference with which to base decisions and choices. Or, in some cases, we may discover why painful memories are running a negative emotional response loop program below our level of consciousness. If you have ever created a negative emotional response loop skit in your mind and played it over and over again, you may have it playing at a subconscious level. It shows up as a feeling that you get when you are around a similar situation or person that the skit is about. Creating positive imagery overrides these skits and dissolves them.

When negative images in our memories are overwritten with understanding, grace, benevolence, and forgiveness it will become a memory that can be called upon for knowledge and understanding so that we may further help others and ourselves. All of our negative experiences of darkness can be turned around to gain wisdom if a positive state of mind is reached and maintained through the consistent creation of positive imagery. Past negative emotional charge fizzles away when you do.

Spiritual progression can take place only when you gain a release from the deep-seated pain that is carried in the heart. This is remedied best with faith in God and forgiveness. To get mentally healthy, it is necessary to get spiritual. Getting spiritual releases us from our fear and pain. Surrender and letting go leads to the dissolution of our illusion of being separate from God. But surrender is a product of faith. It is hard to surrender without sufficient faith.

Counseling Insight

A person who understands these principles can gain the counseling insight needed to get to the heart of a troubled mind by listening closely to what the person needing help asks and states. Upon listening, a concept can be grasped to pinpoint exactly where a person's consciousness is dwelling, as well as what imaginations are prevalent, by keeping one simple perception always in mind: imagine all of the entire spectrum of emotion and imagination as a congress of senators. There are two parties, the negative party and the positive party. A clever person can pinpoint which senator is speaking by the statements and questions asked by the seeker or troubled soul. For they would not ask such questions or make such statements if a senator representing the certain emotion and imagination were not having the floor. This method will give you a lot of insight to the types of imaginations that a person is experiencing even when their emotions are being suppressed.

When you bring a person's attention to their imagery and help them develop an effective imagery management plan, they can discover their own areas of information highlighting and neglect, which will result in an understanding of their own delusions or misconceptions. By helping someone identify their negative imaginings, you can get them underway toward beginning to understand the importance of ceasing to create negative imagery. The best counseling is to teach a person that he or she is a powerful, spiritual, divine being who should take responsibility as being a co-creator with God in the Universe.

Confronting Inner Pain

Those who need help confronting their inner pain should receive that help. Faith is, again, the answer to non-confront. Confrontation of painful memories is of the utmost importance if one *cannot unplug* from the influence of these memories in the negative mind. We all desire to become a co-creator with God. And none of us really desires to be a negative creator in the Universe. When we forgive and realize that there is nothing to fear, we can confront fearful memories. But remember, it is necessary to confront memories only if they are a problem to the present.

Through confrontation and forgiveness, a person can clear their mind of the influences that painful memories of the past cause in today's living. The experience of forgiveness and being immersed in God's love consistently within the present defuses the emotional charge of past painful memories. It is necessary to confront only when the mind consistently drifts back uncontrollably to dwelling in the painful memories or creates negative imaginings based on these memories. Otherwise, just let them go. It is better to *unplug* from the use of the negative mind. We then can be unconcerned about our past to a degree that it no longer justifies creating or dwelling within negative imagery in the present. The negative mind is impossible to *fix* (though its influence can be reduced with conventional therapy) so it is much better to not attempt to deal with it if possible. Consistent replacement of attention on good, wonderful, positive imaginings results in an understanding and level of forgiveness that ceases the need to return the mind to past pain.

When you cannot stop using the negative mind, you need to deal with the thought processes that compel you to continue its use. You need to concentrate on *discovering what past memories contain high emotional charge and are influencing you* rather than on *how* you are being influenced. When you cannot stop dwelling in or creating negative imagery, discovering the negative memories that you are using as a frame of reference helps change the beliefs based on the experience. Incorporating new beliefs such as, *I AM a powerful, spiritual, divine being,* will establish the Truth into your belief system.

Faith is a great part of the equation in improving your belief system. Through an intellectual faith we can realize a deeper spiritual faith. Practicing faith improves the quality of faith. Faith, forgiveness, and understanding are wonderful positive imaginations that add to our portfolio of positive imagery. As powerful, spiritual, divine beings—faith, forgiveness, and understanding are important tools. You further develop the Hebbian connections involved in the neural web and the body learns to produce more easily the chemical messages of faith, forgiveness, and understanding.

There's No Logic in Irrational Behavior

We cannot rationalize the irrational behavior of others when their minds are riddled with negativities. We will never find any logic in irrationality. It simply is not there. This understanding is the first step to forgiveness and letting go. And with faith, understanding, and forgiveness the healing begins.

The senators of the negative spectrum are like demons. The imagery and emotions that originate within us without the consideration of God, as individuals separate from God, are the origin of negative imaginings. Usually, these imaginings are based on the survival or comforts of the individual without considerations regarding the Whole. We can say there are no such things as demons, devils, or the beast, but one thing is certain: there is an appearance of them within the qualities of our negative emotions. The Hebrew word *satan* is rooted in the idea of an adversary. Perhaps our adversary lives only in the imaginations of the thoughts of our heart—within our mind's negative spectrum. Aren't your negative imaginations and emotions your greatest adversary?

Those seeking relief who have buried the memories of past pain and mis-emotion deep into their subconscious mind will exhibit these buried memories through a variety of unwarranted fears, worries, miss-emotions, phobias, and compulsive-obsessive behaviors.

Through consistent positive divine imagery and emotion, painful memories will dissipate. Their Hebbian connections will "rust" and new neurological furrows will become prevalent. I must stress that ultimately we should not concern ourselves with the negative mind. It is best to unplug from it—to ignore it. Focus on your co-creatorship with God as your top priority. Bounce your consciousness to the positive spectrum. If we do not dwell on past painful memories they will have little concern to us. These undesirable image patterns must fire neurons to activate. Keeping them inactive simply stops their effect. You have to tend the fire of your past pain by giving it periodic attention to keep it burning.

When we attempt to rationalize from the negative spectrum of imagination and emotion, nothing will seem to work. The teacher cannot teach, the lover cannot love, the friend becomes an enemy, and strangers seem to be laughing at us, lurking to hurt us or rob us. We inadvertently misconstrue things people say, assign their intentions and motivations, and forget the good and remember the bad. Nothing works out. We are like the donkey with a child upon his back holding a pole with an apple dangling from a string in front of his nose. The donkey walks for miles to bite into the apple and it never gets any closer. We are like the rat in the cage that spins. He runs, and no matter how much effort he exerts he will always be in the same place. This is how the negative spectrum tricks us. This is how the lower nature tricks us. There is no logic to be found in illogical behavior or thought.

The Impervious, Impenetrable State of Mind

I realize that there are those of you out there that have had much more than your share of negativity instilled in you through life's web of hurt caused by negativity. But you must overcome with the help of staying in the positive spectrum of imagination and emotion by placing your faith and trust in God. The book of Job is probably the finest example of a human being entering an impervious state of reverence and loyalty to God. No matter what life cast upon him, he never lost his loyalty to God. His state of reverence and loyalty was IMPERVIOUS, IMPENETRABLE. All things were given to him in the end. Job did become negative in his imaginings many times, and this added to his own misery. When we understand that he was given his every desire in the end, it becomes apparent that his self-induced misery was for nothing. When you achieve this same degree of being impervious and impenetrable within a positive state of mind as Job did regarding his reverence and loyalty to God, you have risen above the lower self. You have attained enlightenment. Everything is OK. You can accept life's dramas and turn things around to your benefit.

Enlightenment is basically an emotion, the spectrum of positive emotion—love. By the consistent practice of expressing positive, enlightened emotion, the brain builds the Hebbian connections that cause it to be come easier and easier to persist in this type of imagery. This also results in the body becoming more and more efficient in creating the chemicals necessary to produce the sensations of love-based imagery, thoughts, and feelings. We have all witnessed people have a fit of temper. During a fit of anger, the body most proficiently creates all the chemicals necessary to instantly transform a person into a seething expression of temper. We can develop our bodies to instantly transform into extremely loving expressions with even greater ease and efficiency. How you choose to respond to situations is your decision. How your body develops its response ability is based on your choice of imagery and its resulting emotion. When you look for every reason you can imagine to be loving and kind, you find them. And you can enjoy persistent peace by being impervious to negative appearances.

No Justifiers

To enter a state of enlightenment, it is necessary to clear your mind of any notion that it is justifiable to resort to any imagination and emotion of the negative spectrum. Spiritual ascension will be inhibited if you do. You can kick and scream like a small child and justify all you want to that you may need to use these emotions and have every right to them, but your ascension toward enlightenment will be inhibited if you do. There are no situations where an expression of love is inferior to negativity.

One lad insisted to me that his very physiology caused him to lust after women and it was quite out of his control due to hormones. He furthered debated that it was natural to lust after women in our youth and that it would be unnatural to suppress these tendencies. I tried to explain that the path of spiritual ascension is not attained through the flesh. I further explained that although it is natural to have the sexual urge, it is not spiritually beneficial to lust after many women and this will work directly against spiritual ascension. Sex need not be eliminated in your life as many priests, gurus, and masters have practiced, but it definitely needs to be put in a proper ethical perspective.

Could a lad not experience the sexual act and still keep his mind in a positive ethical state? I should think so. The sexual act, when founded on honor, respect, integrity, pride, understanding, faith, and trust, takes on the wonder and majesty that God intended it to engulf. Those of you who are participating in sexual perversions are, in reality, trying to find relief from your negative self through the sexual act. I recently observed a documentary where psychologists had captured on film various people committing sexual deviations. These psychologists went on to explain how *normal* it was for two consenting adults to engage in such acts. One scene in particular was of a man and his wife. The man was lying across his wife's lap while she repeatedly struck him with a jockey's horsewhip on the buttocks hard enough to leave small welts. The pain sensations and the talk of him being a bad boy delighted her and him. The psychologists explained how this was a *normal* function between man and wife and should be considered as such by all. All that I could see was two grown adults desperately trying to relieve themselves of their negativity. It's surprising what a person will resort to in order to gain relief from their negative imaginings. This so-called *normal* activity is not mind illuminating activity on the path of enlightenment and is certainly not an expression of the indwelling Christ within us.

YOUR MIND MUST DWELL ONLY IN THE POSITIVE SPECTRUM OF IMAGINATION AND EMOTION AS A CO-CREATOR WITH GOD. IT MUST BECOME TABOO TO RESORT TO ANY USE OF THE NEGATIVE SPECTRUM UNDER ANY CIRCUMSTANCES. YOUR MIND MUST ENTER AN IMPERVIOUS STATE OF POSITIVE IMAGINATION AND EMOTION.

It is perfectly all right to realize the appearance of negativity—briefly. You need only run negative attributes or negative possibilities through your mind *once*. Now that you are aware of the attributes or possibilities, file them as *acknowledged* and then focus your attention on something good and wonderful.

You may ask, "If someone puts a gun to my head should I not fear?" My answer is no, although this is the most difficult end of the extreme. How can this be? If you place all your trust and faith in God, then dropping this body will be insignificant. And, if someone placed a gun to your head and you showed your fear he would feast upon your negativity. If you remained calm and told him that Jesus loved him and you loved him and you were kind to him, the odds of him pulling the trigger would become greatly reduced. He may fall to his knees and ask for help. Things of this nature have been documented. Scream in terror and you may never know. Ninety-nine and nine-tenths percent of the time, what stimulates our negativity are subtle threats or imaginations of threats. The Fight or Flight Response initiates over subtle things such as being told you are wrong, being stared at, facial expressions, or interpretations of intentions or motivations.

Tibetan Buddhism teaches that our journey in the afterlife directly after death is primarily based on the state of mind we are in at the time of death. To be able to die in peace is the ultimate expression of faith in God.

Many of you have been hurt terribly by others. You or your loved ones may have been subjected to murder, mental destruction, or have been involved in atrocities such as rape, the taking of hostages, kidnapping, terrible beatings. Some people are the victims of mean or mis-emotional people who scream in anger as though they were possessed by a demon. Others have been the victims of terrorism, where an individual takes special care to deeply instill fear and terror into your very essence. *These dramas may lead to the illusion that the fear, insecurity, hatred, anxiety, depression, anger, suspicion, mistrust, or worry that has been created should be placed upon an altar from which future choices and decisions should be based to protect you from danger in the future.* Again, I must warn you that this is the mind's way of protecting itself, but anything concluded when in a negative state of mind will cause an extreme lack of consideration of the whole of reality in the future resulting in data being highlighted and neglected.

There are no situations that justify creating or dwelling in negative imaginings. There are no situations where love-based imaginings are inappropriate. Even when it may be necessary to *appear* negative in extenuating circumstances, the imaginings can be based on love.

Challenge Your Imaginings

The mind scans past memories for similar situations it can compare to the present in order to evaluate choices. But the mind may run a negative skit that is based on insecurity, taking things too seriously, taking things personally, making mountains out of molehills, or any number of imagined threats. If your mind's infomercial is not a positive skit, challenge any information that may seem convincing. Most of the time you will find that a clear positive mind can reason away negative (or seemingly protective) information that is surfacing from past fear and pain. The rule of thumb is to think like an angel. Ignore the negative mind if at all possible. It has nothing of value to offer you other than relief from its influence. The memories of fear and pain held in the negative mind make a poor frame of reference on which to base decisions and choices.

Some of you may have erased painful memories of particular incidents and have only phobias relative to the factors involved in the incident. You must untangle the mysteries of your mind by confronting your greatest fears. By confronting I mean acknowledging and giving some attention to the fact that you are afraid, and creating a plan to grow past the fear. For example, if you are afraid of heights, acknowledge that you are afraid of heights rather than exceeding your capabilities and climb up high where you may freeze. Some people may make various excuses as to why they do not want to climb up high rather than admit they are afraid. Acknowledging and accepting yourself as you are is the first step in improving your mental programming. You may never have a need to be in a high place. Yet being afraid to stand on a chair may be too sensitive. There are so many areas to develop yourself that you need not get caught up in forcing yourself to skydive to conquer a fear of heights. Building faith in God is probably the strongest foundation you can work on that will eventually lead to your fears dissolving. Challenge any imaginings that are not based on love or parallel with the intention of God. When you do, you find that you are imagining you are separated from God and have lost your trust in Him as you create negative imagery.

Giving Attention

By giving some attention to your buried fears, your mind may either release the memories or they may become insignificant. But again, I must elaborate that *unplugging* from painful experiences is the preferred method of disconnecting from past pain. Give attention to the past only when you cannot separate it from the present, only when the past is affecting the present with too much influence.

Give some attention to changing your pain to forgiveness. If you were beaten severely, the person committing this act was acting out his own pain. The demons from this pain were in his or her imagination and he or she acted accordingly. A change in imagery results in a change in emotion.

A good perspective to gain understanding of demons is to imagine each and every negative emotion as a demon. The Bible makes many references to evil spirits in this respect, such as the *spirit of jealously, the spirit of whoredoms, the spirit of antichrist.* The entire spectrum of negative human emotion contains nothing more than the qualities of what we humans have conceived as demonic characteristics. Realizing this, we can begin to understand why we need to give full consideration to rebuking the use of these emotions and the imaginations connected to them. I find it amazing that within the collective consciousness of humanity there are archetypes of what a demon should be like. And they are like a magnified version of negative emotion.

As we give attention to permitting our consciousness to dwell in negative imaginings and emotions, what starts out as a mere thought grows into a resemblance of a demonic possession.

People who are consumed with hate, anger, lust, or greed take on a demonic characteristic. People who are giving attention to practicing love, faith, hope, trust, patience, and forgiveness to the point of divinity become angelic in their characteristics.

Within the spectrum of negative emotion everything just goes wrong. The teacher cannot teach, the lover does not love, and friends seem like enemies. We are likened unto a rat in the revolving cage. All our intentions are just out of reach and we are stuck. We may get caught up in immediate gratification, but in the long run we will wind up stuck in ignorance and delusions, miserable, sick, insane, or dead.

Bottom line: PERMITTING THE CONSCIOUSNESS TO CREATE OR DWELL IN ANY IMAGERY THAT RESULTS IN ANY EMOTION OF THE NEGATIVE SPECTRUM IS NOT JUSTIFIABLE UNDER ANY CIRCUM-STANCES BECAUSE THIS LEADS YOU DIRECTLY AWAY FROM SPIRITUAL ASCENSION!!!

- "All loving emotions, like plants, shoot up most rapidly in the tempestuous atmosphere of life." —Richter
- "Emotion which does not lead to and flow out in right action is not only useless, but it weakens character, and becomes an excuse for neglect of effort." —Tryon Edwards
- "Emotion has no value in the Christian system save as it is connected with right conduct. It is the bud, not the flower, and is of no value until it expands into the flower. Every religious sentiment, every act of devotion which does not produce a corresponding elevation of life, is worse than useless; it is absolutely pernicious, because it ministers to self-deception, and tends to lower the tone of personal morals." —Murray

---

[1] *The Random House Dictionary of the English Language,* The Unabridged Edition.

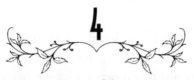

Imagintelligence

A man on Earth is a mortal god, and . . . a god in Heaven is an immortal man.

—Hermes

Emotional intelligence is becoming a major concept regarding the way we handle ourselves in our interactions with others. Daniel Goleman's books *Emotional Intelligence* and *Working With Emotional Intelligence* are perhaps the most in-depth compilations of recent studies and programs that incorporate intelligence into our emotions.

Goleman has well demonstrated that emotional intelligence is twice as important for success in the work place as IQ and expertise combined. Studies by 500 major corporations analyzing the attributes of their star employees concluded that the formula for excellence is one-third IQ and expertise and two-thirds emotional intelligence. When I examined this work, I discovered that emotional intelligence is applied spirituality— though it doesn't mention the spirituality that is actually at the heart of emotional intelligence.

Competition in the corporate economy has now tightened to the extent that the attributes of spirituality have become essential for survival. Emotional intelligence in the workplace results in greater teamwork and less stress, all the more so as we grasp the ways in which spirituality applies to emotional intelligence.

Empathy and self-awareness seem to be at the root of emotional intelligence. Empathy gives us an awareness of the feelings, needs, and concerns of others. Self-awareness gets us in touch with ourselves.

In brief, the body's emotional system relies on incoming data from the senses to activate a suggested feeling or emotional response. To describe this process, I have renamed the emotional system *organic artificial intelligence* since that is exactly what it is. Your entire life experience and the ways you have responded are distilled into an artificial intelligence program to save you the time and trouble of thinking. Thus your first impulse in a given situation is a physiologically-suggested response. We get a feeling or emotion and suggested thoughts. These feelings are a form of *virtual reality* because thoughts and feelings combined create a strong and convincing appearance of reality. All of your negative and positive experiences and responses are distilled and programmed into this first impulse.

The prefrontal lobes of the cortex, where conscious thought enters the picture, responds a second or two after the emotional system puts forth its suggestions. It is after this short delay that we have the option of overriding the emotional and mental suggestions.

When we override with our prefrontal lobes, we extend the development of the neural connection between the lobes and the emotional center of the brain. This override ability is the beginning of emotional intelligence. In her book, *Molecules of Emotion,* Dr. Candace Pert suggests that God manifests through the prefrontal lobes. Can it be that the prefrontal lobes are an organic receiver for The Holy Spirit?

We have the ability to override the emotional system only to a point. The amygdala gland is where emotional memories are stored. When enough threat is imagined or conceived, the amygdala can literally take over the brain and dictate our entire response. This is fine if a snake jumps out at you but it's not so good when we are overreacting or being negative with other people. Since an amygdala hijack, a term used by Goleman, literally renders us a puppet to the response it puts forth, we usually regret such thoughtless and emotional behavior. When you surrender to your first impulses during a negative episode, you then begin to magnify the feelings and emotions with supportive thoughts validating your virtual reality. The more you run supportive thoughts through your mind, the more potent the emotion becomes and the more real the virtual reality appears.

The mind telekinetically moves molecules within the body to create neuropeptides to carry messages throughout the body to the cellular level. These message-carrying molecules are in direct response to our imagery. What we imagine in our minds is created as feelings and emotions in the body. New research demonstrates the mind/body connection. What you imagine or create in your mind is immediately transformed into feelings and emotions. Imagination and emotion are one in the same way that mind and body are one.

Since time immemorial science and religion have failed to acknowledge the full significance of the imagination. More than anything else, the imagination has been thought of as a fantasy faculty or as a creative arts faculty.

Charles Fillmore, calling the imagination one of the twelve powers, emphasized in his teaching that it is a faculty to be developed and utilized in our spiritual growth. Stephen Covey uses the imagination in his proactive model as one of the avenues to intervene in the stimulus/response. Neville, who dedicated his life work to studying, writing, and lecturing about the power of the imagination, taught that it is the Christ within us. A few religions focus on what they call *divine imaginations*.

Current research demonstrates that all thought is based on imagery. Imagery is the foundation, the substrate of all thought—even of our internal dialogue. Imagery is the very tool the body uses to base its neuropeptide response.

Plato said the soul cannot think without a picture. The Bible uses the phrase *the imaginations of the thoughts of the heart* consistently in The Old Testament. Although the Bible never mentions the word *emotion,* some scholars take the phrase *the imaginations of the thoughts of the heart* to mean *emotion.*

Everything you run through your head becomes an imagination. Metaphysics teaches us that we project our belief systems into our interpretation of reality. We see what we are and we are what we see. And all of this is in the imagination.

Perspectives, assumptions, impressions, creative intelligence, and creative imagination make up the lion's share of our thoughts—and it is all within the faculty of the imagination. Anything more than merely being aware is created and processed by the faculty of the imagination.

The imagination is the faculty that we utilize in our co-creatorship with God in the Universe. By taking responsibility for what we dare to create within our imaginations, we take responsibility as a co-creator.

Beyond emotional intelligence is imaginational intelligence. Thus I have coined the term *Imagintelligence*. *Imagintelligence* is utilizing our co-creatorship with God. It is basing what we dare to imagine on values, ethics, principles, character, empathy, and compassion—all of which is spirituality.

Jesus said in Matthew 6:34: "Take no thought for the morrow: for the morrow shall take thought for the things of itself. Sufficient unto the day is the evil thereof." If we change this to say, "Sufficient unto the day are the negative imaginings thereof," an important spiritual principle emerges. Tomorrow will take thought for the things of itself if we consistently create good wonderful imaginings. This means that we do more than act nice; it means we are being nice in the privacy of our own minds—in our imaginations. It means that Jimmy Stewart was right when he said in a movie, "If a man wants to be successful and he's not real smart, he had better be real, real pleasant." Goleman has brought research to light that also establishes this. Successful people with IQs as low as 80 were studied. Their success is attributed to high levels of emotional intelligence. To be emotionally intelligent, it is necessary to be intelligent within the faculty of the imagination. You simply cannot spend your attention on negative imaginings and stay clear-minded enough to be successful.

Aside from being a person you are technically an organism,

and a response organism at that. You have spent your entire life consciously and subconsciously developing your response to life. Your very neurological hardwiring is altered to be "perfect" in the responses you have developed. You have watched others respond and learned to mimic them. Through association, your mind has developed a system to protect you with programmed responses that you and it have developed for the sake of response speed. In other words, your emotions develop to save you the trouble of taking time to think about how to respond. Your response is factored into an emotional urge—an urge to act and think a specific way. The body has supplied you with organic artificial intelligence in the form of feelings, emotions, and thoughts that are a distillation of your life experience.

When you find that you no longer prefer how you respond, you must begin reconstructing your very hardwiring in the neurology of your brain. The prefrontal lobes have the ability to override the engrained emotional response. Every time you respond in a new way, it develops the neurological connections involved. It is your job to "furrow" these new responses into your hardware through repetition and persistence.

What you are up against is a hardwired response development in the form of artificial intelligence that believes it is making the correct choices and causing you to mirror this belief and feel you are responding correctly. Thus you cop a justifier in each situation. Your mind tricks you into "seeing" each situation within the response conditioning your mind has developed—a projection of your belief system. You wouldn't have seen it if you didn't believe it—and you feel it, too.

Until you have practiced *Imagintelligence* for a good period of time, you are always up against the artificial intelligence that has been programmed into your body—an emotional urge or feeling with suggested thoughts that are the result of chemicals created within the body by your past imagery and evolutionary traits. These feelings or urges and thoughts are in response to particular factors found within memories and instincts. This is your first impulse to respond.

The subconscious uses factors within memories to represent the entire memory. If this memory is negative, you will associate the tastes, sounds, smells, touches, sights, and emotional content of memories as factors within this association. The more intense the factors of the past situation, the more serious the present emotional response will be. This organic artificial intelligence is geared toward your unique individual response *to save you the trouble of thinking.*

To a greater or lesser degree, all of this influences you to engage in certain negative imaginings from time to time. The previously conditioned emotional responses literally urge what you begin to imagine and run through your head. A second or two *after* your first impulse, you may intervene at the level of the imagination without automatically responding to the emotional program associated with your body's recorded emotional response.

When you carefully monitor what you imagine and run through your head, the result is a carefully monitored emotional response through the prefrontal lobe override. You feel like the stuff you run through your head. There is no escape. Thus if you want to be happy, run happy imaginings in your mind. And you must have the FAITH to do this in spite of all appearances around you. This is *Imagintelligence.*

Some feel as though this is living in a dream world. Yet I tell you now that we all live in a dream world. The mind not only dreams while it is asleep, it dreams while it is awake. And it is this state of awake-dreaming that we call perspectives, perceptions, assumptions, impressions, and gut feelings. These are fine and even beneficial when they are positive and preferred or when real danger is threatening us or when we are making important decisions. However, the ability to transform negative feelings and thoughts depends upon the ability to ignore these things when they are not aligned with your goals and spirituality.

After you have consistently created positive imaginings for a time, you will have the opportunity to look back and see that you were always living in a dream world. Previously, on many occasions it was a bad dream world. But when you can choose your imaginings and base them on love, values, ethics, and character, then your dream is aligned with God's intent.

The choice is yours. You can surrender to your artificial intelligence that has no program for a total love response, or you can abandon the notion that you are going to sacrifice logic by responding differently, and instead you can begin to install *the total love response program* through *Imagintelligence.* Fear of change is resistance. Resistance brings the illusion that you are logically fine the way you are, all the while hoping the world will change instead of you.

Imagintelligence is thinking before you imagine. It's quickly changing negative imaginings to positive. It's putting the brakes on when your emotional system gives you an impulse that is out of line with your spiritual goals. This is much more important than thinking before you act. God-aligned imaginings result in appropriate behavior without suppressing your negative imaginings.

Imagintelligence can be learned by two newly developed techniques described here as *Imagination Control Therapy* and *Imagery Management. Imagination Control Therapy* is a workable system to avoid The Fight or Flight Response and to create meaningful imaginings on a moment-by-moment basis. *Imagery Management* has been developed to utilize every modern and ancient technique available in order to reprogram the subconscious mind so that it modifies your artificial intelligence or emotional impulses to serve your best purposes.

The greatest advantage to physical health through imagination control is avoiding The Fight or Flight Response. If you succumb to a negative impulse, you will begin the downward spiral of supporting and associated thoughts. Once this process begins, so does The Fight or Flight Response. We pay a high price for surrendering to negative thought. The immune system is inhibited or temporarily shut down. The digestive system is inhibited or shuts down. Blood sugar levels rise. Muscles tense. A host of potentially toxic chemicals (the catecholamines epinephrine and norepinephrine; cortisol, corticosteroids, adrenaline and noradrenaline) are dumped into the body's system. These chemicals were designed to metabolize out of the body within a few hours, but consistent negative imaginings keep them flowing in a steady supply. Thus the over-production becomes toxic.

Mental health has the greatest advantage in imagination control. The mind becomes busy with good, wonderful imaginings and finds peace and bliss. You can be clever and change your perspective on an issue or you can temporarily distract the mind away from negative imagery. It doesn't matter. Avoiding The Fight or Flight Response is the immediate priority. Mastery can be developed later.

There are two of you inhabiting that body—you and God. Let God do the imagining for awhile. If you don't let God do the imagining, it will appear that there are three of you inhabiting your body—you, God, and your emotional system. Every moment, God offers you a way to enjoy the highest quality experience possible—just take the cue. Let go. Have faith while you are remodeling your hardware. And when the day comes that your first impulse is positive and based on love in all situations, you'll have successfully imbedded *Imagintelligence* into your body's emotional system.

Fear

2 Timothy 1:7: *For God hath not given us the spirit of
fear; but of power, and of love, and of a sound mind.*

1 John 4:18: *There is no fear in love; but perfect love
casteth out fear: because fear hath torment. He that feareth
is not made perfect in love.*

The Primary Cause of Fear Is
the Illusion of Separation from God

As we feel separation from God, we become afraid. There
seems to be a direct proportion to the relationship of fear and
this separation. When we feel as though we are in the bosom of
God, we feel comforted and secure. As we experience threatening
situations, we may lose this comfort and security; and as this
comfort and security fade, we begin to fear. We feel separated
from God, and may then find it difficult or impossible to continue to trust God.

These feelings come about as a result of identifying the self
with the body rather than with God. The body has built-in feelings about survival. And if a bear is chasing it, the body is not
comfortable and secure in knowing God. The body experiencing
fear then desires to flee or fight. By identifying ourself with the
body, we permit the body's will to survive to dominate the mind.
We feel separated from God. We think that we are no longer in
the bosom of God. Our security and trust diminishes, and the
separation becomes real to us. Yet, this is an illusion based on the
death or discomfort of the body or mind. From God's point of

view, getting eaten by a bear may not be as terrible as we believe. Yet such a level of mind, where we can surrender to being eaten by a bear, is beyond the scope of this book. Here we are dealing only with avoiding negative imagery and avoiding The Fight or Flight Response. And this alone encompasses the lion's share of our situations.

If our consciousness continues to dwell in the bosom of God, we can endure anything while we are in unison with God. It is that abandoned feeling, that feeling of aloneness—the notion that we are in unison with God when we are feeling wonderful, yet separate when experiences seem negative—that renders us feeling separated from God and subsequently filled with fear in its many forms.

The Fight or Flight Response

The body is literally urging its will to survive through a chemical process influencing our thought processes when we experience fear. Our physiology is quite proficient in creating fear chemicals when we appear to be in threatening situations. These threatening situations may be real or imagined, serious or frivolous. It doesn't matter. The Fight or Flight Response begins. This tremendous chemical response, though initiated for our protection, is far too primitive for most situations in our modern society.

A simple misunderstood look, a critical comment, even too much eye contact, may be interpreted as a threat and initiate this powerful chemical response in the body. Although a low-level response may not carry the overwhelming chemical rush in its initiation as when a bear is confronting us, these lower level chemical activities do urge fight or flight behavior and thought patterns. The mind then focuses on the negative. Strategies of fight or flight are considered. Previous similar situations are scanned for comparison. This may cause us to feel more threatened and raise the level of response. The imagination begins to run away with itself, and as the mind recalls comparable situations of the past the body's chemical response is now building up from a barrage of situations—the present and multiple past situations.

Although designed for a situation as serious as a confrontation with a bear, The Fight or Flight Response is simply not realistic the greater part of the time in today's world. In actuality, we rarely, if ever, will be in a situation where we will need The Fight or Flight Response.

The limbic system can cause a rush from the release of catecholamines for quick action followed by the adrenocortical nervous system activating adrenaline and other adrenal gland secretions such as cortisol, epinephrine, norepinephrine, and other amines, such as serotonin, that trigger central nervous system stimulation. As emotions flare, these and other chemicals, such as corticosteroid stress hormones, along with sugar surge into the body to prepare us for attack or escape. The muscles tense and need more blood, so functions such as digestion, immune system activity, body repair and healing are inhibited or ceased temporarily until the fight or flight situation is over. Then, these chemicals must be metabolized out of the body over the course of several hours. Some break down into other toxic materials while others build up to toxic levels in the blood—especially if there are long term continuous negative imaginings causing low or high level emotional flare ups. This is why it is critical to forgive and let things go. If we don't, we literally poison ourselves.

All negative imaginings are connected to The Fight or Flight Response. It is negative imagery that is used to support the initiation of this chemical response within the body. The emotional system may suggest a first impulse, but, to continue, the impulse must be supported by your subsequent imaginings. *The moment that you begin to dwell in or create negative imagery, you support the initiation of The Fight or Flight Response.* There is no escape. It is mandatory to train your mind to use the initiation of negative imagery as your cue to begin the immediate creation of positive imagery. Otherwise you suffer the discomfort of The Fight or Flight Response.

Fear and Diet

Dietary deficiencies can contribute heavily to the undesirable availability of fear chemicals and the unavailability of chemicals such as phenylethylamine and dopamine, the inhibitors of central nervous system stimulation. Thus what we think—what images we create within our imaginations—is converted into chemicals so we can *feel* what we imagine with our physical body. Eating poorly enhances the negative chemical response in the body, which in turn urges negative imaginings.

It has been recently discovered that high carbohydrate-low fat (and ultimately low protein) diets cause the body's hormonal balance to be insulin dominant which in turn alters your blood/glucose dynamics. High carbohydrate diets usually consist of an overabundance of refined carbohydrates that slam the blood with high levels of sugar followed by high levels of insulin. This condition causes peaks of glucose and insulin that lead to cell receptor damage that over time causes hyperinsulinemia, commonly known as insulin resistance. Once insulin resistance starts, a chain of health damaging events follow such as Type II diabetes, interference of hormonal communication, and the over production of the arachidonic acid family of eicosanoids, which are blood clotting platelets, vasoconstrictors, inflammatories, and promoters of vessel construction during angiogenesis in cancer.

Fatigue, sleep difficulties, emotional instability, mood swings, sadness, depression, and crying for no apparent reason might be signs of insulin problems. Inability to concentrate, irritability, anxiety, brain fog, confusion, and becoming easily obsessed with annoyances may be other signs of poor diet.

It must be noted that insulin dominance over glucagon, the hormone stimulated by protein, is the problem. Sugar levels in the blood may not be high, but levels of insulin dominating in the balance of the glucagon/insulin hormonal axis caused by the consumption of too many refined or high glycemic index carbohydrates and/or insulin resistance cause many problems. It may be requiring much, much more insulin to do the job than it used to. Blood sugar is normal, but glucagon/insulin hormonal balance is way off. This violation of hormonal balance promotes a feedback loop of negative urges, negative imagery, and negative emotions. All this adds to the basic chemicals created within The Flight or Fight Response.

Negative Imagery Chemical Addiction

Chemicals produced by negative imagery can also have an addictive affect. Just as someone may become addicted to caffeine, cocaine, amphetamines, or speed, we can become addicted to any central nervous system stimulant. We have all heard of people claiming they cannot go without their coffee. Some people drive to work eighty miles per hour to get stimulated. Some people are daredevils. Some seek stimulation by acting mean, by criminal activity, or by consistently creating negative imagery. Negative thought itself can be addictive for the chemical stimulation it provides readily and consistently. Those of us who argue or fight a great deal may be doing so out of chemical addiction, a need for adrenal stimulation.

Relax, Take Time to Metabolize

Although central nervous system stimulation may be beneficial if we need to meet an important deadline or are pressured into our best game of handball, if we don't want negative consequences it's necessary to balance these intense moments with adequate relaxation or meditation. It is very important to allow the body sufficient time to metabolize the chemicals involved in central nervous system stimulation.

Modern research demonstrates that meditation in addition to our regular routines lowers cortisol considerably. Two hours of high quality meditation can be as beneficial to the body as four to six hours of sleep.

The Fight or Flight Response's Data Filter

Once the process of fight or flight is initiated, we also engage our data gathering filtration system. This filter is specifically designed to highlight and focus on the negative while lessening the significance of anything positive. The Flight or Flight Response believes that only the negative aspects of the environment are a threat, so the majority of attention is focused on the negative since this is where the possible threat may be.

Body functions such as digestion, immune system activity, and healing are temporarily shut down while the more important threatening situation is handled and we probe and scan for negativity. Muscles tighten for fight or flight. Where there is one threat, there may be more. This may result in tension and stress. If we look for negativities, they aren't hard to find. They're everywhere! Things don't even have to be negative; we may merely imagine the possibility of a threat or completely imagine a threat through misconception. As a negative hunter, we most definitely bag our limit.

Past Negative Situations

We can also react at higher levels of fear when our minds rethink past situations that we are reminded of because of a low-level apparent threat or misunderstanding. We can project that a low-level threat can evolve into a high-level threat, scan our memories for past high-level threats, and then relive them. Worry, for example, can cause as much chemical activity in the body as real and serious situations. Isn't it common to hear someone say, *I've been worried half to death?*

When we do this, we are running a scan of all the earlier times when we experienced a similar threat. For example, we have made an appointment to meet someone on a street corner at exactly 7 p.m. We arrive at 6:55 p.m., five minutes early. At 6:58 p.m. we may begin to imagine our expected party as being late. The mind immediately scans the past for times we have waited for someone who has been late. We recall how these past times have made us feel. We begin to incorporate these past feelings into our present state of mind. At 15 seconds to 7:00 p.m. we may have begun to feel the way we have felt before as we waited for people who have been late in the past. Now, even though the person arrives promptly at 7:00p.m., we have dwelled in our past negative experiences long enough that we are experiencing a negative present time. We may permit this to influence our behavior and our impressions of the party we have just met in spite of the fact that they were prompt. We feel the emotions stored within past events within our imagery and, through association, we may begin to feel other emotion that is stored that is not directly related to the stimulating emotion at hand.

For example, the stimulating emotion may be impatience while you are waiting. But, within previous similar waiting situations where you felt impatient, you may have also felt hurt, aggravated, or upset. These other emotions may attempt to emerge as the mind scans past negative experiences.

There Is No Escape!

The images we create, return to, or dwell in cause chemicals to be created within the body that correspond with the images. There is no escape. As we create our mind movie, our body creates the chemicals necessary to activate our feelings that correspond to the imaginings or internal dialogue. When in a negative state of mind, although we are not actively engaged in creating negative imagery, we may be engaged in negative internal dialogue which mirrors our imagery. Our attention merely leaves the image itself and focuses on the internal dialogue. So we wind up feeling the emotional mode in the way we talk to ourself, too! The bottom line is that we feel like the stuff we run through our minds.

Anger

Each situation we perceive as a threat creates fear. It doesn't matter if the perception is real or imagined; we automatically begin to create our mind movie regarding the fear. We may then greatly exaggerate the perception of the fear. This energy is channeled into The Fight or Flight Response. The Fight or Flight Response channels the energy created by the emotion of fear into a powerful urge that may become active behavior to fight or flee.

When we choose to fight when we are threatened, we will most likely channel our fear into anger. Anger is one of the deadliest negative emotions. Anger makes people kill other people. The passions of anger cause more abuse to others than any other emotion. It causes a person to lose control, to lose respect, to cause great pain to the world. Anger is considered by the ancients to be one of the thieves of the holy temple. From anger comes hate, wrath, vengeance, violence, elevated blood pressure, and increased heart rate. It is disastrous to the mind and body. It can also cause heart attack, stroke, and death.

Anger is a material manifestation which represents, in a general way, the measure of the failure of the spiritual nature to gain control of the combined intellectual and physical natures. Anger indicates your lack of tolerant brotherly love plus your lack of self-respect and self-control. Anger depletes the health, debases the mind, and handicaps the spirit teacher of man's soul. Have you not read in the Scriptures that "wrath kills the foolish man," and that man "tears himself in his anger"? That "he who is slow of wrath is of great understanding," while "he who is hasty of temper exalts folly"? You all know that "a soft answer turns away wrath," and how "grievous words stir up anger." "Discretion defers anger," while "he who has no control over his own self is like a defenseless city without walls." "Wrath is cruel and anger is outrageous." "Angry men stir up strife, while the furious multiply their transgressions." "Be not hasty in spirit, for anger rests in the bosom of fools." Let your hearts be so dominated by love that your spirit guide will have little trouble in delivering you from the tendency to give vent to those outbursts of animal anger which are inconsistent with the status of divine sonship.[1]

Aristotle's challenge regarding anger, found in *The Nicomachean Ethics,* reflects true Imagintelligence. "Anyone can become angry—that is easy. But to be angry with the right person, to the right degree, at the right time, for the right purpose, and in the right way—this is not easy."

Let us gain more insight about anger while examining this concordance search of the scriptures.

- Psalm 37:8: "Cease from anger, and forsake wrath: fret not thyself in any wise to do evil."
- Psalm 38:3: "There is no soundness in my flesh because of thine anger; neither is there any rest in my bones because of my sin."
- Proverbs 14:17: "He that is soon angry dealeth foolishly: and a man of wicked devices is hated."
- Proverbs 15:1: "A soft answer turneth away wrath: but grievous words stir up anger."
- Proverbs 15:18: "A wrathful man stirreth up strife: but he that is slow to anger appeaseth strife."
- Proverbs 16:32: "He that is slow to anger is better than the mighty; and he that ruleth his spirit than he that taketh a city."
- Proverbs 19:11: "The discretion of a man deferreth his anger; and it is his glory to pass over a transgression."
- Proverbs 21:14: "A gift in secret pacifieth anger: and a reward in the bosom strong wrath."
- Proverbs 21:19: "It is better to dwell in the wilderness, than with a contentious and an angry woman."
- Proverbs 22:8: "He that soweth iniquity shall reap vanity: and the rod of his anger shall fail."
- Proverbs 22:24: "Make no friendship with an angry man; and with a furious man thou shalt not go."

- Proverbs 25:23: "The north wind driveth away rain: so doth an angry countenance a backbiting tongue."
- Proverbs 27:4: "Wrath is cruel, and anger is outrageous; but who is able to stand before envy?"
- Proverbs 29:22: "An angry man stirreth up strife, and a furious man aboundeth in transgression."
- Ephesians 4:31: "Let all bitterness, and wrath, and anger, and clamour, and evil speaking, be put away from you, with all malice."
- Colossians 3:8: "But now ye also put off all these; anger, wrath, malice, blasphemy, filthy communication out of your mouth."
- Colossians 3:21: "Fathers, provoke not your children to anger, lest they be discouraged."

My grandmother had a plaque on the wall, a quote by Mark Twain that read, *Whom the gods would destroy they first make mad.* Professional fighters know that if they get angry, they will likely lose control and lose the fight. Nothing is as hard on the constitution as anger. Once we do away with anger, the body can relax. The mind can relax. A great deal of the struggle in life dissipates.

Replace anger with forgiveness, understanding, patience, acceptance, humor, and faith. These positive thoughts will add energy to your constitution rather than drain it with anger. Inasmuch as you may justify anger, you have no right to it. It is only a primitive expression that a basic need has not been met. It is a mental habit pattern that can be broken, and break it you must if you want inner peace.

Kill, dominate, repel (fight), or avoid, (flight), are the life instincts invoked when threatening situations, real or imagined, arise. The negative mind would have us just avoid or flee from potential sources of fear, would have us repel the potential source of fear or pain, kill the potential source of fear, or dominate the potential source of fear. This primitive Fight or Flight Response takes on a multitude of responses.

Fight is most often represented by fear channeled into anger.

Hate may enter into the imagery, which may leave us feeling numb or immune to our fear. We hate to be afraid and we hate to be hurt. If we examine the synonyms of anger and hate, we find a multitude of angry and hateful expressions with all their variations. Flight is most often represented by nonviolent fear expressions channeled into the urge to remove oneself from the situation or area—fast. This may include hiding or simply take on the appearance of becoming aloof. The synonyms of fleeing or hiding also take on a great variety of behavior expressions.

However we may adjust The Fight or Flight Response to fit our situations, we are still being influenced by a chemical behavioral response that has a definite urge programmed into our minds. Once this process is started, the mind begins to filter out all positive aspects of our environment. They are now insignificant because positive attributes are not harmful. Thus the mind begins to catalogue all of the negatives since it is these that pose the threat. Once we begin to examine all that is wrong in our environment, we find plenty. By focusing on the negative and filtering out most of the positive, the negative imagination is given freedom to unlimited realms of creativity. And in a few seconds our entire negative past is called forth, sorted through, compared and considered. A great part of this process is performed subconsciously but a feeling of the total process remains with us.

Still, we may bypass this entire process by refusing to buy into the urge to create negative imagery in the first place. When you see or hear your negative mind, instead of creating negative imagery you have the *choice* to use this as the *cue* to create positive imagery. Scientifically, there is no valid reason not to do this. Spiritually, there is no valid reason not to do this.

Although we are probably not living in the woods where we may be eaten by a bear, our body is still genetically geared for these situations. *The same response that may have been a critical factor in our survival as a primitive species is now working directly against the evolution of our consciousness.* Our rise in consciousness over the past few thousand years is wallpapered over, perhaps, a million years or more of evolutionary developments in survival.

Our modern day *attacks* now come when our boss is yelling at us or while we are contending with anxious drivers, getting fired, paying bills we can't afford, or coping with the children. Even when we merely *think* about these things, we activate The Fight or Flight Response. We can't recall imagery and dwell within it without re-experiencing the chemical response it originally caused—that is until we are immersed in forgiveness. Otherwise the original emotions experienced at the time of the creation of the image are stored within it. When you recall the image, you recall the emotions. This is why it is necessary to let go of our past painful memories. If you don't, you are tending the pain and continually importing it into the present. You absolutely cannot see the present clearly through the eyes of past pain.

The Fight or Flight Response has its place in our survival, but it is primitive at its best. If a hungry lion confronts us, it is useful. Yet we will certainly not have our most analytical wits about us while we are filled with fear. In an extreme situation such as this, it is virtually impossible to control The Fight or Flight Response, at least until you rise above all fear of death, which you may not ever do. Yet, without focusing on this type of extreme situation, there is a tremendous amount of mastery we may enjoy that enriches our lives.

But at the opposite extreme, there are countless low-level situations where The Fight or Flight Response initiates unnecessarily. Many of these are of a subtle nature, yet the negative focus and positive filter are initiated nonetheless. Having awareness of this chemical process being produced in the body is critical in understanding why we think the way we do. This is the ability to understand the thoughts and behaviors of our chemical urges.

An entire behavioral science is forming around the relationship of chemicals and behavior. Scientists are slowly uncovering individual chemicals that urge particular behaviors. Although the bulk of this work is being done with animals, much of this research is opening doors to a better understanding of human nature. Imagery creates chemicals in the body and chemicals in the body urge the creation of imagery, each after its kind. Fear channeled into anger creates chemicals of anger that urge more imaginings of anger. Anger blinds the mind's ability to perceive—and it can be deadly.

Fear of Receiving

Our fears are entwined with our perceptions of receiving. God's intention is to give to us abundantly. This means that it is *necessary* for us to receive. Thus, to receive, it is necessary to develop a state of mind capable of receiving. Too many people have a deep confusion convincing them that they are unworthy of receiving abundance. Throw it out! Just don't buy into it any more. It is a lie. We are all born worthy. The God within us has the full intention of experiencing abundance through us. God is within our each and every experience. God wants no less of a quality experience for us than He wants for Himself. As you think of yourself, incorporate into your self-concept the fact that God is in there with you. There are two entities inhabiting your body—you and God. Now, God does not decide that He desires to promote the experience of misery, poor self-image, poverty, lack, or victimization to share in with you. Absolutely not! His desire is to share a quality, wonderful experience with you, as you. Believing in anything less is believing a lie. In fact, God is always offering us ways to raise the quality of our experience in every situation if we listen and keep our minds open to these Divine Ideas. It is only our misconceptions caused by permitting the influence of past negative experiences that trick us into choosing an experience of lesser quality than God has offered. Each time we choose an experience of less quality than God has offered, the choice is based on fear. Thus we have not received an experience because of fear but have instead created an experience that is a combination of a fear of receiving entwined with God's offer.

Desire

We have, through Grace, been granted an inherent right to the feeling of desire. It is wonderful to desire, yet it is necessary to remain free of our desires. The old school of thought on desire claimed that we must be free of desire by eliminating desire. New Thought teaches us that desire is good. It is God's way of manifesting through us. But, it is important to remain free of the results of our desires. Our freedom from the results of our desires gives us the opportunity to experience desire without involving ourselves with negative mental consequences if our desire remains unfulfilled. To enter into a state of mind where we are anxious or resentful because of unfulfilled desires, or fearful that we will not receive, closes the door to the very state of mind required to attract and receive the fulfillment of our desires. The old paradigm that *having is being* has been replaced by the inversion: *being is having*. So, fear not and enjoy having. In proportion to your belief it will be given to you. Creating the state of mind first puts us in a position where we naturally attract that which fulfills our desires. "But seek ye first The Kingdom of God, and his righteousness; and all these things shall be added to you." (Matthew 6:33)

Incorporate These Ten Virtues

• Forgiveness • Humility • Patience

and The Seven Heavenly Virtues of:

• Faith • Hope • Charity • Fortitude • Justice
• Temperance • Prudence

If we become drawn into a tendency to create negative imaginings, these virtues listed here will restore The Kingdom of God to our consciousness. As the writer of the script of your mind movie, these virtues are wonderful guidelines to *Imagintelligence*. They are your fearless, spiritual, Godlike qualities.

Fear, the Gateway to the World of Darkness

Fear leads us into the world of darkness. We may become angry because we become afraid of something. We may hurt and are then fear more pain. It is a normal response to hate fear and pain. We may become angry when we are made afraid or hurt. We may envy others who have things we fear that we may never have or have soon enough. Fear leads the way into multitudes of variations within negative emotional expressions.

Our world of darkness begins with fear and then unfolds into a multitude of variations as we entwine fear with:

• Hate • Vengeance • Vanity

and The Seven Deadly (states of mind) Sins

• Anger • Covetousness • Envy • Sloth • Gluttony
• Pride • Lust

Fear is the common denominator of these ten basic negative expressions. In our illusion of being separate from God, we may experience these states of mind in our attempt to satiate ourself through our sensual input. When we are void of our unity with God, we miss the pleasure of the wonders of God's magnificence. Within this void is fear in its various expressions waiting to influence our experiences. These misconceptions manifest as variations of the above states of experience.

Fear in Our Illusion of Separation from God Expressed as Hate

Hate is usually the result of repeatedly becoming angry. Things or people that annoy us or make us angry become the object of hate. We hate to be aggravated, hurt, made afraid, or made to suffer losses. We may hate because we fear that we will experience pain, annoyance, or the like, again and again. These things may seem to occur in reality but may merely be within the imagination. Hate may leave us feeling numb or immune to fear, although hate is initiated by fear.

Rather than being the result of becoming angry several times, hate may be the result of only one intense or extreme aggravation, hurt, or loss suffered. In any event, it is the result of an immense amount of energy channeled through The Fight or Flight Response. We may feel as though we have received far too much of undesirable situations or things. "If I wanted to punish an enemy it should be by fastening on him the trouble of constantly hating somebody." (H. More)

A heart filled with love does not hate. An empty heart can hate. A broken heart can hate because it feels abandoned by God. As a part of feeling let down, abandoned, or empty in our illusion of separation from God, we may manifest this fear as hateful imagery, emotion, and behavior.

Fear in Our Illusion of Separation from God Expressed as Vengeance

It is only fear that convinces you that "getting even," experiencing revenge, or inflicting harm back for harm done is the proper channel of imaginings. You have to feel afraid that you will bear the perceived injustice while the "guilty party" may get away with what they have done. When karma is considered, no one gets away with anything. It is the need to control, to witness the punishment that you deem fitting that urges vengeance. There is a higher power at work in the Universe; let it go.

Fear in Our Illusion of Separation from God Expressed as Vanity

The most profound form of selfishness must surely be vanity. For the sake of our vanity one may prioritize almost anything, no matter how frivolous, over more important things. Excessive pride in one's appearance, qualities, abilities, or achievements is overbearing and conceited. One feels as though they are not going to receive enough praise, attention, acknowledgment, credit, or compliments. Though much like pride, vanity is more focused around appearance or image. It also results in lacking in real values, and hollowness. The Bible usage of vanity is usually referring to pointlessness, worthlessness, or trivial. "When a man has no longer any conception of excellence above his own, his voyage is done; he is dead; dead in the trespasses and sins of blear-eyed vanity." (H. W. Beacher)

Fear in Our Illusion of Separation from God Expressed as Anger

When we become angry, we feel that we have been greatly wronged; a basic need or desire has not been met. We fear that we are experiencing something negative unnecessarily or unfairly. We fear that we must experience further unwanted hardships. This makes us angry. We feel a sudden, violent displeasure— accompanied by an urge to retaliate—that may lead us into vengeance. We may fear that we are receiving too much of what we do not prefer. The energy from The Fight or Flight Response may be channeled into anger. Anger is combative fear, a separation from God manifesting in combative imagery, emotion, and behavior.

Fear in Our Illusion of Separation from God Expressed as Covetousness

When we experience covetous we are disregarding the rights of others. We usually desire what someone else has without thinking that something like what he or she has will do. Coupled with a selfish desire, this is another fear of not receiving. We usually covet what we see regularly. Wrongful desire may be channeled in many ways. It is a direct path of descension. "Covetous men are fools, miserable wretches, buzzards,

madmen, who live by themselves, in perpetual slavery, fear, suspicion, sorrow, discontent, with more of gall than honey in
their enjoyments; who are rather possessed by their money
than possessors of it; bound 'prentices to their property; mean
slaves and drudges to their substance." (Burton) Within the
loneliness and emptiness of the illusion of separation from
God, we may manifest covetous behavior, deluded that it is a
way of gaining relief.

Fear in Our Illusion of Separation from God Expressed as Envy

We may experience envy when we fear that we will not
receive something fast enough or may never receive something. This jealous emotion is nothing more than the fear of
not receiving, so we envy those who have what we want.
"Hatred is active, and envy passive, dislike; there is but one step
from envy to hate." (Goethe) We may become extremely angry
which may then become hate if we are constantly envious. In a
world where we are faced with the challenge of overcoming an
abundance of negativity, we certainly do not need to increase
the possibility of negative experience by converting the abundance of others into our displeasure. The more we envy, the
more we our expressing our need for God. Acquiring what we
envy will not fulfill this need for God through a substitution.
Through a fear of separation from God we manifest this
emptiness as envious imagery, emotion, and behavior trying to
fill this void.

Fear in Our Illusion of Separation from God Expressed as Sloth

Sloth is the fear of losing our immediate comfort that manifests in a desire for consistent ease. The need for consistent
comfort is a form of attachment and is the result of a lack of
interest and enthusiasm. We may be afraid of hard work. Sloth is

also a form of selfishness. When we are slothful we are giving priority to our most frivolous comforts over more important tasks. One may fear that they are going to receive what they do not prefer, discomfort. "Sloth, like rust, consumes faster than labor wears, while the key often used is bright." (Ben Franklin)

Behind sloth there may be a feeling of separation from God where one has no passion or zeal for life left. Without God we may hope to feel comforted physically through our sloth. When we are not true to ourselves in pursuit of our dreams we may lose zeal and passion. This may be fear of being stuck in life, perhaps the fear that anything we do will not matter or will turn out disastrous. Without experiencing the mighty works of God we can lose any desire to work. We may feel empty or abandoned within a slothful experience of a fear of separation from God.

Fear in Our Illusion of Separation from God Expressed as Gluttony

Gluttony can be a fear of not receiving enough food. We may fear that we will not be able to eat as much as we would like over a certain time period. Many people who have experienced extreme hunger later experience gluttony. Or we may be trying to gain relief from our own negativity through the consistent pleasure of eating, or by engaging in other pleasures in a gluttonous state of mind. When we seek pleasure through our senses with a gluttonous intensity, some kind of fear is the underlying motive. When physical desires are insatiable it is usually replacing something causing emptiness or hurt; and we are afraid of emptiness and hurt. These things we do not experience when we feel a unity with God.

Overdosing on sensual pleasure is a moment-by-moment example of *having is being* thinking. As long as we are engaged in pleasure, we are masking our true state of mind. This may cause a motive to consistently search for some outside stimulation to give us pleasure because we fear our state of mind without pleasure. Pleasing the senses serves as a powerful mask to cover a feeling of separation from God. But what is left when the pleasure ceases?

Fear in Our Illusion of Separation from God Expressed as Pride

Pride is good—up to a point. It starts out as dignity and self-respect, but inordinate pride becomes what is considered one of The Seven Deadly Sins. This is a vain, conceited pride. This kind of excessive pride is usually a cover-up for fears such as inferiority complexes or insecurity. This is a fear of not receiving enough praise, attention, acknowledgment, credit, or complements. "Pride, like the magnet, constantly points to one object, self; but unlike the magnet, it has no attractive pole, but at all points repel." (Colton)

Fear in Our Illusion of Separation from God Expressed as Lust

Although a great deal of lust is the result of hormonal urges, this many times escalates into a fear of loneliness, a fear that one may never experience intimacy to a preferred degree or not at all. The images we create from lust are basically fears that we will not receive, so we desire without proper or full consideration. "Lust is an enemy to the purse, a foe to the person, a canker to the mind, a corrosive to the conscience, a weakness of the wit, a besotter of the senses, and finally, a mortal bane to all the body." (Pliny)

"In morals, what begins in fear usually ends in wickedness; in religion, what begins in fear usually ends in fanaticism. Fear, either as a principle or a motive, is the beginning of all evil." (Mrs. Jameson) Let us take this quotation a step further and say that fear is the beginning of the creation of all negative imaginations—the world of darkness.

If we begin with the synonyms of fear then include the synonyms of the ten basic fear expressions noted we will largely cover a verbal description of the negative spectrum of imagination and emotion.

The World of Darkness

Fear and its basic expressions: hate, vengeance, vanity, and The Seven Deadly (states of mind) Sins; pride, covetousness, lust, anger, gluttony, envy, and sloth.

Fear

affliction	aghast	anguish
alarm	anxiety	anticipation
anxiousness	appalling	awe
awful	consternation	daunted
despair	direness	dismay
disquietude	distrust	doubt
dread	dubious	foreboding
frightening	grief	horror
incredulous	jittery	misgiving
panic	paranoia	phobic
qualm	rude	shudder
suspense	suspicion	tension
terror	testy	tremble
trepidation	troubled	veneration
worry	hurt feelings	painful emotion
remorse	sadness	suffering
pessimism	**hatred**	antipathy
animosity	dislike	hostility
ill-will	malice	rancor
spite	acrimony	antagonism
aversion	bitterness	enmity
gall	venom	vindictive
detestable	abhor	abominate
desecrate	despise	disdain
dislike	loathe	rejection
bristled	revilement	berate
upbraid	defame	scorn
disgusting	evil	odious
odium	repulsive	revolting
meddling	officious	intrusive

obtrusive	disgrace	disfavor
scared	bewilderment	chaos
complexes	cowardice	curt
cynical	depression	diffidence
discouraging	distress	fleeing
formidability	frantic	frenzied
fretting	hiding	impatience
inauspiciousness	introversion	meanness
menacing	misery	nervous
non-confront	ominous	overwhelm
restlessness	reservation	restriction
restrained	sarcastic	secretiveness
self-doubt	skepticism	snippy
snotty	shocked	tactless
harsh	uneasiness	unnerving
woeful	heartache	regret
agony	bale	torment
travail	torture	upset
argue	bug	taunt
grievous	shyness	sorrowful
strain	stress	suffering
timidity	queasy	wariness
acrimony	aggravate	agitate
animosity	annoy	apprehension
burdened	bitterness	bother
choler	deplorable	despicable
displease	discourteous	disrespectful
disturb	enrage	**envy**
excite	fit	flippant
frenzy	frustration	fury
gall	ghastly	nastiness
plaintive	rile	temper tantrum
cranky	impudence	incense
indignation	inflame	offensive
outrage	sorrowful	regretful
rueful	unpleasantness	surly

impolite	pressured	rancor
rankle	resentment	restlessness
gruff	harass	hostility
doleful	gloomy	**vengeance**
vexation	wretched	wrath
unforgiving	revengeful	unmerciful
huffy	touchy	miffy
petulant	inferior	badger
heckle	hound	pester
provoke	ride	bedevil
beleaguer	harry	hassle
intimidate	jeer	nag
needle	persecute	plague
threaten	goad	bully
coercion	strong-arm	force
constraint	duress	violence
aggression	pressure	pushy
unsteady	unreliable	precarious
shaky	tricky	dangerous
hazardous	unstable	hot-tempered
crossed	feisty	grouchy
irascible	short-fused	sullen
peppery	quick-tempered	impatient
crabby	edgy	fretful
unsettling	wicked	corrupt
fraudulent	iniquity	reprobate
sinful	vile	bad
crooked	deceitful	dishonest
immoral	lying	roguish
scheming	shady	shifty
unethical	unfair	unprincipled
unscrupulous	untruthful	venal
wrongful	adverse	ill-mannerism
vicious	depraved	infamous
nefarious	rotten	ruthless
villainous	base	carelessness

shyness

arrogance

pride

disdain

audacity

insolence

sassy

brashness

cheek

egotism

moxie

aspersion

sarcasm

disrespectful

forward

blasphemous

greedy

avaricious

resentful

enraged

indignant

fuming

hurt

alienated

vehement

hostile

belligerent

militant

lazy

languid

slouch

jerk

dolt

fool

rapacity

prodigious

diffidence

conceit

cockiness

haughtiness

nervy

gall

boldness

brassy

crusty

airs

derision

contemptible

rude

impertinent

fresh

sacrilegious

selfish

grabby

jealous

aggravated

irate

provoked

emotional

savage

terrible

bellicose

combative

quarrelsome

lethargic

sluggish

bungler

creep

dopey

gluttony

excessive

voracious

vanity

narcissism

condescension

loftiness

chutzpah

ridicule

temerity

impudence

presumptuous

pique

scorn

mocking

impudent

irreverent

pert

covetousness

acquisitive

miserly

anger

furious

mad

upset

bitter

fierce

warlike

pugnacious

contentious

slothful

lackadaisical

indolent

clod

blockhead

dullard

overindulgent

inordinate

Fear has its many avenues of expression for us to channel our mental energy into. This world of darkness is a complete waste of our energy, effort, and time. Yet, by experiencing this world, we may learn its pointlessness as well as understand the hows and whys others indulge in this spectrum of imagery. As the writer, director, producer, and star of our mind movie, all we have to do is write the script that pleases us, a script that is pleasing to God, and we will let go of the hold that we've permitted the world of darkness to have on us. Your entire world of darkness is made up of the erroneous imagery you have created within your imagination while feeling a separation from God.

I must again admit that these concepts may be almost impossible to apply to an extremely serious situation such as when a bear is about to make us his supper, but we must give due consideration that the vast majority of our "serious situations" are not so serious. Even Mahatma Gandhi indicated that he would feel quite differently about things if a cobra confronted him. By starting small you can improve your threshold of spiritual response as you rise above your animalistic human nature while imbedding your new, improved *Imagintelligence* into your body.

Concern yourself fervently to discover any traits you may have within the above list. Ask your friends or family about any of these traits you may not know about. When others refer to our faults they usually see our negative traits quite clearly. Those who do not particularly like us usually have labeled us as *being* our negative traits. By finding out why someone may not like us, we usually will discover our negative traits that we have projected to them.

Choosing not to participate in the creation or dwelling in of imaginings within the world of darkness will permit the light of God to shine through us and into our lives.

Here's the deal: You are a co-creator with God. The above list of states of mind is not to be incorporated into your co-creation process. You must write a script free of all these negativities. This is the story of your life. Your life is your mind movie. There are no cues permitted leading to any of the aforementioned states of mind. Any of these states of mind that you may have stored in the memories of your experiences are not to be returned to for comparison or advice. By eliminating the influence of past negative experiences, we are able to choose the intention that God directs us toward without the misconceptions of our past urging a choice of lesser quality. Fearlessly create the mind movie of your wonderful life. And hold that image!

God is consistently bringing forth an ingeniously prepared offer of a high quality Christly experience each and every moment. We are urged to tap into this offer and enjoy the richness of the experience God wants us to have. It is only our fear that causes us to choose anything less for our experience. Yet, we are able to become new each moment. Each moment is a new idea of the highest love experience God can intend within the formless. Join in! Fear not! Ultimately our experience of life and our unity with God is within what we create with the faculty of imagination. Choose the closest imagery that matches God's imagery and you're in the highest quality experience of the Christ consciousness.

"Fear is implanted in us as a preservative from evil; but its duty, like that of other passions, is not to overbear reason, but to assist it. It should not be suffered to tyrannize in the imagination, to raise phantoms of horror, or to beset life with supernumerary distresses." —Johnson

"Present fears are less than horrible imaginings."
                                        —Shakespeare

"There is great beauty in going through life without anxiety or fear. Half our fears are baseless, and the other half discreditable. —Bovee

[1] *The Urantia Book.* Urantia Foundation. 11th printing, page 1673.

The Tree of Life

Proverbs 15:4: *A wholesome tongue is a tree of life: but perverseness therein is a breach of the spirit.*

Galatians 5:22-23: *But the fruit of the Spirit is love, joy, peace, longsuffering, gentleness, goodness, faith, meekness, temperance: against such there is no law.*

All positive imaginations, emotions, and characteristics are attributes of love. To demonstrate this, I used a thesaurus to unfold this concept. I started with the synonyms of love. I then looked up those synonyms. The synonyms of the synonyms of the synonyms of love unfolded into the following list. This list represents the spectrum of positive imagery.

If you will visualize love as the trunk of a tree and the following list of attributes of love as the branches and leaves, you will have the tree of life concept.

This list of emotions and feelings can give you a guideline to using many of our lost or unutilized positive attributes. Remember that each one is attached to and the result of an imagination. Beginning to use the imaginings of all these wonderful emotions and traits is more than adventurous; it is the first mansion of The Kingdom of Heaven. As you read each word, visualize and create the imagery it represents as a mental exercise. If you don't know a word look it up in a dictionary. These are more than words; they are powerful tools. Note how many you have not used for a long time or have never used. Find a way to bring them into your life.

When you willfully create imaginings based on values, ethics, character, and spiritual principles you are applying

Imagintelligence. The Tree of Life is the gateway to the development of *Imagintelligence* into your mind and body.

Love

adoration	affection	devotion
infatuation	tenderness	fondness
admirability	esteem	regard
respect	**charity**	kindness
amour	**altruism**	affinity
attachment	relish	cherish
fancy	idolize	appreciate
enjoy	savor	veneration
worship	warmth	sentiment
piety	**reverence**	**zeal**
allegiance	commitment	dedication
fidelity	captivation	fascination
compassion	gentleness	sensitivity
praise	amazement	awe
wonder	**honor**	revere
value	consideration	humane
benevolence	generosity	thoughtful
intrigue	romantic	munificence
philanthropic	largeness	bigness
magnanimity	contributing	**serving**
donating	perchance	fealty
loyalty	**faithful**	enthusiasm
gusto	zest	prize
treasure	favor	glorify
adulate	**spiritual**	**holy**
fervor	vigor	consecrating
integrative	charming	enchanting
absorbing	engrossing	enthralling
empathetic	**merciful**	considerate
meek	intuitive	**understanding**
aware	receptive	dazzling
ethical	**honesty**	scrupulous
upstanding	decent	fairness

dependability
illustrious
bewitched
liberal
magnanimous
attending
giving
spirited
fervent
religious
blessed
graceful
riveting
hypnotic
affable
tolerance
innate
cognizant
pliant
bright
resplendent
conscientious
noble
respectable
trustful
forthright
careful
incorruptible
suitable
courteous
unbiased
square
solid
reputable
grand
magnificent

reliability
mesmerize
docile
chivalrous
ministering
helpful
devout
ardent
fawning
dynamic
decency
provocative
interesting
clement
amiable
acquiescent
instinctive
enlightening
perceptive
brilliant
accolade
just
proper
upstanding
upright
frank
meticulous
principled
adequate
nice
unprejudiced
reliable
steady
dignified
refined
obedient

distinguished
spellbound
unselfish
attentive
aid
obliging
eager
delightful
obsequious
exuberant
winsome
enrapturing
thrilling
polite
patient
yielding
alert
flexible
intelligent
radiant
acknowledging
moral
scrupulous
trustworthy
virtuous
sincere
precise
modest
accommodating
impartial
pleasant
responsible
credible
elegant
glorious
reasonable

gallant	brave	courageous
valiant	earnest	observant
forgiving	big-hearted	comporting
comforting	assisting	supportive
cooperative	friendly	beneficial
effervescent	lively	blissful
happy	joyous	beautiful
skilled	smooth	poised
alluring	sexy	tantalizing
stimulating	cordial	mannerly
tactful	cultured	fashionable
genteel	polished	eminent
agreeable	good-natured	likeable
gregarious	convivial	merry
jovial	festive	companionable
outgoing	serene	calm
peaceful	placid	tranquil
untroubled	collected	composed
undisturbed	open-minded	broad-minded
accepting	dutiful	relaxing
earthy	wild	instinctive
vigilant	watchful	astute
perspicacious	sagacious	smart
conversant	well-informed	uplifting
illuminating	discerning	shrewd
prudent	discriminating	clever
cheerful	refulgent	particular
meritorious	commendable	laudable
noteworthy	remarkable	tasteful
aesthetic	decorous	seemly
canny	cautious	prudent
vigilant	veracity	candor
genuine	ingenuous	straightforward
guileless	circumspect	decisive
humble	chaste	civil
amicable	refreshing	enjoyable

gratifying	mollifying	soothing
appeasing	capable	competent
efficient	accomplished	incessant
persistent	practical	rational
logical	sensible	regal
softy	palatial	sophisticated
debonair	suave	**divine**
sublime	wonderful	wise
dauntless	intrepid	nonchalant
composed	paladin	bold
diligent	indefatigable	intrepid
vindicating	exculpation	excellence
diplomatic	deferential	optimistic
unique	thorough	exemplary
adroit	imaginative	**hopeful**
harmonious	mellifluous	gleeful
jocular	jolly	halcyon
nonviolent	imperturbable	pristine
unassuming	modest	fun
amusing	thrifty	witty
reassuring	sympathetic	**compassionate**
gay	hilarious	industrious
assiduous	glad	sapient
stimulating	humorous	funny
sweetness	keen	frugal
natural	artful	wily
discreet	chic	robust
gratifying		

Get out your dictionary and start learning these attributes of love. Learning them will help manifest them into your life. You have to admit that God has given us a big enough spectrum of positive imaginings, traits, and emotions to keep us occupied in positive thought with an infinite number of combinations of which to form and refine our personality and handle every situation that may arise in life.

Pick one attribute each day that you are unfamiliar with or do not use.

1. Learn all about it.
2. Meditate on it.
3. Feel the sensation it gives the body.
4. Ask God to help you develop it.
5. Believe that God has helped you develop it.
6. Practice using it in your life.
7. Read the list as many times as you can. This will reprogram the mind as to the possibilities of the positive spectrum.
8. Try to use these words in your speech.
9. Take notice of these attributes in others.
10. Invent any way you can to bring these attributes into your consciousness.

"So he drove out the man; and he placed at the east of the garden of Eden Cherubims, and a flaming sword which turned every way, to keep the tree of life." (Genesis 3:24) Charles Fillmore's *Metaphysical Bible Dictionary* states that "a flaming sword" represents our inner motives that rule our thoughts and action. The flaming sword also can represent the negative sign (–). When the imaginations of the thoughts of our hearts are consistently infiltrated with negativity, the flaming sword moves in every direction, keeping us from the total God realization found in the tree of life. I find it intriguing that the cross can also represent a positive sign (+).

The brain stem is depicted as a serpent by yogis, and scientists refer to our limbic system as our reptile-like evolutionary development. Eve says in Genesis 3:13: "The serpent beguiled me and I did eat." When we succumb to negative expressions suggested by the emotional system, we are beguiled by the serpent. The tree of the knowledge of good and evil can be likened to judgment. Without judgment, we have nothing to get negative about.

The Negative Mind

Jeremiah 7:24: *But they hearkened not, or inclined their ear, but walked in the counsels and in the imagination of their evil heart, and went backward and not forward.*

The mind can be divided into various sections that appear to form groups that join together in association. These group associations seem to work in association and disassociation with our essence as they manifest within the mind. We are bombarded with hundreds or thousands of images or thoughts from which we form our associations and disassociations of the self. We can break these groups down into four basic parts.

We have the conscious mind and the subconscious mind. We also have the positive mind and the negative mind. Our conscious and subconscious minds divide into the two spectrums of positive and negative. We know that input into the conscious mind, through the senses, programs the subconscious mind. We also know that we are aware of our conscious mind and unaware of the subconscious mind. The subconscious mind, in turn, influences the conscious mind. The conscious mind seems to be limited to the choices and decisions that are within the programs embedded within the subconscious mind. This is an important concept to grasp.

The conscious, positive mind is governed by the prefrontal lobes. The conscious, negative mind is heavily influenced by the limbic system. And, the limbic system has an edge over the prefrontal lobes—it is an automatic response urge designed to relieve us of the need to think. The limbic system samples incoming information and the negative subconscious mind creates an independent response urge before we have time to use our prefrontal lobes to think.

When you find that you no longer prefer the ways you are responding to life, it is necessary to ignore your feelings and emotions that are urging you to respond as you have in the past. This can be difficult, but you can't go with unwanted urges and change the way you respond to life. It's a matter of ignoring feelings and emotions long enough to begin the creation of positive imagery. There may be times when you may experience a definite separation between your mind and body. Yet this is exactly your goal when you choose to change your responses. The wisdom within this process is to ignore feelings, emotions, and the imaginings connected with them very quickly, so you can then begin to create positive imagery. Speed means less negative urge. By consistently utilizing the prefrontal lobe override, you are imbedding *Imagintelligence* into your mind/body connection.

Very little of our time track, which contains our life experiences on a moment-to-moment basis, stays within the conscious mind. It is our tendency to consciously remember only highlights. We remember what went on an hour ago, but we do not remember second by second. As time passes, we are conscious or aware of less and less of our life experiences on a moment-by-moment basis. Days, weeks, months, years, and even decades become distilled down to a few memories. On the other hand, our subconscious contains a complete recording of everything.

The positive, conscious mind *attempts* to be analytical and logical. It is also filled with information from our memories, containing an abundance of perceptions and imaginings created by the stimulation of our five senses working together. These memory images tend to highlight information and thus we are not aware of everything contained in each image—much like the conscious mind. For example, we can remember how to calculate the area of a circle but we do not remember all of the perceptions recorded in the image when we learned the equation in math class. Things are highlighted that we feel are important to our existence.

Just as the five senses feed our mental images with information, our creative imagination also supplies data. In fact, the imagination takes the sensual information and creates speculations, assumptions, and conclusions that become the bulk of what we believe to be reality. With a minimum of input through the senses, we calculate, speculate, assume, and create new knowledge for a maximum of conclusions. In an analytical way, we search for validations in reality of our speculations, assumptions, and conclusions. We also play with this knowledge in our minds. In the imagination we create the fulfillment of our wants, needs, desires, or entertainment. Basically, our positive images contain reality as distinct from what we would like reality to be.

Although we are aware in our positive mind that an imagination is not reality, *our body reacts and processes our imaginings in the same manner as it reacts and processes sensual input from reality.* Imagine you are loved and in the presence of the Lord and the flesh will react favorably. Chemicals will then be produced that will enhance our physical existence. Our physical body, being enhanced, in turn, enhances our thought quality.

By contrast, the negative mind becomes confused about reality. It is basically in a state of delusion and is *fear and pain motivated.* The negative mind depends on The Fight or Flight Response, which is our response to fear or threat, whether real or imagined. On chemical cue, our negative mind takes charge of our thought processes once we feel threatened, which may be seriously real or a frivolous misconception.

To the negative mind, fear and pain are the dominant factors in all thought. Living in a civilized, heavily populated society, the negative mind is overwhelmed trying to cope with its own programming. We cannot kill. We find it difficult to dominate, yet try in every way. We attempt to repel, but we are generally stuck in situations where this notion cannot work. We attempt to avoid, but the situations we are trapped in often will preclude this. Subconsciously, we form programs that attempt to implement these urges for us. We may become bossy or controlling, grumpy, mean, or shy so as to implement ways to dominate, repel, and avoid. These are merely civilized versions of the mammal pack's basic urges.

These notions to dominate, repel, and avoid have come about to protect us from fear and pain, but there is not enough space to apply these urges in society and in our households. The negative mind applies these strategies in general to situations projected from our fear and pain memories. *The major factors within a memory become symbolic through association of the fear or pain experienced although, singled out, they may have nothing to do with the past fear or pain experienced. Previous similar situations contribute heavily to these schematic symbols.* These symbolisms are not analytical. They are general, crude associations of fear and pain.

We must begin to become aware of these fear and pain symbols in our reality. Fear and pain symbols justify the creation of imaginings of fear and pain or anticipated fear and pain. This is a somewhat ongoing subtle paranoia that the negative mind creates. The high congestion of people, places, and events in our society today opens the door to an overwhelming amount of possible symbols for the negative imagery process with nowhere to escape.

Once we are afraid or hurt we do not necessarily need to be afraid or hurt again to re-experience the fear or pain. We need merely enter into situations that remind us of our fear and pain through symbols we have created in our imaginations through association.

First, we experience fear or pain, real or imagined, and then it is recorded in our memories. These recordings can become imbedded within the body to the cellular level. Also recorded in our memories is the addition of more imaginings, such as anticipations of more fear or pain that the initial fear or pain has caused. The negative mind gets confused about the imaginations of fear or pain in the same way as the body. The body's heart rate and nervous system will respond to an imagination of fear or pain, or the anticipation of fear or pain, in the same way as actually receiving fear or pain. Fear causes more imaginations of pain. The negative mind sifts reality for validations of these symbols. It sifts information in a very non-analytical way. *It does not consider the entire picture of reality. Rather, it chooses pieces of reality to validate the symbols and imaginations of pain.* This is a mighty web of self-deception the negative mind creates as it filters out the positive aspects of our environment that are deemed insignificant since they pose no threat. The attention becomes so encapsulated that we may fail to consider anything else.

Groups of these painful images begin to form by association. They become somewhat like sub-entities. If magnified, they can take on the characteristic of an entity, an alternate personality. In effect, they cause a reaction to our environment via the *irrational reasoning* of the group or groups of these image associations. We are tricked into thinking these are our own thoughts rather than the sub-will of these groups. Actually, these groups are continuously sifting reality for validation and create a *virtual reality* for us. Unlike our positive imaginings that contain reality versus what we would prefer reality to be, our negative virtual realities contain imaginings of the virtual reality versus what *painful, fearsome realities are possible.*

If a person becomes paranoid, validations of that virtual reality will be found everywhere within reality. When we worry, our virtual reality of worry will sift reality for validations. It would be very comparable to putting on virtual reality gear and installing a paranoid program or a worry program.

Our negative emotions are a direct access to fear or pain images imbedded in the body's memory system. The reason we begin to key into a negative emotion is that the fear or pain symbols contained in reality are evident to the extent that the groups of imaginations are gaining validity and potency by association. The more we dwell in the negative imaginations the more powerful they become and the more intense the emotion. As emotion intensifies we pass a point where we are no longer a human experiencing an apparent human emotion. The emotion actually takes control of us. We have all witnessed people who have become so angry that they seem almost as though they are possessed.

Emotions of terror and rage will do this to a person as fear and anger intensify.

Not only does all of our past fear and pain influence us, but all the imaginations of anticipated pain through fear or imagined pain and fear are contained in these groups influencing our thoughts within the negative mind. This is a very important aspect of analysis. Whether it is self-analysis or therapeutic analysis, the factor of anticipated or imagined fear and pain must be considered in relation to past fear and pain instances. Most of the time it is not the fear or pain that strikes us so deeply as the fear and imaginations of more fear or pain.

Extensive research needs to be done regarding the effects of the imagination on the mind and body. I am sure scientists will find imagination much more influencing to mental and physical well being or deterioration than ever before accredited.

When you experience a negative emotion and you find you cannot bounce over to the positive spectrum, quickly analyze the imaginations you are experiencing along with it. You can grow to understand your own mind and how your negative imaginations are influencing you. Do not be shocked when you begin to acknowledge some strange imaginings you may be having.

The virtual reality we experience directly affects the memory. The groups of fear and pain that influence our present reality also influence our memories of the past. Groups of negative images impose an importance on avoiding potential fear or pain, thereby assigning special significance to certain symbols of past bits of reality that we tend to remember while overlooking the fuller picture of past realities—one reason why so many people experience *selective memory.*

Born of this kind of thought are statements beginning or ending with *every time, everybody, anytime, constantly, everyone, they, they all, every single time, always,* and the like. These introductions and endings to statements display the individual's virtual realities that are dictating conclusions and memory. As these groups of images dictate memory, the individual certainly does believe the imaginings of *every time, everybody, anytime, etc.*

It is somewhat overwhelming to conceive the web of negative imaginings that the average person weaves for himself or herself. To grow past these notions, we must begin to acknowledge that there is a big piece of reality we've been missing by permitting ourselves to be drawn into these kinds of self-limiting image patterns.

If we make the choice to not dwell in or create any negative imagery, we will *unplug* from all influences of the negative mind. If you find that you cannot stop creating negative imaginations, start your self-analysis and Imagery Management Program. Observe your imaginations. Create divine imaginations in your mind movie. Ask yourself, "How would Jesus think? How would an angel think?"

The rule of thumb is this: using negative emotion is comparable to pounding your head on the wall—it feels good when you quit. So quit. Make the choice to create positive imaginations and all that follows will begin to be molded by positive creation.

The actual feelings of past fear and pain are stored within the imagery in our memory banks. By returning to the imagery, we rekindle the fire of these past emotions. It's like tending a fire. You keep the emotions alive by tending them. Let go of them. They are not relevant to your happiness or spirituality. The further they are in the past, the less they can influence you today. But for this to happen you must stop tending them. When you find yourself thinking about past fear or pain, *that's your cue to begin the creation of positive imagery.* By doing this, you are taking responsibility for your co-creatorship in the Universe with God.

The negative mind is like a mirror image of the positive mind. It is a reflection of everything in opposition. It's like an ink blotter; it takes everything in but gets it all backward. The negative mind is anti. It is anti-life, anti-personality, anti-logical, anti-productive, and anti-spiritual. It is the anti-you. The negative mind and all it's "advice" is absolutely unusable on the path of spiritual ascension. Unplug from it. You cannot fix it. The less you succumb to its influence, the weaker it gets.

It is slow progress to attempt to repair the negative mind.

Avoiding using it will bring fast results. As we practice fasting the mind from the negative spectrum, the subconscious negative mind dissipates its influence over us. Unfailing positive imagination, thought, and emotion lift the mind into paradigms of divinity untainted by our animal plane of thought. This simply means that when we stop our fear we are then capable of becoming more loving, and we can see clearly.

Negative imagery is nothing less than a delusion, a trick. It is a virtual reality that your body puts forth in the form of an urge, a feeling, an emotion based on how you have reacted in the past. These urges to act are literally your past negative imaginings that are imbedded into your body returning to haunt you if you no longer prefer to respond the way your have in the past. When you justify dwelling in or creating negative imagery, you are not taking responsibility for your co-creatorship in the Universe with God and you are tricking yourself. It's as simple as that!

8

Reality Versus
Schematic Symbolism

Jeremiah 18:12: *And they said, There is no hope: but
we will walk after our own devices, and we will every one
do the imagination of his evil heart.*

The negative spectrum of emotion has its particular imaginings
that interfere with our ability to identify with reality. Once our
consciousness begins to dwell in this area we lose touch with reality because our mind starts to probe reality's attributes for
verifications to justify the imaginations we have created or
reviewed. These justifiers are often found in schematic symbols.
Schematic symbols are bits of reality based on schemata created
by past negative experiences that the mind may twist from the
true nature of the whole of reality; the schematic symbols are
culled out to form justifiers that are imagined even though they
would not be seen by an objective viewpoint that considered all
factors. Schematic symbols may also be initiators of The Fight or
Flight Response. Complexes, for example, need to be fed with
validations in order for them to exist.

Psychologists know that a complex is a figment of the imagination. Sometimes they are based on reality; sometimes they are
not. An obese person may have a complex about being heavy.
This is based on reality. But the imaginings of this person need
not be based on reality. Previous fight or flight responses also
bring a vast amount of imagery into our memory banks that
contain delusive data compiled by the mind filtering out the positive and focusing on the negative.

An example of a complex would be a situation where an over-weight person is sitting in a restaurant and some people at another table laugh at something. Immediately the complex is initiated by the symbol of laughter and the over-weight person is embarrassed, thinking that the laughing is directed at his or herself. The laughing was symbolic to the complex which has become schema—a reference point.

A schematic symbol need not be this close to the reality of a situation. I once was visiting a friend of mine who had a disagreement with his wife. She was taking a nap in mid-afternoon. The phone rang and my friend answered only to find it was a wrong number. The wife stormed out of the bedroom and accused the man of leaving the window open so the Venetian blinds would rattle to wake her, and that he had probably had a friend purposely call so that the phone would also wake her. She was imagining that her husband was plotting against her because they had had an argument. This stemmed from her imagining that her husband wanted to be rid of her. The blinds rattling and the ringing phone became symbols to prove the plot to her.

People suffering from insecurities continually create symbols to validate their insecurities. A jealous man may see his wife coming home five minutes late as a symbol of her cheating. He imagines her cheating, looks for a justifier to validate the imagination, takes a bit of reality, twists it, and presto, he imagines he has *proof* because she is five minutes late.

A woman imagines her husband does not love her any more or is growing tired of her. He loses a card he bought her for Valentines Day. She immediately starts to cry and say that he doesn't love her. She has her proof. He did not buy her a card. Not receiving a card became symbolic of the validity of her imaginations.

A person who really wants to control his or her mind can forgo this entire spectrum of negative imagery. First of all, there is no need to start having negative imaginings. This is the realm of illogic. It is the world of everything that truth is not. Flip your coin here and you will stop it here. If anyone continues to dwell in negative imaginings after this point, reality is becoming lost and the mind will search for justifiers in the form of symbolisms. Negative imaginations need food and symbols are that food.

Symbolizing pieces of reality causes us to reassign the motives or intentions of others, or place exaggerated significance on the actions of others or on the supposed plot behind events. For example, symbolism tricks us into thinking we have a reason for our feelings to be hurt or for us to feel unloved; we have the proof.

Symbols that justify negative emotions are delusions. As with all delusions, the degree of the symbolic delusion is in proportion to our lack of consideration for the whole of reality. Once your attention is encapsulated on *proving* or *validating* a reason to engage in the creation of negative imagery, you certainly are not going to take the time to devote attention to considering all the information regarding a situation in its entirety. If you did, the result would be creating positive imagery. It is the desire to stay within the positive imagery creation mode that sustains our will to create positive imagery despite all appearances. Through this desire, we take responsibility for our co-creatorship in the Universe with God by becoming a vehicle for His Ideas to flow into this plane of existence. We then cease the search for symbols to justify our negative creations.

By staying connected with God, we lose all reasons to identify with negative appearances. When we consistently associate ourselves with God through a positive choice in our imaginings, we disassociate ourselves with the need to rely on schema devised while in a negative state of mind that leads us into the creation of negative imagery. We need no longer be hunters for validations to prove negative born schema as worthy of our attention.

Developing an ability to reframe the symbolism of a situation reeducates what things mean to us internally. When something appears to validate negative imaginings, this is the cue to begin reframing the situation. Reframing a situation is another form of *Imagintelligence*. From a negative perspective, many people are ingenious in reframing positive things into negative meanings. And this is imaginational illiteracy.

Nothing has any meaning to you except what you give it. This is why it is so important to study the spectrum of positive love attributes listed in The Tree of Life. These are the tools we need to utilize in reframing situations in the quest for the silver lining in every cloud.

9

Reaction:
The Automatic Process

Genesis 6:5: *And God saw that the wickedness of man was great in the Earth, and that every imagination of the thoughts of his heart was only evil continually.*

He made me mad. She made me angry. They made me feel such hatred. You make me sick. You hurt my feelings. He made me worry so much. She makes me jealous. They scare me. They make me feel depressed. They made me act foolish.

When you use these statements, someone other than yourself seems to be responsible for your behavior or the way you feel; you just react. Until we finally realize that the way we behave or feel is our own choice, it will seem as though we are victims of the automatic process. I have repeatedly heard the words *made me, makes me, you caused,* and the like. These words are spoken by the *victim.* In this stage of development, life is happening *to you.* You lift yourself above this stage when you realize that what is happening in your life is happening *because of you.*

No one can *make* you have a particular state of mind; we *choose* our state of mind. It may be true that we can pass our threshold of tolerance or endurance and lose our ability to control our choices, but even our threshold increases by the constant practice of creating only positive imagery. And it is equally true that the body's emotional system may put forth a suggested feeling about a situation that urges certain modes of thinking. But the essence of spirituality is choosing positive imaginings and creating love on the basis of inner feelings despite our environment.

The body's emotional system automatically creates an emotional urge based on your past responses in association with environmental factors. It's an automatic program designed to save you the trouble of thinking about how to respond. These automatic emotional urges or feelings also urge thoughts or imagery within the mind. When you find that you desire to change the ways you respond, it is necessary to ignore these first urges or feelings and thoughts. The body's emotional system is designed to work faster than you can think. But you can still think. And if you do not prefer the suggested response, you can create a new, positive response by creating positive imagery. You have to realize that your undesirable responses are catalogued and imbedded within your body and are the result of your past negative imaginings. To change the way you respond, you must ignore the body's suggested response. If you dwell within the suggested response, you give it more power. Time is of the essence.

Our consciousness must dwell in some area of the *imaginations of the thoughts of our heart.* If we decide that our consciousness will now dwell in hate, we will then hate, create the imaginations that hate leads us into, experience the physiological affects, and then feel as miserable as the emotion of hate denotes. The point is: our choice is not an automatic process when made at the level of the imagination, the first manifestation in the order of mental activity.

If we permit our choice to be negative, then another automatic process soon begins. This is the point where fear or threat begins the initiation of The Fight or Flight Response. So, to remain positive, it is imperative that we make our choice before this process begins. It is true that the body's emotional system responds to environmental stimuli and, by association with the past, creates a feeling or urge before we have the opportunity to consciously think. Yet we do not have to succumb to negative urges, especially if we are attempting to change the way we respond to life. Sure, you will feel a little negative for a few seconds in the beginning, but this, too, will fade with persistence.

If we are hungry and we walk into a restaurant, we see others eating. Even if we are so hungry that we have an urge to take the food away from someone, we override the primitive urge. And if this has happened to you, you probably got a laugh when the thought came to mind. All feelings can be overridden if done so quickly. And with practice, it becomes second nature. Just create good imaginings based on values, ethics, principles, and character—and do it quickly with *Imagintelligence.*

The automatic process has been long termed *stimulus/response* or being *reactive*. Once stimulated, response is strictly a reaction in regard to the stimulation. Practicing *Imagintelligence* raises one above this base way of thinking and conducting oneself. The imagination is the level of choice where urges need not be suppressed; they are changed. When we are in control of our imaginings, we are subsequently in control of our emotions and behaviors. We are then *proactive*. We choose how we respond.

If someone kicks another person in the shins, a man feeling that his manhood is at stake may immediately retaliate with arrogance, return the blow, or worse. Another person may yell violently in anger. Another may become fearsome. The person in control of his or her imagery and emotions knows that there are many, many other imaginings and emotions in the positive spectrum that can be used to respond to and control a situation.

For example, an analysis of the situation may reveal that the person kicking may be having a nervous breakdown, which would call for understanding and compassion. It may become known that the person is having a reaction to medication or the lack of it. Or, of course, the party may just be a bully. Forgiveness, compassion, understanding, hope, and kindness—all can manifest humane, heart-touching results. Flight may be the only option where you can end the negativity. In any event, staying positive is the best option.

Humanity at this stage of development does not nearly enough exercise the responsibility of its co-creatorship in the Universe with God. Nor is the average person in the habit of staying connected to his or her divine self within one's positive imagery such as benevolence, forgiveness, understanding, patience, hope, trust, compassion, and, most of all, faith. We have been conditioned far too often to be petty, unforgiving, without understanding, anxious, hopeless, suspicious, and, especially, faithless. We have our peers to impress. Many people admire the negative qualities in others. Children see drug pushers with expensive new cars, plenty of gold jewelry, and admire them to the point of using them as role models. Children see their parents cursing other drivers on the parkway and actually admire that kind of behavior to the point that the children repeat the stories while filled with laughter. As children, we learn to laugh at negative behaviors. Children become very cruel with each other and laugh as the victim cries. The process appears automatic, but it is not. We are more than stimulus/response, mechanical beings— we are powerful, spiritual, and divine.

We may have a habit of allowing others to make us mad or angry, hurt, anxious, or any other negative response. We must create new habits. The Bible tells us that what we sow is what we will reap. The images of our conscious mind slowly sink into our subconscious. This is sowing. These images influence our existence. This is how we reap. II Kings 3:16-17 reminds me to think positively although the results may not come instantly. "And he said, Thus saith the Lord, Make this valley full of ditches. For thus saith the Lord, Ye shall not see wind, neither shall ye see rain; yet that valley shall be filled with water, that ye may drink, both ye, and your cattle, and your beasts."

We simply must begin to use the imaginings and emotion of faith again as a daily practice. A habit of faith is a power builder. Do not reason that you cannot see it, feel it, hear it, smell it, or taste it; therefore, it does not exist. With practice, you can feel the love and presence of God. When you can feel it, you will begin to see it manifest into your life. If you listen, you can hear the word of God in your heart. The power of faith is permitting the power of God to enter our imaginings and heart. But don't stop there. All the other wonderful positive images and emotions are also there waiting to be used. Get in the habit of being positive. Get in the habit of being happy. That's right! Get in the habit of being happy. The many facets of love are the most wonderful habits we can develop. Too much time has already been spent cultivating the habit of using the negative spectrum of imagination and emotion. Get in the habit of being patient. Get in the habit of being loving. This is the automatic process that we must begin to cultivate, sow in our minds, and allow to become part of our hearts.

We have developed our imagery processes long ago, conceived at times when we were hurt and our minds were in a negative state. Almost all of our erroneous decisions derive from fear. Just like adding a new software program to a computer, we must add a new software program to our minds. The program is simply refusing to use, dwell in, create, or give power to any negative imaginings that come to mind before they become an emotion. Bounce your consciousness over into the positive spectrum immediately when negative images come. Make it a habit.

Perhaps some of you need to study the many facets of positive imagination and emotion because these attributes of love may have been unused for so long, or not even known, that a refresher course is in order. Would you rather have the habit of becoming demonic or the habit of becoming angelic in your imaginings? This is the decision you have to make. If you stay positive the world can fall down around you and you will delight in building it back for the Lord. You can turn Hell into Heaven or Heaven into Hell merely by choosing the imaginations in which your consciousness dwells. When someone flips your coin on tails, remember to flip your coin back to heads. This must become the automatic process.

The reward is the mind causing chemicals within the body to be created that will then enable us to feel the affects of these wonderful images with the added feeling of a growing spirituality as the Holy Spirit becomes more and more prevalent in our hearts and body chemistry. The elimination of the toxic chemicals created by negative imagery then permits the body to restructure its chemical messages throughout itself, opening chakras.

When Jesus was transfigured with the Holy Spirit, His body was undergoing a re-chemicalization process due to divine imagery. In other words, His mind's illumination chemically changed His body. It is amazing that we all have the blueprint within our bodies for this to occur if we can continually keep our minds in divine imaginings through *Imagintelligence*. With a little practice, this, too, can become an automatic process.

Positive Imagining

Philippians 4:13: *I can do all things through Christ which strengtheneth me.*

Believing In Yourself

Create and hold a mental picture on your mind of yourself succeeding. How true it is that the subconscious mind will develop this picture. When you understand that your imagination is your greatest power, you can perceive the importance of the imaginations that you create of yourself. This cannot be stressed enough. If you consider that your subconscious mind has the power of God within it to manifest your thoughts into reality, you must take special care concerning what images you create throughout your day within the conscious mind. Loving yourself and creating a mental image of yourself as succeeding, being productive, ascending spiritually, and evolving is the foundation of your growth.

You can begin to really believe in yourself when you consider that you are a divine being having the human experience. Believe that you are like an angel. "What is man, that thou art mindful of him? and the son of man, that thou visitest him? For thou hast made him a little lower than the angels. (Psalms 8:4-5) When you visualize this in your mind, an angelic responsibility automatically aligns in your thoughts. Though we may have trouble living up to this responsibility, we at least know what it is and have begun to consider it. When we consider these things, we begin to practice them and walk in the correct direction.

Visualize Jesus or a deity of your choice telling you that you are now an angel or a saint. Repeat this imagination every day so it begins to sink into the subconscious mind. Practice conducting your behavior with the assumption that these imaginings are true and factual. And true they are. If you do not know it yet, you soon will through self-realization. You are a powerful, spiritual, divine being.

Visualize yourself as the person you have the potential to become. We all have great potential. Visualize attaining this level of your highest self. Keep this image of yourself consistent.

Holding Negative Imagery Drains You

Nothing can drain us of energy as efficiently as negative imaginings. Hate, anger, worry, fear, depression, and the rest of the negative spectrum are like an energy black hole. It takes an immense effort to become stressful and ill at ease. Our positive spectrum of imagination and emotion is easy, relaxing, and entertaining. When the dramas of life tell us, "You have every reason to be angry, you have every reason to be depressed," we can remain calm and at ease, blissful with little effort, and solve our problems with a clear, calm mind. A peaceful mind does not jump to conclusions; it gives full consideration to situations.

Once you stop using your negative spectrum of imagination and emotion, you can go a step further than the personal peace found in positive imagery. When Jesus said to judge not by appearances, there is an important reason for this. When you judge by appearances, for example, "John is lazy," you are creating a mental image of John being lazy. When this image of John being lazy is created in your mind movie, the image *urges this behavior.* And subsequently, the way you respond to John may also urge this behavior. When Jesus said that when you must judge, use righteous judgment, He meant the image created of the individual who is the object of your judgment should be of an ascending quality. "John has been behaving lazily, but he will certainly grow past this quickly." This way, the behavior is urged toward positive action and the *essence* of a person is not judged.

This is the responsibility of the peaceful mind. This is the powerful urge that a peaceful mind can generate in others.

As we interact with people, others need our positive imagery urging them toward the light. Practice this daily and you will witness the Holy Spirit pour from you into all who interact with you. It may not show immediately, but the seed has been planted.

As we interact with others, those who are the most aggravating, the rudest, and the most unlikable are the ones who need our uplifting positive imagery the most. And when we pour the Holy Spirit through us into them, we are giving our peace to those who need it most.

The workable uplifting themes of positive imaginations are unlimited. Visualize love beams emanating from your heart into their heart. Create an imagination of them growing, ascending spiritually. Visualize yourself breathing in their pain and fear, removing it from them forever. The power of these imaginations is amazing and it is scientific.

We simply cannot create too many wonderful imaginations about people and life. The time spent doing so by a powerful, peaceful mind is time spent in the greatest, most admirable way.

Energy

Without the constant drain of negative imaginations and emotions your body not only relaxes but generates energy that may be utilized purely on the positive spectrum of mind/action. As your mind dwells in The Kingdom of God, your energy builds like a storehouse of usable power as the negative subconscious mind's influence fizzles away.

The positive spectrum of imagery opens your enthusiasm toward life. There is no greater energy builder than an enthusiasm born of positive imaginings. Through this parallel of imagery with the God-Mind, we are in constant contact with God. We become intensely interested and are filled with enthusiasm as God's divine plan incorporates us into our self-realization.

The imagination is unlimited in what we can create as energy builders. Visualize beams of pure God-energy coming from the heart of Jesus or Buddha and penetrating your heart. Visualize true enthusiasm and zeal filling your body. Or visualize being completely engulfed in God's light surrounding you, filling you. The possibilities of these imaginings are infinite and the body will create the chemicals necessary to make you feel the images you hold in mind. What could make us feel more energetic than the Holy Spirit growing within us? And share the Holy Spirit. Each time we share our insights and a person sees light because of us, we feel wonderful.

It is also necessary to eat correctly. The most recent research on the hormonal stimulation of food within the body shows that the government approved Food Pyramid is WRONG for anyone with syndrome X (insulin resistance). The AMA revised the Food Pyramid in July 2000 for insulin resistant people. Every farmer knows that you fatten stock by increasing grain and trim stock by reducing or eliminating grain. Research now shows us, through scientific fact, that insulin is our greatest enemy. The high carbohydrate diet recommended by doctors and nutrition "experts" is causing a high insulin level in the blood. Insulin is a hormone that tells the body, *Store fat and hold on to it.* Higher levels of insulin with little glucagon, the hormone stimulated by protein, causes us not only to store fat, it causes a metabolic situation that promotes disease.

The discovery of eicosanoids, (pronounced eye-kah-sah-noids) powerful hormones created within the body's cells, has confirmed the harm to the body from insulin and glucose spikes—higher levels of glucose and insulin than the body was designed for. There are good and bad eicosanoids. We need both. But the good ones must be dominant. High carbohydrate eating results in high insulin levels and promotes bad eicosanoids. Bad eicosanoids promote hardening of the arteries, heart disease, respiratory problems, cancer, fatigue, and other metabolic problems.

The best ratio of protein, fat, and carbohydrates has been

established by Barry Sears, Ph.D., in his 1,000,000+ copy best selling book, *Enter The Zone*, as 40% carbohydrates, 30% protein, and 30% fat for a perfect metabolic balance. If you want to enter the zone of optimum health, reading this book is a must. Eating this ratio of macronutrients promotes the highest energy level you can attain. I believe that the more active you are, the more carbohydrates you can eat without harm. Activity inhibits insulin stimulation.

Three to six grams or more of methylsulfonylmethane (MSM) per day can give an abundance of energy. Amino acids, enzymes, vitamins A, C, D, E, co enzyme Q10, pantothenic acid, selenium, calcium, manganese, and germanium are all sulfur bonders. The FDA has never compiled data on our need for sulfur because it is found in all food. But, refining, processing, and cooking food removes vast amounts of organic sulfur leaving us sulfur deficient.

Most of us are short on enzymes from not eating enough raw fruits and vegetables. Many of us have parasites. We all know to worm a new dog, but our doctors assume that we all can go through life without contracting parasites. Yet we tell our children not to feed ice cream and candy to dogs and cats because they will get worms.

Candida yeast overgrowth in the gut from antibiotic medicines cause many side affects. Antibiotics kill off the good bacteria that the body needs. Mainstream doctors do not treat people for candida. Candida suppresses the immune system by allowing food to enter the body without being bonded to the proper enzymes. This may lead to food allergies.

Many of us are short on tissue salts from not eating enough raw vegetables. When the body has all the tools it needs, it naturally has an abundance of energy and a strong immune system.

We can conquer anger and a vast array of negative imaginations and sometimes feel our vitality sagging. As a foundation, we must eat well. It is very difficult to feel vibrant without eating the whole foods God provides us. We can eat processed foods with enzymes and nutrition destroyed, and then take vitamin, mineral, and enzyme supplements, but God created the *proper combination* of these in His whole foods. Study nutrition and learn about the most recent research. It will be years before recent findings on diet and nutrition trickle into the medical and nutritional world. Refined white flour, refined white sugar products, beer, white rice, and potato-based foods zap the body's system the hardest with high levels of carbohydrates that quickly convert to glucose. Fresh fruits and vegetables are high carbohydrate foods with slower entry into the blood due to fiber and the type of sugars they contain.

To control insulin and eicosanoids, balance your metabolism with the correct balance of carbohydrates, protein, and fat every time you eat.

Salts are used throughout the body to the cellular level. Many people take tissue salt supplements for this reason. We must give full consideration to the nutritional needs of our body's cells. Rid your mind of the illusion that you are feeding you. *Eat for the sake of the body's cells.* The extra energy the body wastes working to convert the poor nutrition we take in is a tremendous drain on our vitality. The conversion process highly depends on activity. The less exercise we get, the more the body must live on the poor nutrition we get. Eat well; feel well. We don't put water in our car's gas tank or sand in the engine, yet we can easily do the likes to our body. The body is the temple of the Holy Spirit. Love it, respect it, and cleanse it. Too many people do not have a clue about what the body needs for optimum health. Too many people think they are eating well because they eat a sufficient amount.

The food we take into our bodies is chemicals. These chemicals urge thought in the same way that chemicals create the feelings we call our emotions, which in turn urge more thought in regard to that emotion. Whole foods urge pure thought, while heavily processed and junk foods urge negative thoughts. This manifests as our behavior. Studies of prisoners have revealed that the average criminal has had a poor diet high in junk foods.

To gain strength, we must first weaken. Thus we must exercise until we feel ourselves weakening. To gain energy, we must expend energy until we feel it running low. Thus we must become as active as we can be. A healthy person needs about three hours per week of vigorous exercise or about seven hours of walking. If you are handicapped, have your doctor work with you so you can do what you can. Intense interest is the best substitute for exercise. When we are filled with enthusiasm and zeal, we feel energetic.

Mentally and spiritually, negative imaginations and emotions are an energy drain. The mind becomes deluded and the anti-world of thought grows. The unlimited positive images we may create can bring energy flowing into us in the same way negative thought drains us. Visualize God's pure energy in the form of light entering your body. Practice this in unlimited variations. Tap into the unfailing energy of God. Visualize it, see it, make it part of you in your mind. Just as we can become filled with worry as we create worrisome images, we can become filled with energy as we create energy filled visions of God and His power flowing into us.

Prayer

When you pray, every problem can be solved. As you pray to solve problems you must be careful of your imaginings. We cannot pray and then, when we are finished praying, create the images of worry, being trapped, or whatever problem we are experiencing as having no end in sight. The movie we create on the screen of our mind will equate to the sum mathematically. A positive imagination and a negative imagination will cancel each other out.

Prayer is wonderful, beautiful imagery. After the image is created, we must not only place it in God's hands for deliverance, we must put forth conscious effort with the image. Most importantly, we must believe that God has answered our prayer. Give thanks that the prayer has been answered even if you have not already witnessed results. If you believe it has been answered and have not witnessed results, it is in the making. Results are coming. Give thanks. Visualize your prayer as being answered. Create a clear picture in your mind movie of the answered prayer. This is truly tapping into The Kingdom of God within you.

Creating Happiness

First of all, chemicals within the body produce the actual feeling of happiness. Of course, these chemicals are produced as the result of imaginations of happiness. As a happy person can project happiness into his or her reality and see many reasons to be happy, an unhappy person can project unhappiness into his or her reality and see countless reasons to validate this mental state.

Appreciation is a sure happiness builder. When you appreciate what you have, yourself, and life itself you see many reasons to be happy. How can a person who controls one's imaginations and keeps one's imaginings in the positive spectrum be unhappy? Unhappiness is caused by the use of the negative spectrum of imagination and emotion. Fasting the mind from negative imaginations is a wonderful way to be rendered happy. The natural blueprint of the body's re-chemicalization through the positive spectrum of imagery creates happiness.

Just as a wizard creates a brew of elements to achieve alchemy, we too are the wizards behind our physical bodies. The elements we must use are the vast array of positive imaginations, all essential to our brew of chemicals produced by the body, leading to emotion, and experience. When the Christ consciousness is tapped by our minds, we now have the main ingredient in our re-chemicalization.

At the first thought of any unhappiness, we need only visualize Jesus (or the deity of your choice) standing next to us beaming us with pure love. Through this kind of imagination control we will not only feel happy, we are changing our existence to dwelling within the Holy Spirit. This is happiness and beyond.

Stop Fuming, Fretting, and Worrying

When we permit God to run the universe and our lives, we learn acceptance and surrender. Most fuming, fretting, and worrying are the results of our bullheaded notion of needing to control. When we need to control and cannot control, we fume, fret, and worry. The more we need to control, the more our fuming, fretting, and worrying is magnified. Just kick back and let God run things while we do our best. Remember that God has a much bigger picture of life than we have. He sees things we miss. Talk to God each moment you can. Every time I find myself struggling with something I'm trying to accomplish, I can always stop and realize that I'm not consulting my partner, God. And God is everyone's partner. Don't try to do things all by yourself when we all have a partner like God. Accept the way things turn out when they turn out differently than we may think they should. He is working within the big picture. We are working within the little picture.

We all need to be concerned. Worry is over concern to the point that we begin to create negative imaginations about sinister situations about to befall others or us. By creating these imaginations, we are inadvertently praying for the very thing that we do not wish to happen. Thoughts held in mind produce after their kind. The movie we imagine in our minds must have God as the star. It is very easy to get drawn in by the worry habit. This also stems from a need to control. We conquer worry when we turn life over to God and try to do the best we can. As with all habits, worry can be broken with God's help. Tap into the indwelling Holy Spirit and you have nothing to worry about.

Create wonderful imaginations about your day, the ones you love, the community, and the world. Be so *unrealistic* as to become what others may label as eccentric. Keep producing the uplifting movie in your imagination with God as the star. Realize that worry itself is a red flag warning you that your faith is slipping, your ability to succumb unto acceptance may be dwindling, or you are trying to control. Stop as soon as you catch yourself. You will soon find that what you rationalized as *realistic* was merely an illusion born of your worldly thought conditioning.

Expectation

Jesus taught us the concept that if we can believe, all things are possible to he that believes. Fire your heart with expectation; feel as though it has come to pass and it will. Through the insight that we receive from Chronicles 28:9, we learn the proper order of mental creation and physical manifestation: " . . . the imagination of the thoughts of the heart of thy people . . . " This is the proper order for firing the heart. Visualize and expect the best, the best for you, the best for humanity, the best for the universe. After you imagine these things, they become the thoughts of your heart. Fire the heart with imaginations of zeal, enthusiasm, interest, God's work, and God's word. And expect! Expect in the purest, most unselfish way possible.

Self-Doubt Leads to Defeat

Self-doubt is the greatest obstacle to success. The second that we begin to believe we are defeated, unto our belief it will be given to us. Rather than even slightly considering defeat, we must, at the very most, consider what appears to be defeat as a temporary setback, a delay. God is likely to have a good reason for this. He may want us to pursue a different path. Things may work out better in the long run. We can, at best, only speculate about what we think we know. Through faith we learn the patience we need to accept and await God's answers and plans for us.

Our tendency to create images of many seemingly insignificant negativities undermines our positive imagery. Once the major negatives such as anger, greed, hate, vengeance, and other high level negatives are conquered, we find an almost infinite amount of little, even tiny negativities. All these little self-doubts add up. Negative words in our speech, "I hate it when I run out of gas," little negative assumptions, "I knew he would be late," seemingly insignificant negative thoughts, "Why is everyone too lazy to do dishes but me," all add to the sum of our positive and negative math equation of imagination. Changing the way in which we express ourselves is critical. "Running out of gas causes unnecessary delays. I will try harder not to do so." "I believe he will be on time. If he isn't, I'm sure he will improve." "I thank you Lord that I have dishes to do. I hope everyone else in the house will appreciate doing dishes as much as I do." It's just a matter of changing your words to uplifting images.

When you judge, judge with righteous judgment. Picture everyone ascending in your mind movie. In this way we are constantly sweeping the dust from our minds that may be accumulating rather than defeating our purpose. To do otherwise is to assume that people have an evil purpose rather than that they are divine beings. When the behavior of one of my children was undesirable, I never thought that this was symbolic of the child's essence. It was a temporary problem. So it is with us all. This is why we must create the same uplifting image of everyone and ourself. You aren't defeated until you imagine you are.

Solving Problems

Every problem has a solution. By keeping a calm, cool head and not permitting negative imaginations and emotions to enter our hearts, we are able to think clearly. The moment that we allow our consciousness to dwell in negative imaginations and emotions, we begin to fail in our ability to consider the whole of reality, all the facts. The less we consider the whole of reality, the more delusive our conclusions become. Full consideration with a clear mind opens our hearts to the indwelling Holy Spirit to guide us through our problems.

Write down the facts concerning the problem, pray about them, and then visualize them as becoming solved. Sleep on it if you have the time. Use the power of your imagination. Visualize enlightened souls beaming you with a knowledge ray.

The imaginations are unlimited, and they stimulate the Holy Spirit within you.

Faith and Healing

When you are sick, see your minister as well as a doctor. We can't deny that the physician, as well as the Holy Spirit, plays an important role in healing. Shamans are many times playing both roles. A modern doctor who incorporates God into his practice can always attest to witnessing miraculous healings. The placebo factor has become a high consideration in the testing of new drugs. The most important thing an ailing person can do is to create an image of God healing his or her body. The more people incorporate faith, the more conscious effort and attention is put forth toward healing one's own body. When we join in the healing endeavors of others by creating the divine movie on the screen of our mind, our conscious effort and attention reinforces the healing endeavor of the other individual. Believe, believe, believe, imagine, imagine, and imagine. And remember, our beliefs will equate positive/negative until the sum of all imaginations and prayer are distilled down to the positive or negative remainder of the whole.

We must clean away our doubts, our fears, our worry, and our depression. Although we can say this is truly difficult, in actuality it is much more difficult to experience negative imaginations and emotion. Especially when we consider that by dwelling in the negative spectrum we are inadvertently praying for these negative things to happen through the power of sustained negative imagery. Always consider that the very first thing you must do to manifest something into the physical world is the creation of an image in the mind. Control the imaginations, incorporate God into them, and we can do mighty works. Do not limit imagination! The Kingdom of God is within you and so is the power of God when we create the image of Him performing mighty works through us. Through acceptance, surrender, faith, and imagination we truly capture the mysteries of The Kingdom of God. And through imaginings of total faith, we can heal others and ourself.

New Positive Imagery Renews You

We have the ability to change our very existence through our thought processes. The inflow of new thoughts definitely remakes us, but it is as equally important to eliminate old negative imagery and old paradigms that lead to negative imagery. If someone slaps us in the face, we have been conditioned to take this as an insult. The urge is to become angry. Yet, if we grew up in a culture where a slap in the face was a gesture of friendship, our urge would be that of affection. So it becomes necessary to rethink and unlearn our conditioning. In order to justify negative imagery, we have our lower self speaking to us, "Only a fool would not be angry after what he did to me." "You hurt my feelings. I have every right to be mad." "I have had one stroke of bad luck after another. How can I feel any other way than depressed?" These are examples of worldly, negative imaginings. Through fear and pain, we justify our negative imaginations. We have the illusion that we have every right to feel this way, that only a fool would not feel this way, yet nothing can be further from the truth.

There are no legitimate justifiers that can validate the use of the negative spectrum of imagery. The second you believe there are appropriate times and situations to dwell in or create negative imaginings, your consciousness has passed into the anti-world. If we consider that these negative justifiers and thoughts are actually the anti-Christ manifesting through us, we can grasp how very critical it is to keep our consciousness in the positive spectrum. II Corinthians 10:3-5 states: "For though we walk in the flesh, we do not war after the flesh: (For the weapons of our warfare are carnal, but mighty through God to the pulling down of strongholds;) Casting down imaginations, and every high thing that exalteth itself against the knowledge of God, and bringing into captivity every thought to the obedience of Christ." So when we create negative imagery, we are going against the indwelling Christ within us.

As we eliminate our old thought processes, it becomes necessary to create new, positive thought processes. Affirmations are a wonderful positive thought and faith builder. Explore the Scriptures by a concordance search on faith in the chapters Matthew, Mark, Luke, and John. By affirming faith it will become part of the subconscious mind. Subconscious mind cleansing is the point to conscious spiritual thought. We are told that we use only a small percentage of our minds. But this is what we use consciously. The greater percentage of our mind is very active. Our subconscious mind contains the power of life, the indwelling power of God within us. Keeping the consciousness within the positive spectrum in our imaginings throughout the day programs the subconscious mind with positive uplifting images. Just because we are not aware or conscious of the subconscious mind's influence and activity does not lessen its power. Our entire existence stems from the projections of the subconscious mind. It shapes and forms our reality. We can work on renewing our conscious self, but the subconscious remakes our reality. So our entire existence is remade through our conscious imaginings. And it all starts in the imagination.

Create an imagination of yourself being reshaped by the hand of God. Produce the most fantastic mind movie of this life you can muster through the limitless imagination. Wisdom, understanding, pure love, faith, enthusiasm, strength, and power through God await you. Control the imagination and you have the secret to life. What better way is there to constantly renew the mind than to consistently engage in the creation of positive imaginings?

Relax—Let God's Light Shine Through Your Face

There is no greater way to relax than through surrender to God. Stop trying to control something. Just do your best and let it go. When we try to run things, we will cave in under the strain.

A critical place to focus our positive imaginations is at work. Too many of us get caught in the trap of loathing our job. Yet, how many third world people would trade places with us in a heartbeat and feel like a king? If you would like to advance in your work, create the imaginations that will take you there. Do what it ethically takes. But be careful in choosing what you want to do. We cannot serve God and mammon. All wealth needs competent stewards, but the true wealth is found within The Kingdom of God within us. When we focus on material gain, we lose sight of spiritual ascension. Material gain can be experienced as a result of spiritual ascension. The more we are determined to serve God and the brotherhood of man, the more material things we will have at our disposal to help us on this quest. This is the Lord providing for our needs rather than for our wants.

You are important in your job. Create ways to fulfill this truth. Attitude, ability, attendance, and a loving, positive, responsible nature on the job will lift your job spirit as well as open the door to the possibility for advancement.

Within God's divine plan there are endless possibilities for advancement through His never-ending synchronized coincidences. Imaginings such as "I'll never get anywhere working here," place limitations on God. Millions of people have advanced from the most humble of positions in their work. Everything is possible through the imagination when God and faith are prominent in our mental images. If we can only realize how many opportunities we miss while our consciousness is engulfed in the negative spectrum, we will soon learn the importance of a clear positive mind.

Relax the body. Relax the mind. Surrender your imagination to God. The most powerful form of active meditation we can practice is letting the light of God shine through our faces. When we disconnect from God long enough to experience negative imaginings, it shows up in our faces. Look at your face in the mirror. Relax every muscle. Think of the love of God and let it swell in your heart. Notice how it beams through your face. Project this face to everyone you come in contact with. This is witnessing the word of God at its highest. People will see your face and know you are onto something. They will notice how you carry yourself, how you behave. They will become curious. They will want some of what you appear to possess. Then, when you speak the word of God, they will listen because they see it manifesting in the loving glow of your face. Believe me, you cannot express the light of God through your face if your imaginations are not within The Kingdom of God. And equally, as you physically project the glow of God's light through your face, you will urge divine imaginations in your thoughts. The body urges the mind; the mind urges the body. At the first sign of negative imaginings, focus on projecting God's light through your face and the mind will follow. Just as we see what we are and we are what we see, we feel as we look and we look as we feel. Mind and body are one. Relax the face and you are relaxed. Project the light of God through the face and you are directly in touch with the Holy Spirit. This is easy power.

Getting People to Like You

Since we store information in the form of mental image pictures, create a picture about each person's name. Everyone is flattered when you remember his or her name. Be pleasant. Don't you like being around pleasant people?

Aside from being positive, it doesn't hurt to be interesting. Better yet, be an inspiration. When you inspire someone they love being around you. There is no greater inspiration than the feeling of being uplifted spiritually. Sharing any insights at all will create affinity for you—if you have listeners. Never force your point of view on anyone. People carry a lot of pain. If you initiate a healing within them, they will be appreciative.

Most importantly, love people. Let the spirit in you flow out to those who need it most. Any of us can love the lovable. Those who appear unlovable are people who have been hurt to the point that they project this hurt into their personalities. If we consider that negative behavior is the absence of the Holy Spirit, the Holy Positive Spectrum of Divine Thought, we can see the responsibility we have to pour out our positive spirit into those who need the light. Darkness needs light so we can see. When the spirit awakes within us, it is our responsibility to light up the darkness. People are attracted to light. Everyone wants to come to the light. And they will appreciate you for lighting their life.

Be empathetic and make people comfortable while you do this. Don't force your beliefs on people. When people feel comfortable around you, they like you. In this way, you can be an inspiration to them without appearing to be forceful in your beliefs.

Heartache

My mother used to tell me anytime I was depressed or had an aching heart, "Get busy. Do something and you won't have time to feel miserable." I was well over thirty before I could understand the wisdom in such a statement. When we are hurt, the mind naturally tends to dwell on the hurt. We can sit idle and dwell on our hurt indefinitely, but this will make matters appear worse. We are creating chemicals of hurt within the body, which are in turn urging more imaginings of hurt. The cycle continues with the imaginings of hurt creating more chemicals within the body, which urge more imaginings of hurt. This can be like falling off an emotional cliff.

It can be almost impossible to control your mind when you are involved in an intense situation involving heartache. Your only hope is to distract the mind. You can do this by busying yourself. Simple household chores, which we neglect first off when we are heartsick, can greatly improve your state of mind. This may not be enough action or may not fully occupy the mind as much as is needed to distract it. If so, try doing something more important or do something for another person. Help someone. If all this involvement does not distract the mind enough, if you are healthy, run or work out. The more active you become physically, the less the emotional pain can influence you.

Most importantly, you must control your imaginations during times of heartache, grief, mourning, and all serious trials and tribulations. You may deem this as difficult, but once again I will state that it is more difficult not to do so. The shortest verse in the Bible is John 11:35: "Jesus wept." It is quite natural to mourn over the death of a loved one. Jesus wept over the death of Lazarus. But Jesus created an image of Lazarus being raised from the dead as He wept. We need to do likewise. Though we may not be able to raise the dead, it is necessary that we create a positive ending to these scenes in the movie of our mind. If we do not, we will become lost, separated from God, and the pain can grow to undesirable proportions. Stay connected with God in times of heartache. Keep the heartache divine. Experience it, then let go of it. If you hold onto it you will be placed in the position of having to let go of God in order to remain attached to the pain. This is where you must draw the line. This is where a genuine positive heartache experience becomes a negative heartache experience.

The highest levels of spiritual imaginings permit us to feel bliss throughout an experience of heartache due to death and tragedy. As the writer, producer, director, and star of the movie in our minds, we can write the script any way we choose. Visualize loved ones who have died as ascending to God, becoming an important person in God's Kingdom, as becoming a positive force in helping humanity, as becoming liberated through death. These positive thoughts will even have an influence on the deceased person after his or her death.

Sogyal Rinpoche, author of *The Tibetan Book Of Living And Dying*, discusses this in great detail. The deceased need our positive imaginings for direction, for help in their possible liberation or direction after death. I strongly urge everyone to read this book.

A Higher Power

One of the basic criteria for twelve-step programs is the belief in a higher power. Through our imagination we not only have the ability to tap into a higher power, we can become this higher power within our unity with God. The imagination is limitless. When God is the leading element in our imagination, we are united with Him; we are paralleling His thoughts or will. As eccentric as creating love beams, power rays, light beams, and visualizations of Jesus or other deities performing miracles may seem to be, creating them within our mind movie breathes life into the power of God within us.

Within our concepts and understanding of angels, we believe that they help us on this plain of existence. Since angels are not in physical form, they use the power of their imaginations to manifest the changes necessary for our help. We can do the same. We have this same power. The more we practice consciously and willfully using our imaginations, and humbly include God as the power source, the more we become angelic in thought. The power of God is within us, within our imagination. Tap into it; use it. Use it to heal and bring the Christ into the collective consciousness of humanity.

The Power of Negative Thought

Proverbs 6:16-19: *These six things doth the LORD hate: yea, seven are an abomination unto him: A proud look, a lying tongue, and hands that shed innocent blood, an heart that deviseth wicked imaginations, feet that be swift in running to mischief, a false witness that speaketh lies, and he that soweth discord among brethren.*

To deepen our understanding of positive thinking, the power of negative thinking needs to be brought to the attention of everyone because it has an even greater power than positive thought. This is not to say that the power is a good power or that it can be used productively. But it is necessary to make perfectly clear the powerful *anti* effects negative imagery has in our lives and how it works against God's Divine Plan by closing doors that would be opened or remain open when we continually create positive imagery.

The mind has a dual nature, positive and negative. The negative images we create are the *undoer* of our positive thoughts. They are the anti-you, the anti-life, the anti-love, the anti-divine, the anti-good, the anti-logic, and, most of all, anti-Christ. In effect, the creation of negative imagery reflects fear through the desires of the flesh that manifest the beast in us.

Negative imagery is the opposite, mirror image of positive imagery. Negative imagery is the cowardice of valance, the suspicion of trust, the hopelessness of hope, the foolishness of wisdom, the fear and hate of love, the pessimism of faith, the anger of bliss or compassion. Name any positive imagination and it will have opposing negative imagery when there is an absence of God.

When you are once again in a positive state of mind after experiencing a negative emotion, look back and analyze what took place and you will find that it did little good to create the negative imagery the emotion was based on. The only good that will ever come of the creation of negative imagery is the knowledge of realizing its disastrous effects. It's like pounding your head on the wall and realizing it feels so good when you quit. Acknowledge the imaginations you were experiencing while you were in the negative state of mind. You will always find that you were of the illusion that you were without God.

When we say "I," we are referring to the positive "I." None of us views ourselves as the negative self. We know it is there, but who wants to view his or herself as a hateful, faithless, cowering, depressed, anxious, greedy, lustful, fearful, or worried soul. We know these qualities are there to a greater or lesser degree, but this is not "I," it is the flaw or shortcomings of "I." None of us really wants to be negative. We just fall for the automatic process—the illusion that we must respond to the hand life deals us with the seemingly fitting imaginings and emotion. If this were true then we could not be happy unless life was going smoothly with nothing going wrong. We would need to live in utopia. Most people fall for the illusion that money is the problem but we all have heard, witnessed, or experienced that this is not so. If you are a negative thinker, no matter how much money is in your life you will still be a negative thinker. I have seen my share of power-hungry, ulcerated millionaires. I have also witnessed happy souls who were quite poor financially but rich in spirit. Some of the world's greatest saints are renunciates. They are happy.

If you are a creator of negative imagery, you can create your own Hell out of Heaven. If you are a co-creator with God and a creator of positive imagery, you can create Heaven out of a hellish situation.

As I now believe that my mind is in Heaven and only my body is here on Earth, I look around me and think how amazing it is to discover that life on Earth can be Heaven for all of us if only we will let it be. Once, my imagination drifted to the would-be thoughts of a soul a thousand years ago. I could see the imaginings of such a soul dreaming what Heaven would be like. As I became this soul, I imagined a place where there is beauty and wonder. Where we no longer needed to walk or ride animals. We had magic carriages to propel us along to anywhere we wanted to go. We could make passage through whole countries in a single day. I saw a world where we no longer needed to build fires. We had heat that just warmed us in our homes with no effort on our part. We had cookeries that were magic and heated our food with a wave of the hand. We no longer needed to slave for hours just to make a few garbs for us to wear. These things were provided already made. We no longer needed to burn fires or lanterns to see. Light just happened.

There, in this place, we all pitched in to build a world for God and the newcomers so they too could have the gifts of God. Anything we wanted was provided. We could wave our hand and see anything we wanted, hear anything we wanted—beautiful music, plays, education, wonderful scenery. In this place, everyone could even fly. It was a place where we could learn anything we wanted. There were schools and great libraries filled with thousands of books.

This daydream of the past really describes the here and now. We have all of these things, but our negative imaginings create an illusion that everything is not enough. Life on Earth really is Heaven, but the negative imaginations of the inhabitants of this wonderful planet are causing the hells to manifest. If no one had any negative imaginings, this world would be Heaven. We need rules, governments, police, armies, court systems, psychiatrists, and the likes only to control man's negative imaginations.

The Bible says that God repented that He had made man because every imagination of the thoughts of his heart were evil continually. Our evil imaginations are what stand between Earth being Heaven and the hellful existence that so many people live. The homeless, the starving, the sick, the hurt souls of this world are all products of the overwhelming power of the negative imaginings of the multitudes. If we all take responsibility in our co-creatorship with God as creators of positive imagery, through the power of the mind of each and every one of us, the world will change to Heaven.

A friend of mine, Lee Farmer, wrote a story that tells of such negative thoughts and how they affect us.

Once upon a time a young wanderer came upon a great sage sitting alone atop a mountain. "What are you doing?" asked the young one. "I am helping save the world," replied the great sage. The knowing sage saw confusion on the young one and began to explain how THOUGHT was the most powerful thing in God's Universe. "Thought," he said, "is of the highest vibration. If one slows that vibration it becomes light and if one slows it even further it becomes matter. My teacher called it coagulated thought. The greatest gift God gave humankind was free will. We choose to make our thoughts positive or negative. Unfortunately, thousands of our brothers and sisters are consumed in negative thoughts. They are like steampots filled with so many negatives that they spread those negatives every time they open their spouts. As time goes on, those negative vibrations slow and are manifested in the Universe as evil. Through the ages, there have been hundreds of great masters who have spent every waking moment overcoming the negative thoughts of thousands."

The young wanderer pondered this for days and told his parents of his encounter. His father, being a wise man, noted how much better this world would be if all people focused on the positive. These great masters could then spend their time creating wondrous miracles. This young wanderer was so moved by what the sage and his father had said that he spent the rest of his life focused on positive thought, giving no weight to negatives.

After years of practice he is now a great sage on his

own mountaintop. Though he didn't save the world while traveling on his path to that mountain, the seeds he planted along the way are growing into the next generations of great sages.

You can make a difference! Spread some positive thought.

Negativity manifests into the Universe through the imaginations of the thoughts of our hearts. It manifests as darkness. From domestic violence, child abuse, and petty hatreds to power hungry, greedy leaders of nations, the negative imagination is the culprit behind it all. We breed it, instill it, create it, and perpetuate it with our everyday imaginings. We instill it into our children. They watch us use it. We use it on them. We take positive actions for granted, but negativity spreads like a juggernaut of some outbreak of a powerful virus. When you stop and think about it, the concept of Satan becomes obsolete. With all the negative imaginations of six billion people manifesting into the world, why do we think we have a Satan willing his evil into this world? When we realize the power of the accumulated negative imaginations of the multitudes, we can then see that there is no need for a Satan concept. Without God being the source of our imaginations, mankind can appear quite evil enough on its own. We need no help from a devil.

You can be positive for a week and one hour of negativity will undo all the positive accomplishments. You can be positive for a whole lifetime and undo all the positive accomplishments in a day. All the world's positive accomplishments can be wiped out in a few hours if our leaders start pushing the buttons to the nuclear missiles. The power of negative thought is much greater than positive thought. Positive images are each little brick in a wall. Negative images are the bomb that blows the wall down in a few seconds.

This is why Jesus said in Matthew 6:34: "Take no thought for the morrow; for the morrow shall take thought for the things of itself. Sufficient unto the day is the evil (negative imagery) thereof." Get it through your head; you are contributing to the absence of God if you think negative, even if it is just worrying or being depressed. Evil (negative imaginings) takes on all shapes, all sizes and accomplishes deeds blatantly or subtly. The absence of God's light renders Grandma to worrying herself to death, it results in kids picking on each other, it leaves us feeling depressed, it leaves us feeling greedy, it results in our lusting. How many marriages have failed after one day of lust creeps in and takes control. Years of marriage go down the drain. Years of trust fade with one act.

There are few congratulations for positive actions, but our negative actions can be limelighted and destroy us. A man can spread the word of God all his life and be considered by all to be the greatest of men, but find him doing one horrid act and years of positive deeds are lost to our sight. Think of everything that has went down the drain that took years to accomplish after a few moments of negativity. It is astonishing. Great minds quit learning after years of study and sacrifice. Great musicians quit after years of practice. Governments and nations collapse. Everything can be traced to negative imagery. It is the weak link in the chain, the straw that breaks the camel's back, the fray in the rope, the flaw in the diamond, the limp in the walk, the blindness in sight, the darkness in the light. It is truly the anti-life.

My father used to tell an interesting story. He told it to illustrate the importance of doing a good job in any project to which I turned my hand. Apparently, it is a folk tale that parents tell children in various styles that evolved from a Benjamin Franklin quotation that he borrowed from the seventeenth century religious poet, George Herbert. So, this is my family's version.

Long ago, there once was a mighty kingdom ruled by a mighty king. Everyone in the kingdom was happy and all loved their fair and just king. All the workers in the kingdom took great pride in their work and each performed his trade with diligence. The kingdom was filled with great craftsmen who were proud of their work. The craftsmen had all apprenticed under the older fine craftsmen and learned the art of doing the best job a person can do.

One day a lone traveler came into the kingdom looking for work. This traveler seemed to have no real skills. He went to the king's palace looking for work in the kitchen and asked if he could work there, but the head cook had many apprentices and feared that the traveler would be too much trouble to supervise. Another apprentice had spoiled one of the king's meals and the cook was watching out for the king. The traveler went on to the head servant, but he had many apprentices and was fearful because one had dropped a tray at a meal and embarrassed the king. The head servant was watching out for the king. The traveler went to the king's gardener, but one of his apprentices had knocked over one of the king's flowerpots and the gardener was afraid to supervise any more apprentices. He too, was watching out for the king. The traveler then went to a bench to eat a humble portion of food he was carrying. The head cook was there with the head servant, the head gardener, and the blacksmith. They all were reasonable men and began to talk among themselves about helping the traveler find work.

The cook said he was afraid for the sake of the king's food. The servant said he was afraid for the king's image. The gardener said he was afraid for the king's priceless garden pottery. They reasoned to the blacksmith that the traveler could work for him and no one need fear for the king, for what harm could the traveler cause working with the king's blacksmith? The blacksmith agreed and hired the traveler.

The blacksmith's shop was beside the king's stables because he made all the shoes for the king's horses. The first job the smithy gave the traveler was shoveling out the stalls in the stable. The traveler was glad for the work, but was very unhappy about the job shoveling manure.

His mind filled with resentment and frustration. Later in the day the smithy called the traveler to begin teaching him how to shoe a horse. The smithy prepared the horse's hooves and had the traveler observe the shoeing process. When he had completed three shoes he told the traveler that he was to now do the forth shoe and afterward he was to finish shoveling the stalls. The traveler's mind filled with resentment at the thought of any more manure shoveling. The smithy watched as the traveler pounded the nails into the last hoof and was satisfied with the new learned skills of the traveler. Before the traveler had finished the shoe, the smithy was called away do something important and told the traveler to finish the last shoe and he would check it later. The traveler's mind was so filled with resentment about shoveling manure that he did not put in the last nail. He then led the horse back to the stable and disappeared from the kingdom rather than shovel manure.

A messenger appeared to the king exclaiming that an evil army was closing in on the kingdom that would surely conquer the king's army if he did not appeal to a nearby king for help and join forces. The general of the approaching army would conquer both kingdoms if they did not ally forces. The king immediately dispatched his son as a messenger to go to the nearby king and ask for help. When the prince went to the stable to get a fresh horse, the stable hand gave him the horse the traveler had just brought back knowing the horse had just been shoed.

The prince rode like the wind toward the other kingdom to warn of the approaching conqueror. As he was riding the horse, the shoe that the traveler had not put the last nail in began to loosen. Finally, the loose shoe made the horse stumble and fall. The prince was killed by the fall. The message was never delivered. The evil army closed in and conquered the kingdom.

For the want of a nail, the horse did stumble. For the

want of a nail, the prince was lost. For the want of a nail, the message was never sent. For the want of a nail, the kingdoms were lost.

This story epitomizes the power of negative thought. One negative imagination can have this much power. Doors can slam in our face that would be opened if we did not create that negative imagery and do that negative deed.

Visualize a big city with all the negativity of a day. Intoxicated people beating their kids and beating their spouses, crack heads with their crack missions of paranoia, deceit, and robbery, neglected homeless people, hateful people, depressed people, thievery, plots, arrogance, perverts looking for victims, gangs looking to kill someone. It's all in a day's negativity.

There is hope for all this within the resurrected mind, a mind that rebukes all notions of the negative spectrum of imagination and emotion. This is a mind that is in touch with the indwelling Christ, a mind in touch with spirituality, with God. This is the dawn of the twenty-first century. As a species, we no longer need The Fight or Flight Response. We no longer need to use our negative spectrum of imagery. It is impossible to use to any benefit. No good can become of its use except the relief we experience from stopping its use. Negative imaginings are primitive. We are not the beasts of the jungle although we have made a jungle of the world.

There are poisonous snakes, hungry lions, herds of stampeding elephants, alligators, and black widow spiders out there in the asphalt jungle in the form of corporate executives; people with hearts full of competition and cut throat greed; criminals lurking, plotting, scheming; lying politicians plotting for gain; bankers laundering money for murderous drug pushers. The beasts are out there just as in the jungle. The strong survive. The weak are prey. Greed rules. Negative imaginations are truly demonic in quality. Negative imagery brings out the monster in people; the lust, the hate, perversion; the horrid, selfish acts on the world that bring murderous, grievous, heartbreaking effects into life.

One of the greatest examples of negative imaginations is the crucifixion of Jesus. Imagine thinking a man who preached only love, a man who manifested so many miracles being accused of consorting with the devil because He performed miracles or dared to pick an ear of corn to eat on the Sabbath. Many Jews were so afraid of God that they followed the scriptures to the letter so much they lost the concept, the spirit of the scriptures. Negativity was so strong at the time of Jesus that even miracles would not convince the negative minds of that era of the presence of God within Jesus.

Fearful was their point of view. Until Jesus, man's state of mind was as described in the Old Testament: man walked in the evil imaginations of his heart continually. Mankind continued to do so at the time of Jesus. Jesus was born into a very negative world. Many Jews had a mammoth fear for God so powerful that they became a people with hearts filled with suspicion, ready to kill anyone that disagreed with or broke the law of the scriptures.

The imaginations of fear and suspicion laced with greed, superstition, tradition, and a lust for power are what crucified Jesus. These were negative thoughts so powerful that, to many Jews, killing Jesus appeared to be the logical thing to do. It appeared to be a service to the people.

Jesus suffered the cross to show mankind that no matter how many miracles you perform negative thinking will totally justify any deed, even killing the Christ. What an amazing viewpoint that was. Eyes looking at things through suspicion see suspicious things. The crucifixion was negativity at its highest level, a level of ignorance filled with fear and suspicion that was perpetuated and magnified after the death of Jesus. Millions of people were killed in the name of Jesus. The killing started with the Christians as the victims, but the Christians then killed as conquerors spreading this doctrine of love. There have probably been more people killed in the name of God than for any other reason.

Today, different denominations of Christian churches feverishly declare that only those belonging to their church will be granted salvation. I once heard a sermon from a preacher declaring that the devil has spirits in little statues, tarot cards and

Ouija boards, and to stay clear of these satanic articles. He then followed up this concept by accusing Hinduism, Yoga, meditation, and Buddhism as being religions of the devil. He believes all these wonderful age-old religions are of the devil and damnation is coming to all who practice them. It is fearful, suspicious thoughts like these that lead to religious wars.

I have read that Spanish soldiers arrived upon strange shores and read from a scroll to the people there to now profess their souls to Jesus Christ as their personal savior. If these poor souls did not understand Spanish, they were sometimes put to death for noncompliance.

After the crucifixion of Jesus, a river of blood did flow in His name. How could man murder in the name of a teacher of love? This viewpoint can only be understood when you look through the imaginations of suspicion, fear, and other forms of pure negativity. Only the negative mind could reason such atrocities.

When you realize that The Kingdom of Heaven starts with your consciousness dwelling continually in the positive spectrum of imagery, you will begin to see God's Divine Plan unveil to you. Permit your mind to dwell in negative thought and your consciousness leaves Heaven and enters a hell where you begin to do the so-called devil's work. God's divine plan is immediately inhibited. For the sake of a nail, the kingdom is lost. The veil of ignorance shall remain as long as you use your negative imagery spectrum. Remember, it is not the very thought that counts, it is our allowing our consciousness to dwell in negative imagery that creates the destructive force within these imaginations. The longer we dwell on negative imaginings, the more power we grant our negative emotion to manifest darkness onto this Earth through us. This manifestation is the undoer of life's perfect interaction through God's divine plan.

It is necessary to stay positive for quite some time to see God's divine plan unveil with the abundance intended. We will see the immediate results of becoming positive, but it takes a while for the negativities we have propelled into the Universe to make their cycle and fizzle out. This is the unfailing boomerang of action-reaction in the laws of the Universe, karma.

When we persistently dwell in divine imagery, we can become liberated from karma. The transformation, the renewing of the mind breaks the necessity of the action/reaction within karma. As we rise in consciousness, we experience a karma that is in accordance with the higher level of consciousness.

12

Parallel Universes

I Corinthians 15:45-49: *And so it is written, the first man Adam was made a living soul; the last Adam was made a quickening spirit. Howbeit that was not first which is spiritual, but that which is natural; and afterward that which is spiritual. The first man is of the Earth, earthy: the second man is the Lord from Heaven. As is the earthy, such are they also that are earthy: and as is the heavenly, such are they also that are heavenly. And as we have borne the image of the earthy, we shall also bear the image of the heavenly.*

Plato speculated that there are really two worlds, the physical realm that we know through our senses, and the world of pure ideas. He implied that we see things in their true form only in the idea realm. Today, the image is considered to be a mental picture of an idea or concept. What we create as an image in our mind is our interpretation of the realm of pure ideas, a reflection of our perceptions and belief system. Plato's understanding of pure ideas is similar to the metaphysical concept of the ideas of the Formless. Considering Plato and metaphysics, the image can still be considered the primary manifestation in the order of mental activity. It is the first step from the formless to the form, the first manifestation of the expression of the formless from the Mind of God to the human mind. Since the realms of the formless, pure ideas, and the image are all intangible, it can be said that they occupy the same Universe. We can call this the Intangible Universe.

The physical world is the realm of form, the material world.

It is a result of the ideas and intentions of the formless. We can call this the Tangible Universe. Positive emotion is the first manifestation of the Intangible Universe in the Tangible Universe. Negative emotion does not originate in the Intangible Universe. Rather, it is the result of a feedback loop originating or appearing to originate in the Tangible Universe.

Our consciousness and awareness are able to travel freely between theses two Universes by the focus of our attention. The Tangible Universe usually has a great deal of our attention because we are linked to it through our five senses. We keep track of what is happening in the Tangible Universe. We have work to accomplish, responsibilities, things we have to do, and things to move. We are forever rearranging matter. Yet, inasmuch as the Tangible Universe has a great part of our attention, we naturally bounce our attention to the Intangible Universe regularly. In fact, we tend to spend as much time in the Intangible Universe as we can afford. Even though we have a limited capacity for processing incoming information through the senses, our attention drifts to the Intangible Universe where we imagine things. We imagine the intentions and motivations of others, daydream, plan ahead, and on and on. And although we are only part-timers in the Tangible Universe, and we only believe what we see, we really only see what we believe as we busy ourselves returning as quickly as possible to the Intangible Universe where we are free to create anything we choose—instantly.

Oh, how dangerous we would be, as the gods we are, if our imaginings manifested immediately into the Tangible Universe. Even the consequences of our feeling the misery caused from negative emotions resulting from our negative imaginations has not been a deterrent from the urge to create negative images with our co-creation gift from God. Yet, the effect of negative imagery does not stop there. Disease, poverty, confusion, and fear all manifest, directly or indirectly, as we have created it within our negative imaginations.

It is by the grounding or rooting of our attention in the Tangible Universe that we persist in the first stage of existence—

everything is happening to me. Within this belief system is the notion that the Tangible Universe is our first concern and what we possess in this Universe will then cause us to enter into a desirable state of mind. Yet, by grounding our attention in the Tangible Universe, our imagery faculty becomes vulnerable to the situations and dramas that unfold within this Universe. We literally place our state of mind, the way we feel, in the care of the weaknesses of others and the dramas of our life experiences. Our five senses become input channels to our consciousness for the sole purpose of a feedback loop that originates and ends in the Tangible Universe, initiating our imaginings, creating the way we feel. We then feel like our environment. Some people are so vulnerable to their environment that they permit even the weather to affect their state of mind. We hear statements like, *I feel gloomy when it rains. When it's sunny, I feel wonderful.*

Sensual input reports directly to the faculty of our belief system, another member of the Intangible Universe. Our belief system is heavily governed by the image we hold of ourself. Who and what we believe we are affects our beliefs in general. Self-image greatly affects what information we deem important, what information gets ignored, and what choices and decisions we make based on the information we choose to accept or ignore.

It is necessary to keep in mind that we do not have the mental capacity to take in all sensual input, acknowledge it, remember it, and conclude from it. To cut down on the amount of information we think we need to consider, we develop information filters in accordance with our core belief system. This filtration system renders us vulnerable to seeing what we believe and failing to consider the rest of the information. Literally, what we conclude is going on in the Tangible Universe is a product of our core belief system through the "eyes" of our self-image. Sensual input is filtered through our belief system formulated by our self-image and then goes on to influence our faculty of imagination within the Intangible Universe—that is, if our attention is grounded in the Tangible Universe. As you involve yourself in this feedback loop grounded in the Tangible Universe, it becomes evident that you are interpreting your sensual input with great bias. You see what you believe you are. Physiologists know the very fact that we convert the physical world into organic interpretations gives way for much margin of error. Add the self-image and core belief system as governing information and we are subject to any number of highly erroneous interpretations.

Even physical pain may travel through the imagination, although much of it may bypass it. Yet the imagination may take the physical pain, enhance it, assign a meaning to it, anticipate more, fear more, speculate what more pain may feel like, and fear that as well.

The Intangible Universe is a one-way street. Ideas flow forth into the Tangible Universe. Although the Tangible Universe may attempt to give feedback to the Intangible Universe, the feedback information travels only to the edge, the imagination, and is returned through the self-image belief system.

But, what about grounding our attention in the Intangible Universe? The immediate advantages are:

- **A connected feeling with God.**
- **A connection to the Intangible Universe where we may tap into the Source of all Pure Ideas.**
- **The ability to create the type of imagery we prefer to manifest into the Tangible Universe rather than to permit the material world to create our imagery for us, which may be negative and result in a negative feedback loop.**
- **Our creations of positive imagery appear in the Tangible Universe as:**
  a. Positive feelings and emotion
  b. Positive moods and states of mind
  c. Spiritual ascension
  d. Abundant reality

With time as a consideration, emotion is an on the spot appearance of our imagery. Moods and states of mind become the summation of our imagery and emotion over a period of time. Our spirituality is a product of our imagery, emotion, moods, and states of mind over a period of time. Our reality is a product of our imagery, emotions, moods and states of mind, and spirituality over a period of time.

> Psalms 82:6: "I have said, Ye are gods; and all of you are children of the most High."

> John 10:34: "Jesus answered them, Is it not written in your law, I said, Ye are gods?"

If we remove time from the consideration of our ability to manifest, perhaps we could see more clearly that we are gods. It is only our impatience caused by our preoccupation with the illusion of time that creates the illusion of the control level we have over the Tangible Universe. Some imagery manifests quickly, while other imagery takes a long time. We can easily be drawn into doubt as time passes and we see no results of the imagery we are holding. And too many times we discount secondary thoughts of doubt as our impatience mounts. The doubt created by unexpected and unwanted time undermines our ability to manifest what we want. Yet the Tangible Universe is a result of imagery we hold whether or not we consciously choose our imagery or permit the Tangible Universe to create it for us out of the influence of appearances. Time is transcended by faith when we do not wear faith away with resentments and doubts.

If we consistently hold an image in the Intangible Universe, it will manifest in the Tangible Universe. Though emotions are manifested on the spot, the rest appear to take time. By returning to an imagination time after time, we solidify it in the physical realm. (Thoughts held in mind produce after their kind.) Running the imagination over and over just before sleep allows the imagery to slip into the subconscious mind where the picture is developed into the Tangible Universe.

The subconscious mind is our God-like power. All that we imagine during the day sinks down into the subconscious mind where it creates our Tangible Universe. Positive creation programs us to tap into the depths of the Intangible Universe where pure ideas can be found. Negative imaginings inhibit our ability to tap into the pure ideas of The Formless.

Our imagination is the interpreter of the ideas of the formless Intangible Universe and converts them into the world of form in the Tangible Universe by holding the image in mind. As God attempts to express through us, our imaginations interpret His Intention and thus pass His expression through us. God has nothing to do with our negative imagery. It is separate from God, just as we feel separate when we experience fear. And all negative imagery is founded in fear. God is cause. The Intangible Universe cannot cause God. But The Intangible Universe can cause us to create and experience positive imagery—if we allow it, if we surrender to it.

The Power of the
Subconscious Mind

Isaiah 55:7: *Let the wicked forsake his way, and the
unrighteous man his thoughts: and let him return unto the
Lord, and he will have mercy upon him.*

The constant use of our spectrum of positive imagination and
emotion has a direct effect on our subconscious mind. The
imaginings of the day sink into your subconscious mind where
they become the essence and product of the sum of your conscious imagery. In effect, your conscious imagery becomes your
reality through your subconscious mind. Your beliefs are
ingrained into your subconscious mind. Imaginings, beliefs,
thoughts, assumptions, and impressions all form the subconscious program that imprisons the conscious mind. Thus our
conscious freedom is restricted to the limitations we self-impose
through the subconscious programs we form throughout our life
as we create and dwell in negative imagery.

When someone is deeply under hypnosis, the hypnotist is
speaking and dealing with only the subconscious mind. A person
under hypnosis can be told that they are cold and they become
cold. If she is told to support herself with her head on one chair
and feet on another chair and become rigid, she will do so. Great
strength can be displayed. The hypnotized person's reality
becomes, through the suggestions of the hypnotist, whatever the
subconscious believes.

Our daily thoughts affect the subconscious mind in the same
way. We form images in our mind, sift reality for validation of

these imaginings through symbolism, and then these thoughts sink into our subconscious mind. The subconscious then is a product of our imaginings whether or not our conscious imagery is valid, invalid, evil or good, positive or negative. It does not matter to the subconscious mind. Our imaginings become imprisoned within the limitations we engrain into the subconscious through consistency. Whatever we give our attention to, we get more of. Whatever we consistently imagine becomes increasingly real.

Experiments with placebos demonstrate that whatever the conscious mind believes strongly enough, the subconscious acts upon. Conscious belief can override subconscious programming and limitations. Throughout the ages, many miraculous healings have taken place. Many of these miracle healings have been initiated by fraud. People have been duped into thinking the bones of dogs were the bones of saints, and yet healed. When it is believed that the bones of saints have healing powers, it does not matter to the subconscious mind weather the bones are actually bones of saints. All that matters is that the person wanting the healing believes that the bones are the bones of saints and that they have healing powers.

In the book, *The Shaman,* by Piers Vitebsky, there's a story of a man named Quesalid, a Kwakiutl man from Vancouver, Canada. By apprenticing as a shaman to learn the tricks of the trade, Quesalid set out to prove that shamans were conjurers and frauds. He indeed did learn many tricks to make it appear that he was conjuring up the help of the spirit world. This man became a practicing shaman who healed so many people with such success that he would not stop his charade. He continued because he was healing so successfully, even though he, himself, thought he was a fraud. Quesalid's conclusion in the end was that ultimately he did not know weather real shamans existed. He did know that people who believed in him and his tricks were healed. Quesalid sparked the people's imaginations, and their subconscious minds ordered their bodies to heal.

Although this kind of healing may appear to be the result of conscious healing, what is happening is that the conscious mind believes so deeply that eventually the subconscious mind creates a new program; thus the previous limitations are removed or extended. And that, of course, is the object of this book, to remove or extend subconscious limitations through conscious endeavor. It can be a slow process or it all can hit you so that you are enlightened in the twinkling of an eye.

The power of our subconscious is not limited to our own mind and body. Others can and do influence us with the power of their conscious and subconscious minds. Prayer is a powerful example of this influence.

There are many healing methods based on the belief that within the imagination there are realms where the separate imaginations of people can unite or meet. The possibility that one person's imaginations can directly affect the imaginations of another person hold profound implications in healing the mind, body, and spirit, as well as for learning experiences.

The Silva Method, developed by the late Jose Silva, has been taught in more than twenty languages in more than a hundred countries. This thought system promotes the utilization of the imagination for healing yourself and others. One of the techniques is The Mental Laboratory, a fascinating concept where you construct a laboratory in your mind equipped with everything you need to heal yourself and others. You create the imagery of the appropriate healing taking place in this laboratory under the appropriate circumstances. You can also have expert advisors in the lab. And it works.

Cardiologist Randolph Bird studied 393 patients who were admitted to the San Francisco General Hospital coronary-care unit. Neither doctors, nurses, nor patients were aware of who was being prayed for by home prayer groups.

The patients being prayed for had astonishing results. The patients receiving prayer were reportedly five times less likely to require antibiotics and three times less likely to develop pulmonary edema, a condition where the lungs fill with fluid because the heart is not pumping properly.

Experiments such as this interested Larry Dossey, M.D., who has since become one of the world's experts on the effects of prayer in medicine. In more than one hundred controlled experiments, Dr. Dossey has shown that "prayed for" test tube bacteria grow faster, "prayed for" yeast resisted the toxic effects of cyanide, and "prayed for" rye grass grew taller.

Dr. Dossey has been quoted as saying, "I adore these experiments. Because they don't involve humans, you can run them with fanatical precision and you can run them hundreds of times. It's the best evidence of all that empathic, loving, compassionate intentionality—in other words, prayer—can change the world. And it operates as strongly on the other side of the Earth as it does at the bedside."

Science has proved that the one thing faster than light is thought. In an experiment with identical twins with the psychic ability to feel each other's pain, one twin was sent to the opposite side of the planet. When pain was induced on the first twin, the pain was transferred to the twin at the other side of the planet at a rate faster than the speed of light, when compared by atomic clocks and electroencephalogram readouts.

Prayer is the most divine use of the power of the subconscious mind. When we pray, we are creating an imagination of divinity in our conscious mind that sinks into our subconscious mind where it then unites with the cosmic power of God. As we believe and have faith in what we pray for, our thoughts materialize into reality through the power of the subconscious mind, which is in unison with the power of God. This is why faith is the most powerful resource a human being possesses.

We've all heard the saying that we are what we eat. In exactly the same way as our body becomes what we eat, our spiritual essence becomes what we think. Actually, what we eat also affects our imaginings. Poor nutrition and poor eating habits will not lead to a sound mind for divine imagery. The more pure and balanced we make our body, the more pure the mind.

Our reality is distilled to our imaginings of each day inasmuch as our consciousness can be likened to a vast self-hypnosis.

As we continually have conscious imaginings we are experiencing many repetitive image patterns. Anger or peace and joy are the result of continuous negative image patterns. Tell yourself something enough times and you will believe it. Your subconscious will manifest what you believe and make it your reality. Our self-esteem, whether high or low, is a result of our imagination patterns. Our reality becomes exactly what we believe it to be; or, in other words, what we imagine it into. By consistently applying *Imagintelligence* to our thought processes, we create new response programs within the subconscious mind. After some time, the body's emotional system may start suggesting positive urges as the first feelings and thoughts even when you appear to be in a negative situation.

14

Imagination Control Therapy: The New Software Program for the Mind

Matthew 18:21-22: *Then came Peter to him, and said, Lord, how oft shall my brother sin against me, and I forgive him? till seven times? Jesus saith unto him, I say not unto thee, Until seven times: but, Until seventy times seven.*

Basic Imagination Control Therapy Criteria

To unplug from the negative mind it is necessary to install a new software program in our thought processes so, as in the analogy of The Parable of the Coin, we can flip our coin (consciousness) from tails (negative) to heads (positive). There are several criteria to orient yourself with to understand and activate this new consciousness in learning to apply *Imagintelligence* in our everyday interactive responses.

• When you desire to change the way you respond, it is necessary to ignore the immediate feelings, emotions, urges, and imaginings that come over you so you can stop and consciously override your body's first impulse.

Every negative imagining you have ever created has been recorded within the mind/body connection in the fashion of an organic artificial intelligence program that is based on past responses and through associations of incoming sensual data with the past. The body's emotional system samples incoming data and suggests a response. This suggestion is in the form of feelings, emotions, urges, and imaginings that suddenly appear. To change the way you respond, it is necessary to ignore these impulses until you can willfully and quickly begin the creation of positive imagery.

The body's suggested urge comes first to save you the trouble and time of contemplation. This urge may also be an evolutionary animal instinct. The impulses come first. Ignore them. Follow up immediately with the prefrontal lobe override—willful and conscious thought. Doing this consistently literally builds more neural connections and reconstructs your brain hardware to respond more and more to willful conscious thought rather than allow it to succumb to the emotional system.

• Develop the knowledge that you are a co-creator with God AND that your imagination is your co-creation faculty.
• Develop faith in the logic of positive imagery to the point that you feel good about creating it despite all outside influences that appear to dictate the notion or urge to create negative imagery.

This faith begins with an intellectual faith, the knowledge and logic where we are able to rationalize that dwelling in negative imagery results in negative consequences to others or us and that all divine and positive imagery is grounded in love and parallels the intention of God. As you practice intellectual faith, your spiritual faith develops far beyond your intellect. Through this faith, you assume responsibility as a co-creator of good in the Universe with God.

I have seen a few people argue that they would feel foolish having blind faith to the point of creating positive imagery when things are in chaos or in moments of serious misfortune. I can only respond by saying that creating negative imagery in any situation will always seriously inhibit our potential to handle the situation with a clear mind and thus usually causes us to justify doing something foolish or worse. You absolutely must come to terms with rebuking the urge to dwell in negative imagination and emotion. If there is a single doubt in your mind about this, you will continue to justify using your negative spectrum of thought.

• Assign less value to the information you receive through your senses.

When you believe everything that seems apparent as you receive information through your senses, you are most likely neglecting to have your consciousness connected with God and you are judging only by appearances as Jesus has instructed us not to do. Righteous judgment extends beyond appearances. "Judge not according to appearance, but judge righteous judgment." (John 7:24) This may be the most difficult mind training effort you will undertake. You have spent your entire life believing what your senses of sight, hearing, touch, smell, and taste have brought to you. *But our spirituality is not limited to information received by the senses.* You have the faculty of *imagination.* This faculty, with its creative ability, consistently exceeds the input of information by the senses and when aligned with the God-Mind brings love, clarity, and righteous judgment.

We also have the ability of *direct knowing.* As you keep your consciousness connected with God, you are also connected to the Universal Mind. You can suddenly just *know* something. Most familiar are the terms: *intuition, insight,* and *instinct.* Being connected to the Universal Mind, the imagination that utilizes creative intelligence with intuition, insight, and divine instinct combines into powerful additions to the information received through the senses. When we neglect information that may be received from these sources and judge solely by appearances, we are very much limiting the data on which we may be basing our decisions and choices.

• Don't take anything personally.

Although this may seem to be a tough perspective to train

your mind to, refusing to take anything personally stops The Fight or Flight Response from initiating. It also gives you the opportunity to realize that the people you interact with are acting out their own perspectives and their behavior has nothing to do with you. Even when they insult you, it's nothing personal, it's their own perspective manifesting. Once you catch on to this, you eliminate considerable stress in your life. And when you internalize the behaviors of others to have no negative content that relates to your character or essence, that's *Imagintelligence.*

• Realize that appearances are usually based on a projection of your belief system. You wouldn't have seen it if you didn't believe it.
• Develop a sincere desire to develop and improve your self-image.

At the heart of the urge to create or dwell in negative imagery is the lack of positive belief in your self-image. *The very image you hold of yourself forms your belief system.* Your belief system influences your choices in your decision making process. Your choices determine your actions.

In the school of New Thought, it is fundamental to believe that we are divine beings having a human experience. All beliefs that we are born sinners, unworthy, conceived in iniquity are to be dissolved. We are born a perfect creation of God. We are powerful, spiritual, divine beings. We are all worthy, good, wonderful, compassionate, kind, gentle, loving people. To believe anything less is to believe a lie.

Orthodox Christianity has pushed the dogma of the original sin of man. For the past few millenniums it has been drilled into many minds that we are worms of the dust, miserable sinners. And this mind virus spread globally. At the center of this concept, the fifth verse in the 51st Psalm has been limelighted: "Behold, I was shapen in iniquity; and in sin did my mother conceive me." This was David in a depressed, lamenting state of mind after he came to terms with the greedy and thoughtless act of sending

Bathsheba's husband to the front lines of battle to die so he could have her for his own.

At a time when David was in a high state of consciousness, he wrote the 8th Psalm. Here is Truth for us to believe about ourselves. Versus 3-5 say: "When I consider thy heavens, the work of thy fingers, the moon and the stars, which thou hast ordained; What is man, that thou art mindful of him? and the son of man, that thou visited him? For thou hast made him a little lower than the angels, and hast crowned him with glory and honor."

How about Genesis 1:27: "So God created man in his own image, in the image of God created he him; male and female created he them." Or Psalms 82:6: "I have said, Ye are gods; and all of you are children of the most high." Didn't Jesus quote this verse when He said in John 10:34: **"Is it not written in your law, I SAID, YE ARE GODS?"** Using these truths as guidelines, we can feel good about believing we are masters—divine, powerful spiritual beings.

If you do create and dwell in negative imagery, when you are back in a positive state of mind look back and analyze the emotions and imaginations you experienced. You will find that dwelling in negative imagery seriously inhibited your potential. It seriously inhibited God's intention for you to have the highest quality experience that He intended. Observations such as this should confirm to you that the negative spectrum of creation is futile. Realize that when you create negative imagery you are surfacing what is in your belief system that reveals the area of your self-image that needs work.

In our conversations between our higher and lower self, sometimes called The War in Heaven, we hear our lower self telling us, "You have every right to be angry." "Who wouldn't be angry if this happened to them?" "Anyone in there right mind would want to choke a so and so like that." If there truly are justifiers to create negative imagery, then why do so many of us hold the illuminated, enlightened mind in such high esteem? Can we believe that an enlightened being would justify creating negative imagery if they were in our shoes? I think not. *There is a price for total peace in our lives. That price is ceasing to create negative imagery.* This is a small price to pay for a continual inflow of God energy and bliss and a consistent feeling of unity with God.

It is imperative to understand that there is a difference between dwelling in negative imaginations as compared to imagining negative consequences of decisions or pondering negative possible results that may occur. *Dwelling* in negative imaginations creates a mind movie that in turn creates the negative chemicals of which negative emotions are dependent. Acknowledging the negative long enough to avoid it or create something positive out of it is quite different than dwelling in the negative until the undesirable chemicals are created in the body causing negative emotion.

Once you come to terms with justifying the use of your negative spectrum of creation, you can now begin to run a self-analysis concerning any negative images you may continue to create because you cannot seem to stop yourself. It is progress to become negative, acknowledge that this is an area that needs improvement, and to then try to stop or prevent further episodes by considering the development of an Imagery Management Plan, rather than justifying the whole episode. When we admit that we have no justifier to create negative imagery, we can begin to layout an effective Imagery Management Plan.

Unplugging from the negative mind, through a realization that we are co-creators, manifests a major leap in self-development and spiritual ascension, allowing total faith, the logic of the bigger picture, and a sincere desire to develop our self-image. A true seeker will immediately know that this is a streamlined path to enlightenment, self-realization, total God realization, or divinity; say it as you will. To rebuke dwelling in or creating all negative imagery and emotion—while developing the mastery of creating positive life experiences—feels right and has an immediate effect on the mind and body through re-chemicalization. As you practice this thought process, your faith will progress from an intellectual faith to a spiritual faith. You will become a vehicle for the faith expression of the indwelling Christ. You will know who you really are.

Keep in mind that I say to rebuke negative imaginings. This is not saying that they will never again come to mind; it is saying that we must not permit our consciousness to create these thoughts or dwell in them for any length of time. When negative imaginings enter into the mind, acknowledge them and then, very quickly, choose a positive imagination to replace them.

• Understand the very fact that when you find yourself beginning to create or dwell in negative imagery *this must become your cue* to immediately create positive imagery.

It is necessary that you invent ways on your own that you can achieve the perspective of finding something positive to create. This mastery is to change your viewpoint or perspective to an angle where you can find something positive. There are many ways to find the silver lining in the cloud. Here are a few.

• Humor is a wonderful way to change things around. It is better to laugh than to cry. It is better in general not to take life too seriously.
• In more serious situations, look for wisdom and lessons.
• Each situation is an opportunity to express (and teach you) who you really are.
• Look for the bigger picture.
• Acceptance and surrender are other necessary considerations for the big picture.
• Use your powers as a powerful, spiritual, divine being in combination with your faculty of imagination to create imaginings parallel with the intention of God.
• Reinforce your positive imaginings with your physiology. Your mind and body are one. The way you carry your body, your facial expressions, your vocal tones, your internal dialogue tone, your body language, your posture, and breathing all have a subconscious association with emotions and mind states. Imagine positive scripts and create a positive physical appearance.

As you learn a spiritual lesson or insight and forego the misery of the negative emotional experience each time you rebuke creating or dwelling in negative imagery, you feel more and more comfortable with letting go of your urge to dwell in or create negative imagery. *Thus, by learning to bypass your present belief system and to create positive imagery **despite what you may believe, despite what you may hold as your self-image, despite appearances, despite how you feel**—you are assuming the responsibility of your co-creatorship with God.* Witnessing the results of continuous positive imaginings as you conduct your co-creatorship builds your self-image and redefines your belief system. Thus, by acting the part in your divine imaginations through faith and a higher logic, you become the divine role you are playing.

The priority of ceasing the creation of negative imagery and its subsequent emotion has far more importance in relation to your spiritual success than the amount and quality of positive imagery you create. It is through your ceasing to create negative imagery that you fulfill the principle of Matthew 6:34: "Take therefore no thought for the morrow: for the morrow shall take thought for the things of itself. Sufficient unto the day is the evil [creation of negative imagery] thereof." In other words, channel all your energy into ceasing the creation of evil (negative imagery and its manifestations of internal dialogue, speech, and deeds) and tomorrow will take care of itself. Simple, isn't it?

This is a paradigm shift from the conventional approach regarding positive thought that focuses on techniques for developing and evolving positive thoughts and concepts, but more typically neglects direct techniques to avoid being drawn into negative thought. In basic Imagination Control Therapy, the focus of your attention is on techniques for ceasing to dwell in and/or creating negative imagery and its subsequent emotion and action. Once you discover that you can avoid negative thought, you are able to progress in a more stable spiritual ascension. You become more grounded. *Your positive creations naturally unfold and bloom without the handicap of continuous periodic intervals of negative imagery.* The result is a continuous renewal of the mind and self in your co-creatorship with God and a continuous elevation of the quality of your life experiences moment-by-moment.

The Basic Imagination Control Therapy Software Program

• *Something happens, a situation develops that appears to urge the creation of negative imagery and emotion.*

• *You then discover that you have a negative imagination in your mind or your feelings are becoming negative.* There may be times when you are engaged in internal dialogue, speaking, or action when you may not have your attention on your imaginings, but your body will feel the imagery. *This is your cue* to initiate a change toward positive imagery. Your body's emotional system has made a suggested mode of feeling and thought. The prefrontal lobes of the brain are on a second or two delay.

• *You then acknowledge the imagination or feeling and ignore responding to it.*

• *At this point, you must accept this challenge by exercising your responsibility as a co-creator, faith, and a desire to improve your self-image.* Despite any appearance, despite any way you may feel, you become loving and create positive imagery. Love makes the difference in who you are. Through faith and knowing who you really are, and by understanding that the creation of positive imagery will not be inferior to the creation of negative imagery, you will come to terms with any risk you may attempt to reason, such as feeling foolish. Acknowledge that this faith and awareness is how you are renewed in mind and self.

• *Next, search out and find a **realistic viewpoint** or perspective where you can choose to create positive imagery through your own creativity. Or, **distract** your mind away from negative imaginings by purposely abandoning the situation mentally* *until you can handle it with love.*

Actually, by directing your attention to remaining unified with God, you are influenced by His creativity. Your Mother/Father God always creates a direction for your imagery to form, offering you the opportunity to create the highest quality experience possible. All we have to do is surrender to His Idea.

This change in imagery will automatically change your emotional urge. Keep in mind that emotions are manufactured on the spot by your imaginations. Even if you delay until a negative emotion begins to develop and strengthen, you can reverse the process by creating positive imagery as quickly as possible. This is similar to making a wrong turn when driving, realizing the mistake, and then turning around. A negative emotion means it's time to turn around—you're going the wrong way.

- *Lock in these positive imaginings with faith, a higher logic, the satisfaction and pride that you are representing God with all of your mind and heart, and the realization that positive images are productive while any negative images are counter-productive or destructive.* And, acknowledge that you are avoiding The Fight or Flight Response initiated by negative imagery.
- *Consider your physiology and change it to an appropriate representation of positive imaginings.*
- *Continue to create positive imagery, **ignoring all negative appearances.*** Find ways of improving the quality of your mind movie creation. Creating the highest quality experience possible is the goal.

Having completed this sequence (which may happen in a fraction of a second), you have fulfilled your responsibility of co-creatorship. Each time you are successful, notice how much better you *feel* as a result. Give some attention to becoming aware of the options these imaginations bring forth since you have retained your clear mindedness. Each time this is accomplished successfully, the sum total of your self, in terms of experience, is renewed to a higher state.

This is the basic Imagination Control Therapy technique. As you practice this technique it will become second nature, *as easy as flipping a coin.* Make this thought process a *habit.*

I have added the concept of imagery and emotion in paraphrasing the saying:

> Sow an image—reap a thought,
> Sow a thought—reap an emotion,
> Sow an emotion—reap an attitude,
> Sow an attitude—reap a habit,
> Sow a habit—reap a character,
> Sow a character—reap a destiny.

Your *image creation habits* create the quality of your life experience. Through the imaginations of the thoughts of your heart you create your attitudes, your habits, your character, your destiny, and the quality of your experiences. Oh, what mastery it is to develop your faculty of imagination! Oh, how the quality of experience grows and grows as you learn this mastery! Quality of experience is governed only by the limits of your imagination and perspective directed by an ever-growing attitude.

By practicing the Imagination Control Therapy thought process, it is possible to ascend spiritually in leaps and bounds and ground yourself to God through a stable thought process. It is this simple, if you can cultivate enough faith to *prioritize* your responsibility as a co-creator with God into your self-image to the point that it changes or overrides your present belief system. It is your self-imposed limitations within your self-image that project the appearance of justifying the creation of negative imagery and the experience of its subsequent negative emotion. You are well able to solve the challenge of keeping mentally connected with God and, within this unity, of dissolving all fear of creating positive imagery in spite of any appearance. You are blueprinted for it and it feels right.

Within this new software program for the mind, all truth

unfolds naturally. You find answers to questions, the path of love, and the wisdom of the masters. Your powers begin to awaken and you become established within The Kingdom of Heaven where your desires and needs are added unto you. These things were always within you blinded by your own negative imaginations, which are rooted in fear. *Without the delusions caused by the negative spectrum of thought, you develop the ability to give reality the further considerations that you have overlooked, since your **negative imagery is no longer consuming your ability to see the whole of reality by encapsulating your attention**.* And we only have so much attention to go around.

Delusive Conclusions and the Negative Imagination

There is a direct correlation between delusive conclusions and the negative spectrum of thought. I cannot emphasize this enough. We reach many conclusions within seconds. We have all heard of the expression, *jumping to conclusions,* yet the majority of the time we feel that we are not guilty of this when just the opposite is usually the case. Time after time this can be observed in human behavioral patterns.

These patterns are expressed in the behavior of all people, to a greater or lesser degree, no matter how intelligent or accomplished. Once the negative imagination is permitted to emerge, situations are misread, the actions of others are misinterpreted, complexes may dominate the mind, motives and intentions of others are misinterpreted, and a vast amount of information is filtered out. A productive critique may be taken as a slur against our essence or the importance of events may become exaggerated. Our life experience becomes greatly influenced by what we imagine with the mind's negative spectrum of thought in our negative creation process. Life becomes a pretense of darkness. Rebuking the negative imagery creation process opens the door to the possibility of a higher level of thinking through the creation of positive imagery based on realistic thought habits. When the foundation of our self-image and belief system is a projection of ethics, values, and virtue based on our inherent status as a powerful, spiritual, divine being we have no reason to be drawn into creating negative imagery.

Keep in mind that running possible negative results through the mind or acknowledging negative aspects of the environment are not dwelling in the negative imagination. It is the dwelling in relation to your *intent* of these imaginings that begins to activate The Fight or Flight response and its thought filtration system that leaves the positive aspects of reality unacknowledged. It is also necessary to consider which particular beliefs within your belief system have urged you to create or dwell in negative imagery, emotion, and feelings. You will then discover your limitations projecting from your fears and complexes that have provided these delusions.

Although thinking something positive, even if it is nonsense, may be better than creating negative imagery, finding the silver lining in every cloud is a challenge that takes creativity, effort, and a desire for higher levels of thought. Basing your imaginings on ethics, compassion, altruism, high values, virtue, and the many other attributes of love provide an avenue of thought that is spiritual and a reflection of your connectedness to the Mind of God. These higher levels of thought lead to spiritual ascension through insights and the practicing of faith. A key is to find a realistic positive imagination to replace any negative imagination that *seems* to be appropriate with an imagining from the Christ consciousness or higher self. You cannot go wrong if you do.

Self-image

Improving your self-image is the most powerful shift in imagery you can take in relation to the cessation of your succumbing to an urge to crate negative imagery. Your delusions are founded in buying into the lie that you are less than a divine being, a child of God with full inherent birthrights. You focus on the appearance of your world and conclude your self-value and how you fit in to the picture. Few of us have been taught that we are powerful, spiritual, divine beings. One might easily infer from our standard teachings that we are inherently violent, rude, selfish beings and that positive qualities and virtues are something developed above our animal urges rather than as our deepest and truest inherent qualities. And, orthodox Christianity has done more than its share to cultivate the thought that as our true nature, we are lowly sinners, worms of the dust. This belief has permeated our society, our minds, and our hearts. It is simply an untruth!

Do you think that God is dwelling within us for the experience of being a lowly sinner or worm of the dust? No! His offer and intention is for us to participate with Him in the highest quality experience that He ingeniously creates out of the far less than perfect circumstances of the experiences we have chosen in the past.

The most profound step you can take toward ceasing to create negative imagery is to stop buying into the lie that you are anything less than a powerful, spiritual, divine being. Of all visualizations you may practice, holding the self-image of a powerful, spiritual, divine being is the single most important factor in your development.

- *Powerful,* because we are made in the image and likeness of God. And, God just happens to be dwelling within us. He is there always. At any time, we can tap into this mighty power.
- *Spiritual,* because we are a part of God, and we are in God as He is in us. It is how we are designed. It is how we are made. It is who we are!
- *Divine,* because we are powerful, spiritual, have God dwelling within us, and are created with no less than this status in the Mind of God.

Reflecting on this visualization of yourself many times a day has a profound affect on everything you ever thought that you believed. This is who you really are. Discovering this Truth, how can you behave or think in ways that are any less than who you really are?

The Lower and Higher Self

It is necessary to come to terms with our having a higher self and a lower self. Until you come to terms with your spirituality, these two selves are at constant battle. The lower self is the disassociated paradigms we have of our limitations. Your animal nature, your fears, your conceptions of lack—all work together to form this perspective of yourself that seems to instruct you and offer you advice. But you can always ask yourself before you accept this advice, "Is this based on the Truth that I am a powerful, spiritual, divine being?" If the answer to that question is no, then it's a lie, a misconception, an illusion! I cannot emphasize this enough. The quality of your very existence depends on your reconstructing your belief system on this basis. The more you believe this, the less reason you have to justify the creation of negative imagery. This being the Truth, it is necessary to orient your entire learning process, your studies, and your goals toward cultivating this Truth into the depths of your soul.

Fake It 'Til You Make It

One approach is to act accordingly whether or not you have this Truth ingrained to your depths. I once heard a student reason, "Fake it 'til you make it." And this is a good approach. You assume the role of a character who is a powerful, spiritual, divine being. You act and think accordingly. You take on the physiology of your desired state on mind. This may seem superficial, yet behaving, thinking, and physically appearing as anything less is the ultimate superficiality of your inherent birthright.

Within this approach, you are privileged to witness a good amount of God's intentions manifesting through you despite your handicap of self-doubt. You become what role you assume. It gets easier with time and you witness positive changes in your life and heart.

I have read where actors who are portraying the part of a depressed or angry character begin to feel the depression or anger of their character. The imaginary world is this powerful to the body. And the body is this powerful to the world of imagination.

Inversions

In all action-reaction Newtonian physics there are inversions. For example, electricity creates magnetism and magnetism creates electricity. Our *beliefs create imaginations* and our *imaginations create our beliefs.* So we have the option of the pure logic of the bigger picture to urge us into a perpetual creation of positive imagery in spite of any appearances.

We all have said, "I wouldn't have believed it if I didn't see it." Yet, you wouldn't have seen it if you didn't believe it. People may not have much love in their life, so they long for love. Yet by giving love they attract the love they long for. Thus giving becomes receiving.

Many people fall for the illusion that they will *be* happy if they *have* acquired certain material things or the love of a certain person. They feel miserable and place their happiness in the future to be gained *after* the acquisition of what they desire. To them, *having* equals *being.* Cultivating the feelings of how you will be if and when you have the desired things will cause you to naturally attract these things into your life. Thus, *being* equals *having.*

The imaginings we have created in the past create emotions, moods, and states of mind. This all manifests within our physiology. This process also has its inversion. Our physiology is subconsciously associated with our mind states, moods, and emotions, and urges the particular imagery patterns that created, perpetuated, and built upon them. So taking on the physical appearances of desired mental states urges the associated mind states, moods, emotions, and imaginings associated with the physical state assumed.

Because physiological expressions are universally the same, assuming the physical traits of our past desired mind states is not the only powerful tool available in tapping into past beneficial powerful states that we have developed and may not be utilizing. We can mimic or model other people who are already successful. Merely by modeling the physical attributes of these people sends the same signals to your brain as these traits are sending to their brains. It's all in you waiting to be developed and utilized.

Disassociation

Your higher self is a disassociated paradigm where you view and judge from your true self, the powerful, spiritual, divine being. Although you may demonstrate lower degrees of your higher self in your imagery, thoughts, emotions, and actions the perspective of thinking from the highest level of consciousness is available to you always and continuously. This is the basis of the concept of disassociation. The thought processes are available to you, but you may not associate yourself with them. Many psychologists attribute the phenomenon of channeling to the idea of what I have termed disassociated paradigms (known to them as merely disassociation).

It is easy to quote great wisdom and advice, but hard to associate yourself with the idea that this is "I." But this is exactly what you must do. You must begin to associate yourself with the highest levels of imagery and thought that you can conceive while at the same time you must *cease associating* yourself with the thought processes of the lower self.

If you find yourself in dialogue with the higher and lower self, believing what the lower self advises is falling for trickery and believing in a lie. Your higher self is the most highly developed part of your thought processes, filled with your greatest knowledge and wisdom. Believe what it says. It is this higher self that we endeavor to completely become, eliminating that within us that justifies the creation of negative imaginations.

Researchers have found that an entire cabinet of characters, perhaps Einstein, Emerson, The Dalai Lama, and Mother Teresa can be imagined and a disassociated paradigm created for each person, especially if you read about them and understand somewhat how each of them thinks. These cabinet members can then act as your advisory board in a visualization exercise where you meet with these people. Our minds are capable of taking on the disassociated viewpoints of as many people as we can imagine. We can receive advice from these individuals that can be as good as coming from them in the flesh. These disassociations are so profound that research has born speculation into the probabilities of our ability to tap into these personalities in the Universal Mind as if we possess a holographic mind.

Or we may visualize completely imaginary beings of a powerful, spiritual, divine nature. It can be an image of our enlightened self speaking to us. It does not matter. Our mind has the ability to form new perspectives of disassociated paradigms. And, of course, we can ultimately relate to the Christ consciousness within us in this way.

Suffering: The Urge to Create Negative Imagery

Perhaps our suffering or delusions of suffering cause the greatest urge we have to create negative imaginations. Paradoxically, our creation of negative imagery is the greatest cause of our suffering. Suffering is another example of inversions in the law of action/reaction in Newtonian physics. *Negative imagery causes suffering and the perspective of suffering causes negative imagery.* This is a rapid spiral of descent. **"... I beheld Satan as lightning fall from Heaven."** (Luke 10:18) Satan, a Hebrew word rooted in the idea of an *adversary,* can be thought of as our negative self. For we have no greater adversary than our negative thinking, our negative creation process. And the second we choose to create negative imagery, our mind falls from its heavenly positive state to the hellish state of negative emotion. Not only do we feel as terrible as the emotion we are experiencing, but, thanks to The Fight or Flight Response's thought filtration system, we now are provided the disassociated paradigm of this mode of imagery. Now there are the appearances of countless reasons to justify the existence of the negative imagery.

If we had to find a common thread of experience between all sentient beings, it is suffering. Despite anything you know to the contrary, despite all of the training you may have had to the contrary, and despite of all your spiritual development, gaining a perspective on suffering may be the single most important clue in discovering your urge to create negative imagery. This is a great problem to solve. A person may achieve a high level of education, training, and spiritual development, yet may experience regular periodic negative moments—as though possessing none of the aforementioned qualities—and resort to dwelling in and creating negative imagery and negative emotion.

We find it difficult to surrender to the intention of God, yet we may surrender easily enough to causing our own suffering and beginning the creation of negative imagery. We do this because there is an appearance that we have become separate from God—that He has abandoned us into suffering. If we pray while we suffer, we again feel connected to God and our feeling of abandonment begins to dissolve. Yet we may return to a state of abandonment as soon as our prayers are finished. Have you ever prayed and then thought that praying will never do any good as soon as you were finished? We probably all have. "Where is God while I suffer?" you may ask yourself. It is clear that we don't feel as though we are safe in His protection in the midst of suffering.

Suffering and Perspective

Although we do not want to suffer and can think of every reason why we shouldn't, contemplating why we need a certain amount of suffering in our lives can change our perspective of suffering and life itself. People with nerve damage and lepers who have lost feeling in their limbs have reported that they feel as though the limb is no longer a part of their self. It is now only a tool. Physical pain gets our attention and it gets it quick. We are then compelled to protect our body.

A wonderful exercise for the mind is to contemplate what we would be like if we had no physical pain ever in our lives. At first this may seem like a good idea. But without any pain at all, we are vulnerable to every lesson we have previously learned about pain. Imagine if you had never felt fire, if sports or play had never injured you, if you had never been spanked, if you had never fallen, if a bee had never stung you. All of us may not have experienced each one of these situations, but *the point is to imagine not having the experience that our pain has taught us.* To exist in complete naïveté is as dangerous as having the awareness of a baby our entire life. Take time to reflect on the necessity of physical pain. So, as you can see, pain is a guide, and a good one at that.

All this seems insignificant in the event we are in extreme physical pain. To most of us, extreme physical pain is experienced very seldom—although this may not be the case for a few people involved in extreme circumstances such as war or rough, violent environments. And there are many people who suffer from chronic pain. If we are not involved in a legitimate cause or the military, we have the option of choosing to leave a violent environment. The point is that the average person is exposed to only rare occasions of extreme physical pain. Knowing this, we can enable ourselves to be more accepting of physical pain. Generally, extreme physical pain lasts only until the next morning. I once severely sprained my wrist. I was amazed that the unbearable pain was gone by the next morning. A doctor had prescribed a pain medication that helped me to fall asleep. Although the wrist was very sore and painful when moved, the unbearable pain was gone in the morning. Choosing to immobilize the arm, I was no longer in pain at all. In many cases, the body seems to have a built-in system to relieve the intense pain of severe injury. In this case, my body required immobilization of my arm and I complied.

Tragedy and extreme pain have catapulted many minds into the highest levels of thought and spirituality. There are countless stories of people who have accomplished mighty feats of greatness with pain as the catalyst.

Generally speaking, extreme physical pain is rare. So, after contemplating extreme pain, it is necessary to contemplate on the average pains of life that are not extreme. The way we perceive moderate physical pain has everything to do with how we perceive our suffering. A friend of mine who is a guitar player and a roofer has a different perspective on hitting a finger with a hammer than his coworkers who are not musicians. An injury that may not affect his ability to perform roofing may well affect his ability to play a guitar. I have seen a gruff construction worker rejoice after getting hurt on the job, looking forward to a vacation. The same injury to a child would seem disastrous.

It has been my observations that people who have experienced many lumps and bumps in life tend to be more accepting of pain. Construction workers receive minor injuries consistently. Pinched fingers, little cuts, bangs and bumps, as well as exposure to the elements of weather are common. Just as a construction worker learns to accept minor pain and discomfort as part of the job, we all need to accept minor pain and discomfort as part of life.

A big part of our suffering is the intention we assign to others that may cause us pain. For example, if someone is cleaning a wound we may have received with alcohol it will burn, but we do not assign an intention of malice to him or her. The same amount or even much less pain received in malice is taken in a different perspective and may hurt much more. Our urge to retaliate arises in the form of the creation of negative imaginations and perhaps then becomes action. Whether or not we act on our negative imaginings has little to do with the chemical response to these images within the body. And, negative images resulting in negative emotion adds to our suffering. You see, aside from the times we are experiencing physical pain, discomfort, or hunger our mental suffering is usually a creation in our imagination due to our perspective.

It is true that we need to mourn when our loved ones pass on, but there is a balance and spirituality to be considered in mourning. Too much is no good, too little is dispassionate. The point is that we rarely experience mental pain legitimately. Aside from atrocity and the death of loved ones, we need not suffer. For most of us, truly legitimate extreme physical and mental pain is rare. Using minor pain or discomfort as a spark, the undisciplined mind projects its belief system into this pain or discomfort rationalizing the reason for it or what it means. The person projecting this may rationalize this pain or discomfort as a symbol of another's intentions or motives. They may perceive it as a true and factual feedback of their own unworthiness, a sign of failure, or a violation of their body. Thus suffering begins through justifying the creation or dwelling in of negative imagery and its resulting emotions. More so, the undisciplined mind may completely fabricate suffering that is based on nothing but a perspective based on a disregard for an abundance of information.

Resistance to change is another avenue to suffering. As we create imaginings of the negative aspects of change, we induce suffering. The antidote is to contemplate the positive points of changes that are inevitable or necessary in our lives. The Universe is in a constant state of change. And so are we. By ceasing the creation of negative imagery we become ever-evolving, powerful, spiritual, divine beings ever-renewing ourself, moment-by-moment, from experience to experience.

We may feel abandoned by God—alone in our suffering. We forget that there are so many others who are now suffering and have suffered similar experiences. Our focus turns on ourself. As this happens, we increase suffering through the imagination. All this is unnecessary and can be eliminated by a change of perspective. You change your perspective by uncovering the considerations you have neglected. When we are injured, this is an opportune time to extrovert our thoughts into the common suffering of all humanity, all sentient beings. We are not alone in our pain. And although it is a bitter fruit, it is necessary and can be a challenging opportunity toward self-mastery.

Acceptance

When you cannot accept something, the mind begins to create a scenario where you "straighten out" the situation. The mind forms a skit where you are the star of your mind movie, putting everything right. This has been termed the negative emotional response loop by Dr. Frank Young. It is a loop because the mind tends to run the skit over and over in its attempt to relieve your inability to accept. When you can't accept something, you suffer. To break the loop, you must distract the mind by focusing your attention on something else, preferably something positive.

An inability to accept things can also influence you to lash out, grow very angry, become upset, or be depressed. Behind the feeling of the unacceptable is fear.

Surrender: Negative or Positive?

In our quest for enlightenment, illumination, liberation, say it as you will, it is necessary to come to terms with the realization that no situations serve as a cue to begin the creation of negative imagery. *An enlightened mind is a mind clever enough to find a new perspective, a new viewpoint, or just create a positive imagination despite any appearance.* It has been my observation that too often we are like the racehorse waiting for its cue to run, but we race into the creation of negative imaginations. But this is mostly habit and a learned or conditioned response. These are responses we have witnessed and learned. Again, it is buying into a lie! No matter how many times you have seen negative reactions, they are inappropriate! Not one of the people you ever witnessed acting negatively are acting out of the belief they are a powerful, spiritual, divine being. When we are around people who respond to life's challenges from the perspective of a powerful, spiritual, divine being we witness God in action manifesting through the human form at a high level, at the Christ level.

Where does the blind, seemingly automatic surrender to the urge to create negative imagery come from? The only answer I can offer is that it comes from a combination of ignorance, delusion, self-absorption, learned or conditioned response, or habit—all based on fear. It's true that the body suggests a response before you have time to think, but you don't have to go with it and magnify it as though it's a great idea. Aren't the antidotes for these character flaws study, unity with God, compassion, values, ethics, principles, character development, and rethinking our role models? It is necessary that we begin considering powerful, spiritual, divine people as our role models. Why do we think we need our positive imaginations to be built on firm foundations of compassion, forgiveness, patience, and love before we can thoughtlessly create them?

As intelligent as we have become, isn't it strange that we require no firm, sound, logical foundation to justify negative thought? What a phenomenon it is for so many educated, even spiritually developed people to throw away their intelligence and be drawn into the negative spectrum of nothing less than irrational thinking by the creation of negative imagery. Why are so many so helpless to the urge to create negative imaginations and experience negative emotion when there are *so many reasons not to,* while in contrast there are *so many reasons to* create positive imaginations? Isn't it intriguing that beings who possess as much intelligence as humans surrender so easily to the discomforts and misery of dwelling in and creating negative imagery? And isn't it even more intriguing that we need a firm and solid foundation of study, mental discipline, faith, logic, and security to entice us into the splendor, bliss, and peace of mind that comes with the creation of positive, divine imagery?

We learn behavior responses as we grow and develop in life. We witness negative responses in our family, friends, and community members. We see negative behavior on TV. It is also quite a phenomenon that we are drawn in by these negative behaviors and responses to the point that we begin to mimic them whether or not they are destructive in the long run. Just as a criminal sees only short-term reasoning, we may be drawn into this same trade-off of short-term gratification for long-term disaster. We all see the long-term problems that develop for angry people. We see the long-term problems that develop for hateful people. But do we conclude that it is imperative to our happiness and success in life that we avoid these emotions or the imaginations that cause them? And how many of us realize that negative emotions are directly correlated to our imagery?

Memory: Our Image Records

We all realize that we have a memory to record and store what has happened in the past. Our memories store a complete recollection of what has happened as well as what we had anticipated or planned would happen. Few of us realize that memories are stored as imagery containing a record of countless combinations of the sensual perceptions of each moment. For example, we don't just hear, we hear the volume, the direction, the estimated distance, and the tones. These perceptions are all recorded in or associated with an image.

Each memory image also contains the emotions experienced during the moment it is recorded. When we recall these past images, their emotions also return. I have observed people who exhibit signs of a variety of emotions while telling stories. For example, an older woman I know was telling me stories of her life. She recounted how she had emigrated from France, some of her grandest times, and some of her terrible times. As she told her stories, she very much so relived and exhibited the emotion that was imbedded within each memory image. I felt as though I was witnessing a medley of her emotional life as well as hearing her stories. Although most people don't exhibit stored emotion to the same extent as this passionate French woman, we are quite vulnerable to being influenced by our stored emotion. This is a great part of the reason that we feel threatened when we become involved in a situation that has many of the same sensual perceptions as a past situation where we have recordings of fear or pain.

Current research demonstrates that much of the potency of our emotions is recorded in the amygdala gland. When situations develop that contain similar factors that are recorded within our memories, the amygdala might stimulate potent emotions similar to these past recorded experiences through association.

Keeping in mind that the majority of the time when we recount the negative past we have created our own suffering, we seem to reenact the disassociated paradigm that originally persuaded us to create the imagery and emotions in the first place. Even when the fear or pain being recounted is legitimate, the majority of the time we have created countless negative imaginings about the situations and the people within them. This is why it is important to avoid creating negative imagery at all costs.

A Change in Emotion Is a Change in Belief, Perspective, Viewpoint, and Paradigm

A shift in imagery and emotion causes a shift in belief, perspective, paradigm, and viewpoint. At the very moment we choose to begin the creation of negative imagery, we throw away our positive perspective, our positive paradigm. Our belief system changes—at least for the time we are in a negative state of mind. When in a positive state of mind, most people believe that hate, revenge, anger, and violence are states of mind that they wish to avoid. Yet when negative creation begins, these same people justify a shift in paradigm and perspective to negative. We literally possess a distinguishable personality for each emotion. Thus each image we create has the potential within it for its related emotion, personality, paradigm, and point of view. When you observe this objectively, the creation of negative imagery has the distinct qualities of literally causing a person to appear almost as though he or she is demonically possessed as each shifts his or her perspective, belief system, intentions, and motives in relation to the negative imaginings being created. And time spent dwelling within negative imagery magnifies the emotion.

Priority

Perhaps another reason we buy into the delusion of creating negative imagery is having the wrong priorities. Wouldn't you cease justifying the creation of negative imaginations if the very top priority in your life is bliss, if your co-creatorship with God leads you to manifest good; if it is your priority to feel wonderful, to be connected to an exuberant joyous feeling of unity with God; if you value love and compassion; if you desire to flourish, to experience abundance, and to have the highest quality life experience possible. The more we consider our priorities regarding the display of negative emotion, the less we justify exhibiting them even if we are creating the imaginations. This is suppressing emotion for the sake of an incident requiring a priority of controlled behavior. As opposed to our situation in our home or at work, our priorities are different in a courtroom where we may be asking for mercy. We may act differently in front of our mother, father, or minister. We may take more care in not exposing a behavior response to a friend that we may openly express in private with our mate. When we look at ourselves this way, we seem quite fickle as a species. Yet, most of us do have our priorities. Why not incorporate God as a priority? Why not incorporate bliss, peace of mind, kindness, charity, compassion, and joy as priorities?

We experience physical pain in many ways and to many degrees. Most of this pain is minor. How we perceive our pain dictates whether we suffer from it or not. If you have a sincere desire to rise above suffering, to achieve a higher level of consciousness, to experience life in the highest quality, spirituality, and love—then create positive imaginations despite any appearance. Ignore the urge to create negative imaginings. Developing indifference toward negative impulses is the key to transformation.

Reasons Why Not to Create Negative Imagery

• Negative imaginations create negative emotions.

- The urge to create negative imagery is based on delusions.
- Creating negative imaginations undermines your purpose as a co-creator with God.
- When you create negative imagery and enter into negative emotions, you are being irresponsible to your co-creatorship with God.
- Negative imaginations are uncomfortable.
- The more you dwell in negative imagery and emotion the stronger they get and the worse you feel.
- Negative imaginations have no legitimacy to your being a powerful, spiritual, divine being.
- When you create negative imagery, you initiate The Flight or Fight Response in the body.
- The Fight or Flight Response causes a flood of toxic chemicals to release in the body.
- The Fight or Flight Response's toxic chemicals cause a variety of negative symptoms in the body.
- Negative imagery and emotion cause diseases in the body.
- Negative imagery and emotion cause the mind to be disturbed.
- Negative imagery and emotion cause the heart to be troubled.
- Negative imagery and emotion inhibit the development of your self-image.
- Negative imagery and emotion are destructive to your relationships, your spirituality, your work, your efforts, your goals, your state of mind, and your health.
- When you are in the midst of creating negative imagery and emotion you are in the process of becoming everything that you are not—your anti-self.
- In a negative state, you temporarily lose any new perspective you have developed regarding compassion, forgiveness, tolerance, understanding, and spirituality. Your renewed self is then temporarily regressed into the worst or lesser selves you have been.
- When you are in a negative state, you focus on everything negative and do not consider the positive attributes of your environment, as they now seem insignificant.

• When in a negative state, you focus on the problem rather than the solution.

• When you are in a negative state, you are convinced that you are seeing things clearly although the mind is filtering the majority of information being sent to it and processing only the data that is significant to maintaining the disassociated paradigm of the emotion you are experiencing.

• Creating negative imagery is a sure-fire way to undermine your efforts in the long run.

• Negative imagery and emotion are like a weak link in a chain. They have the potential to break the success of a long line of positive effort in very destructive short-term ways.

• In order to begin the creation of negative imagery, you have chosen to buy into a lie, a lie that you are limited and less than who you really are, a lie that seems to validate picking and choosing certain data to highlight while eliminating considerations of other data. You see only what the emotion permits you to see.

• Negative imaginations inhibit your ability to be a kind and loving person.

• Negative imaginations inhibit your wisdom, its development, and application.

• During the creation of negative imagery, you have chosen to disconnect from God to a greater or lesser degree.

• There is no faster or more efficient way to reduce the quality of your life experience than to enter into the creation of negative imagery.

• Although God is consistently creating an abundance of ingenious offers of ways you can have the highest quality of experience moment-by-moment, entering into the creation of negative imagery is the most efficient way to reduce the quality of your moment-by-moment experiences and interfere with your ability to constantly renew yourself.

• Your ability to perform at your highest level is greatly inhibited by the creation of negative imagery and entering into negative emotion.

- As you become negative in your state of mind, you individualize and alienate yourself from God and humanity. You begin to feel alone.
- The greatest part of suffering depends on the creation of negative imagery to perpetuate the paradigms necessary to self-induce suffering or cause suffering to others.
- While in a negative state, you are not clear minded.

We can all write down hundreds of reasons why thinking positively is superior to thinking negatively. But try to write down some reasons that it is necessary to think negatively. If you can list any, look again and you will find some beliefs that are in great need of a foundation of love. Otherwise, there are no legitimate reasons we can list.

The Spiritual Blueprint

The body is literally blueprinted to respond to the cessation of negative imagery within the mind in conjunction with the consistent creation of positive imagery by enhancing our mental and physical health. The more we avoid the creation of negative imagery, the more efficient the body becomes at creating a format of physical and emotional health. Once negative imagery ceases, consistent positive spiritual imagery, thoughts, emotions, moods, internal dialogue, and action result in the body going through a re-chemicalization process. The positive thinker affects the body while the re-chemicalization brought on by the positive and divine mental state affects the thinker. Thought patterns affect the neuron cell circuitry in the brain by *furrowing* these thought patterns. Consistent positive images create positive image neurological furrows (Hebbian connections) that make it easier to repeat this process. We become what we think. We feel the way we think. Life becomes what we think it is or what we think it into through the perspectives and perceptions we develop and maintain by our imagery and the disassociated paradigms of the emotions they cause.

As our neuron brain cells die each day and are never replaced, the living neuron cells continuously grow dendrites to further connect the surviving cells to compensate for the loss of the unreplaced cells. *This dendrite growth is in response to your thought processes, your imaginings.* This is an important concept to understand. As the new dendrite growth consistently incorporates your new knowledge and imagery patterns, insights develop or old insights deepen in response to this growth compensation. Inevitably, a shift in paradigm occurs. Newer and more in depth insights are formed. But these insights are relative to your negative or positive image patterns and your belief system. Thus we find a balance in the mind/body connection as the emotional system puts forth suggested feelings and thoughts based on the past tempered by our new experiences and new responses that become hardwired with our new dendrite growth.

Negative imaginations create the appearance of a paradigm of insights of darkness and inhibit the transformation process you are blueprinted to achieve. The creation of positive divine imagery results in a paradigm of insights within the Light, the promotion of health, and a realization of who we really are— powerful, spiritual, divine beings.

Endeavoring to create more positive and less negative imagery must lead to the cessation of dwelling in the negative spectrum altogether for re-chemicalization to become profound. Short-lived negative thinking (up to a minute) cannot disrupt this process much. When your negative response to life is merely on the surface and has no penetration to the depths of the mind through your consciousness holding the imprint of the negative state, you are blocking the toxic Fight or Flight Response chemical process that promotes disease to the mind and body. For example, expressing anger in a way that is merely a form of communication where you can laugh at any time is a negative response that is just on the surface. Many of us have put on the face of anger to correct children, and then ducked around the corner to chuckle. Even Jesus flipped over the tables of the money-changers in the temple. But I speculate that He was only putting on the mask of anger to communicate to those whose attention He could not otherwise get. I doubt that Jesus actually experienced the chemical release of The Fight or Flight Response. I doubt that He actually felt threatened in any way. Yet, Jesus was intelligent enough to know that sometimes you need to get the attention of the people.

The chemicals in your body resulting from negative imagery block the flow of energy in your ganglionic nerve centers and redirect it to your physical systems for fight or flight. When negative imagery ceases, these ganglionic nerve centers, known in the East as chakras, open the channel for your spiritual energy to flow where it may enhance your state of consciousness.

Is Heaven on Earth Possible?

To some it may seem quite eccentric to believe that the mind can be in Heaven while the body is on Earth. Nonetheless, the body has the capacity within itself to create the chemical response to physically manifest your heavenly imaginings in just the same way as it creates a response to all imagery that results in your entire spectrum of emotions and feelings. The human body is considered by many yogis to be a perfect vehicle for the expression of consciousness. I agree fully. The blueprint for extended consciousness through the body's re-chemicalization and dendrite growth, the very fact that we can feel a divine experience, the fact that we can reach higher levels of thought, throws a monkey wrench in any theory of evolution that denies God's active participation. We have been created with this blueprint although it is near dormant in most people, waiting to be developed, to be resurrected.

Act and feel the way you would if you were in Heaven and this becomes your reality. If you were in Heaven, you couldn't feel as though you were really part of Heaven if you continually created negative imagery. There is a certain responsibility involved in your thought processes if you are to be a child of the light, a child of God. You are more than human; you can be and feel as though you are a child of God. You are blueprinted for it.

Make your reality Heaven and you will *feel* it. The brain, body, central nervous system, and endocrine system guided by the subconscious mind will assure this occurs.

Meditation Affirmations and Denials

- I AM capable of creating only positive imagery.
- There are no appearances that justify creating negative imagery.
- I AM capable of becoming only positive emotionally.
- There are no situations that justify the negative emotions.
- I AM co-creating the Universe with God.
- As a co-creator, God's intention for me is to create only positive things in the Universe.
- I AM a positive co-creator.
- Negative creations are adverse to the intentions of God.
- I realize that my positive spectrum of thought is parallel to the intention of God.
- My faith is deepening, progressing toward becoming an expression of my indwelling Christ consciousness.
- I always find the silver lining in every cloud.
- I AM consistently creating only positive imaginations and they are keeping me connected with the Christ consciousness within me.
- Through consistent divine positive thought, I AM a child of God walking in the light.
- I AM a powerful, spiritual, divine being.

Children

A prudent adult or parent will closely observe the imaginations of children. There is no greater way to develop a child's mind than to consistently review their imaginings. Usually, when children are troubled, they will blurt out their negative imaginings. "They all hate me," or "Nobody will let me play with them," are expressions said often by children learning to interact.

Educating a child about their imagination and talking about what images the child is creating will form insights within the child that will be of the utmost benefit in growing up and developing.

Psychology teaches us that we develop our personalities, thought processes, and many of our schemas within the first four or five years of life. These are formed, validated, and used as reference points from the images we have created during this critical time period. So, this is the most important time to form the ideal images in our memory banks.

Teaching children to love, share, and most of all, create positive imaginings of others and the world will pay huge dividends in their mental and spiritual development. Focusing on the imagination cultivates a self-awareness of what imaginings a child is creating and will allow the child to develop in an environment where there is no eluding the fact that the imagination is the primary manifestation in the order of mental activity. Basically, this means that a child can be aware of when their mind is creating negative misinformation and learn not to give the misinformation validity. Children can easily learn to stop the process of creating undesirable negative imaginings. At the same time, a child can develop the faculty of the imagination and perhaps begin to enter into the gateway to the Whole. Keep in mind that there are windows of opportunity for learning by children where they may express their true genius. And true genius is a product of imagination.

Children who are born into a world where they are taught to create loving, wonderful imaginings about others and life will build a new world through developing the gateway to All Knowledge and Experience—the imagination.

A great resource for emotional development in children is The Collaborative to Advance Social and Emotional Learning. CASEL is an international collaborative of educators, scientists, human service providers, policy makers, and concerned citizens who are working together to promote social and emotional learning (SEL) as an integral part of education in schools throughout the world. CASEL seeks to provide a forum that fosters the exchange of educational ideas and practices that support the development of knowledgeable, responsible, and caring students. CASEL's mission is to establish social and emotional learning as an essential part of education from preschool through grade twelve. For more information on CASEL, visit their website at http://www.casel.org.

General Exercises

All of the aforementioned practices contain an abundance of mental exercises that are wonderful and beneficial. Discover and use as many as you can. You will feel wonderful. Here are a few I practice. I highly recommend discovering the love chemicals in the body created when we dwell on wonderful, loving imagery. Love is the most wonderful, gratifying experience we can have. Being one with God is the experience of love in its highest form. These imagination exercises will develop this wonderful feeling.

Tonglen

A great part of meditation training in Buddhism and Tibetan Buddhism is imagery. A student of meditation is taught to use visualization and the imagination for countless ways of development. I am particularly moved by the practice of Tonglen as described by Sogyal Rinpoche in his acclaimed spiritual masterpiece, *The Tibetan Book of Living and Dying*. The practitioner of Tonglen breathes in the pain and suffering of others or his self then exhales thoughts of blessings. Tonglen truly develops our compassion. And there are many more variations of this exercise.

The Buddhist practice of compassion instructs one to imagine the suffering that an animal or other human being experiences in various situations. Meditators are encouraged to visualize many wonderful divine visions such as light beams radiating from their masters and the presence of living or passed-on masters.

Love Exercise

- Relax in a comfortable place. Close your eyes. Begin to imagine yourself in a wonderful place. This can be anywhere you feel close to God. A beautiful mountain scene, a flower garden, a magnificent church, or anywhere you feel good. It may be somewhere you have been before or somewhere you wish you could go. It doesn't matter.

- Lock the scene into your imagination. Work on details. As you visualize, try to get sound involved. Hear the sounds of your scene. Feel as much as you can. You can imagine a warm breeze, the sun warming you, feel the earth or whatever you visualize yourself sitting or laying on. Smell what you are visualizing. Smell fresh air, clean sea air, flowers if there are any, incense if you want it. Smell trees or plants. You can be chewing on a weed. Taste it. Taste what ever you can incorporate into your imagination. Now, lock in all your senses in this wonderful imagination.

- Now visualize someone or something you love or loved very deeply in the picture. Let the love fill your heart. Embrace the love. Bring someone or something else into the scene you love or loved. Embrace this love. One by one bring everyone and everything you have ever loved into the picture. Your old bicycle, your first dog or cat, family, friends, those who have passed away or are still alive . . . All the love you have ever experienced is now in this picture. Embrace this love. Celebrate this loving adventure. Hug and kiss them. Tell them if you miss them.

- Focus this love within your heart. Feel your heart swell and swell with love.

- Feel the Spirit of God in your heart. Hear the Spirit of God telling you that you are His son or daughter, who He loves very deeply. Embrace this wonderful feeling of God's love. Know that God is love and while you hold this wonderful, powerful feeling of love in your heart, you are one with God. Know that you are a powerful, spiritual, divine being.

Love Bubbles, Lights, Rays, and Beams

Since there are no limits to the imagination, we can create images of anything we choose. Love bubbles are a wonderful way to imagine capturing and holding love within a space. Start your meditation by visualizing a love bubble surrounding you. Expand the bubble of love larger and larger until you engulf your home, neighborhood, city, state, country, the planet, and then the Universe.

If someone is in need of love, create a love bubble around him or her. Love bubbles can be greatly intensified. Visualize the light of God, love rays or beams, direct them at the bubble then penetrating and filling the bubble. Stuff it abundantly. We can then imagine that the lights, rays or beams are held and collected inside the bubble where they become more and more dense.

During the day, we can use bubbles, lights, rays, or beams to give love to others around us. If we are in intense or non-preferable situations, we will feel much better when we beam someone with a love beam or circle rays of love around their heads. This kind of imagery not only results in our feeling better, it distracts the mind from negative imagery while keeping our minds clear for higher levels of thoughts or insights to surface. Creating positive images about people urges positive behavior. Keeping our mind clear enhances our chances of not overlooking positive options that will improve the situation.

Rewriting: Changing the Past

Most of us have images we hold from the past that influence us today. Psychologists and layman informally call this *baggage*. Through Imagination Control Therapy, we have the ability to create new, more preferable images in addition to the old stored images we do not prefer—creating a preferred outcome.

Each time we recall images of the past that have had an undesirable outcome, all we need do is create a more desirable ending by creating the preferred outcome. We are the writer, producer, and star of our personal mind movie. Rewrite the script. Past images of hurt and pain often surface during sound and light sessions. Each time they appear, rewrite a new ending. This practice embeds the new ending with the stored past images. Thus the past hurt and pain are replaced with new image memories.

I have found it very helpful to imagine meeting someone with whom I have experienced an undesired outcome on the astral plane. There we apologize and forgive each other, hug or shake hands and admit the error of our thoughts.

Great personal growth and a profound understanding of unconditional love result form this practice. Rewriting apologies into our past images and actually working out situations with those who have hurt you or those you have hurt relieves us of a great burden. Just change the script. This may take several sessions of rewriting, but the new images will embed into the old memories. The "baggage" is removed. In this way, we forgive in each past instance as well as in the present. Also, when there is a positive outcome the new ending changes the negative emotional charge imbedded in past painful images to positive. Do this only if these memories keep coming up or if you cannot avoid negative thought and these memories are at the root of this problem.

Anthony Robins recommends a form of rewriting where you change the attributes of the person, people, or place within a bothersome memory. For example, if someone has yelled at you and said hurtful things, you rerun the scene in your imagination and—by changing the person's voice to that of Mickey Mouse or a little kid, or making the vocal tones render the person sounding silly and harmless—you change the way you represent the memory to yourself.

Developing Compassion

In developing our compassion, Buddhism exercises the imagination by recommending we attempt to imagine the suffering of an animal or human in a particular situation. This develops our understanding of the suffering of other sentient beings. It gives us an avenue with which to express compassion through a sharing of suffering, based on the inherent rights of other beings, in the context that suffering is as undesirable for them as for ourself. American Indians express this compassion for their prey when hunting, extending compassion by honoring the spirit of the animal for contributing to human survival.

A consistent endeavor to see yourself as part of the whole of humanity rather than as an individualized part of it gives us a new perspective. If we focus our attention on our individuality, we then struggle to gain our basic necessities, money, or other material things to save ourselves from the pain, suffering, and fear of having to go without these things. We cause others the feelings of pain, suffering, and fear when we neglect the considerations necessary for compassion by focusing our attention on only our individual needs and desires. Compassion is more than a concept or action; it is an emotion. And without it, we sacrifice a perspective that rewards us with an abundance of joy in life.

With compassion comes empathy. As strange as it may seem, empathy is now finding its way to the top of the list of importance in our corporate worlds. It's a simple matter of financial efficiency. Corporations are teams and they are discovering that emotional intelligence is the most important factor in team efficiency. And empathy is the greatest part of the foundation of emotional intelligence. Being aware of what is going on in the consciousness of others is the greatest gift we can contribute to our team interactions.

Playing the Role of an Angel

Try imagining that you are an angel as you go throughout your day. If someone behaves less than preferably, use your angelic powers to create and will a visualization of them acting blessed, kind, and loving. If you see limitations of imperfections in others, use your angelic powers to correct the deficiency. Visualize it, will it, assume it to be true. Feel like it has manifested.

As you walk around, wherever, create an imagination of each

person you see being perfect in mind, body, and spirit. Repeat this to yourself as you pass them. Imagine they are being healed, simply by passing you, of any ailment of which they may be afflicted.

Visualize cleanliness where there is filth, order where there is chaos, love where there is fear or hate, and abundance where there is lack.

Always Ask, "What Is My Responsibility in Each Cause and Effect?"

In any human interaction that we perceive as undesirable, we can exercise our faculty of imagination to discover possible ways in which a percentage of the situation may be owing to our own erroneous thinking. Try to imagine all perspectives in any given situation. Ask yourself if the behavior of this person can be modified by your changing something about yourself. Is there any thing about you that may be contributing to this person's action toward you? Is there a possibility that you may be misinterpreting this individual's facial expressions, motives, or intentions? Could it be that there's something going on in this person's life that may be affecting his or her behavior? Is this behavior really directed at you? How can you change your perspective to assume some responsibility for a change toward a positive situation?

Asking yourself these and other questions opens the door to more and more options in how you handle yourself in situations. Isn't the point of higher levels of thought an ability to respond in a beneficial way that will take you closer toward your goals and desirable mind states? We find this ability in *Imagintelligence.*

Imagery Management

II Corinthians (10:3-5): *For though we walk in the flesh, we do not war after the flesh: (For the weapons of our warfare are not carnal, but mighty through God to the pulling down of strongholds;) Casting down imaginations, and every high thing that exalteth itself against the knowledge of God, and bringing into captivity every thought to the obedience of Christ.*

In the event that you simply cannot help yourself from surrendering to your body's negative emotional impulses, it is helpful to begin some serious work in these areas of weakness. You do this by preparing an Imagery Management Plan. The idea behind an effective Imagery Management Plan is to change the belief system and our organic artificial intelligence programs in our emotional systems by improving the self-image; that is, coming to terms with the truth that you are a powerful, spiritual, divine being—a child of God. Choices and decisions are based on the self-image as a reference point. Using the self-image as schema, you have no other pathway of choice or decision other than what you believe to be true about yourself. If you find it hard to accept the truth that you are a powerful, spiritual, divine being—a child of God—your belief system, programmed by your subconscious mind, is imposing these limitations.

An effective Imagery Management Plan tears down these limitations through reprogramming the subconscious mind and teaching you to ignore your body's first suggested response from the old programming if it is not what you prefer. This reprogramming is accomplished by restructuring your conscious imagery and developing your ability to override emotional impulses with the prefrontal lobes so that you no longer contribute to more subconscious negative programming and, by directly reprogramming the subconscious mind with the positive images and thoughts you prefer, utilizing the most profound tools and systems that technology has to offer today.

Our goal is to realize that we have an organic artificial intelligence program in the form of feelings and emotions, and then to retrain this program. If you do not learn to ignore your negative feelings and emotions, you will be stuck with the mere memorization of spiritual, imaginational, emotional, and social values and principles. You are not merely an organism—you are a response organism. Your entire life experience is imbedded within your personal mind/body connection, shaping and justifying your responses. This organic response within you believes—and projects—the illusion to you that it is the perfect response. Thus, our minds use such justifiers to rationalize our imperfect responses. If you did not want to change the way you respond to life's dramas, you wouldn't be reading this text. But memorization alone is to no avail. Imagery management and Imagination Control Therapy are systems designed to imbed *Imagintelligence* into the mind/body connection, into the organic artificial intelligence system, into *the imaginations of the thoughts of your heart.*

Criteria for an Effective Imagery Management Plan

- **Understanding The Emotional System and Prefrontal Lobes**
- **Understanding Fear, and The Fight or Flight Response**
- **Identify Your Limiters**
- **Prayer**
- **Study**

- **Affirmations**
- **Denials**
- **Meditation & Visualization**
- **Tools and Aids**
- **Desire for Spiritual Ascension**
- **Diet, Vitamins, & Supplements**
- **Alpha, Theta, and Delta**

The Emotional System and Prefrontal Lobes

The emotional system is your body's artificial intelligence system. It is geared toward survival and quick response. It runs ahead of the executive prefrontal lobes where willful conscious thought originates. Your feelings and emotions suggest a response and certain imaginings. A second or two later, you have the option of overriding this impulse. When you receive an impulse, you can surrender to it with supporting thought or you can change the mode of thought to something else. If your initial impulse is inappropriate in regard to your goals and spirituality, a response you desire to change, it is necessary to ignore the impulse for the next couple of seconds so you can begin the willful use of your prefrontal lobes. This may seem a bit uncomfortable, but it is necessary if you are going to be successful in transforming yourself.

As you practice ignoring your first impulse, you develop your prefrontal lobe override ability by furthering neural connections. You are literally restructuring your brain hardwiring. Be patient; have faith. Your first impulse may seem quite real, but it is only a virtual reality created by your body's emotional system to save you the trouble of thinking. Here you are not only going to think before you act, you are going to think before you dare imagine.

All Wrong Choices Can Be Traced to Fear

Our every wrong decision can be traced to fear. We can be

afraid of being alone or that no one loves us, or that we are inadequate or inferior. The lower self can think up a million reasons to be afraid. The truth is, there is little to be afraid about. Excluding fear caused from legitimate threatening situations (and even this is an illusion based on the fear of death from too much identification with the body), the mind imagines most fear. Again, this is owing to perspectives derived from beliefs stemming from self-image. The less you realize you are a powerful, spiritual, divine being, the more limitations you impose on yourself and the more you permit The Fight or Flight Response to govern your choices and decisions. You make all of your decisions and choices based on what you believe to be true of your self-image. Anyone who begins any statements with the phrase, *I'm afraid that . . . ,"* should affirm a thousand times, *I AM a powerful, spiritual, divine being.* Until you get this through your head and imbedded in your subconscious mind as your true self-image, fears and visions of your supposed limitations will plague you.

People express their fears many ways in their speech: *I'm afraid that I don't look good enough, I'm afraid I won't get the job, I'm afraid they won't like me, I'm afraid they will laugh at me, I'm afraid that I won't be able to do it well enough.* The bottom line is: saying *I'm afraid* reflects a self-image of lack or limitation.

The antidote is prayer, affirmations, denials, visualizations, and study. By observing your internal dialogue and imaginings, you can analyze your internal conflict regarding your two basic disassociated personalities, the lower self and the higher self. If you had a script of the lines the lower self portrays in this dialogue, you have the key to discovering what affirmations, denials, visualizations, and studies are necessary for you to formulate and practice. Let's examine this conflict.

The War in Heaven

It has been said that The War in Heaven may be conceived as the constant battle that we experience between the higher self and the lower self. Many people will not acknowledge that they are having this internal dialogue where the lower self points out their every limitation or advises them. This scene has been somewhat depicted in the movies as an angel sitting on one shoulder and the devil on the other, both advising us. Some of this internal dialogue is so absurd that we try to ignore it, tune it out, and pretend that we are not so irrational as to have such outrageous thoughts. And some of these thoughts appear to be quite irrational. But the real insanity is that many times we buy into them. It's almost like having our very own little rotten demon pointing out our every imaginable weakness, limitation, fear, anxiety, or inadequacy. And we listen and believe as though this is the voice of truth. Ironically, even if our self-esteem is not very high, we invariably have a high regard for our own opinion. And too often we buy into believing the lower self since it appears to be a reflection of our own opinion rather than merely that of our lower self advising us out of fear.

This is the imagination running away with itself. The more you listen, the more a floodgate of this kind of malarkey opens. This is a disassociated personality that we develop throughout our life by lending an ear countless times each day to the most fearful, angry, insecure part of ourselves. Yet we don't have to listen. We have the option of ignoring such malarkey.

The hit TV series, *Northern Exposure,* once did a wonderful portrayal of this kind of internal dialogue. Ed, a shaman in training, was confronted with his demon, a little green dwarf who ran circles around him constantly telling Ed his every fear, weakness, and insecurity. For a while, Ed buys into the talk, but he soon learns to ignore the demon. When the demon realizes he has lost Ed's attention, he vanishes.

When our demon says things that are totally ridiculous, we usually ignore it and pretend that we didn't hear such insanity. Secretly, we don't want to admit to ourselves that we even carry on such dialogue. But the second the demon hits on an insecurity that is remotely credible, we instantly lend an ear. But now you are going to lend an ear only to understand that what the lower self has to say reveals the issues you need to work on—your limiters.

Listen and Identify Your Limiters

Listen to what your internal dialogue is saying. Identify what the lower self is saying and what negative imagery it may be urging you to create. Just as you learn the traits of a character in a TV series or a book, by listening you will learn about your lower self, what it has to say, how it thinks, and the things it says. It will be obvious that these things are not coming from the higher self. In this way, you can begin to identify your limiters—the beliefs that limit your consciousness.

Lay out the script. Once you identify with the character, you pretty much know the script, and you know the lines the character will be likely to say. When the lower self says, *You'll never make it on time, you know you're always late,* this reveals that you need to start seeing yourself in a new self-image of being "on time." Affirm that you are prompt. Deny that you will ever be late again. Apply the I AM principle. This is all simply a matter of familiarizing yourself with your disassociated lower self by listening and identifying. Thus you begin to release the occasional or frequent associations that you form with the lower self as it advises you.

Most of us try to project an attitude of professionalism at work. Applying this same attitude of professionalism toward our spiritual and personal development goes a long way. Admitting that you have a herd of disassociated personalities in the form of paradigms and subconscious programs is the first step toward rising above it all. The only difference between these disassociated paradigms and a case of true multiple personalities is that the latter loses awareness of the other personalities, or actually appears to believe that this is an alternate entity during the occupation of each paradigm. As long as all this internal dialogue between your higher and lower selves is going on only in your head, you're normal; unenlightened, but normal; struggling and possibly tormented internally, but normal.

Apparently the biggest problem with the criticisms and advice of the voice of our lower self is that many times we believe what we are hearing since, after all, it is ourself who is saying this.

If we would hear the same thing from an outside source, the first thing we'd most likely do is consider the source. When you say these things to yourself, the considered source is you. And you hold your opinion in high regard, don't you? Maybe we don't hold ourselves in high regard but we hold the opinion, itself, in high regard. *Each negative image we create has its own disassociated paradigm that we immediately begin to associate with.* That is why if you want to keep a clear mind it is of the utmost importance to cease the creation of negative imagery.

Each and every time you dwell in or engage in the creation of negative imagery there is a flaw—a limiter—in your belief system that needs to be identified. You will know your flawed belief by the justifier that you use to convince yourself that the choice to engage in negative imaginings is correct (or at least appears correct under the circumstances). When you identify your justifier, you can develop your Imagery Management Plan to remove and replace the erroneous limiting belief. Any belief not based on the truth that you are a powerful, spiritual, divine being—and not founded on love and its many attributes—is erroneous and needs to be corrected. These beliefs are nothing more than erroneous programming in the subconscious mind reflecting into the conscious mind.

Prayer

When you don't like the situation you or others are involved in, pray about it. Ask God to help. God is your partner. He and you are living within your human body. Tap into this mighty internal power that is with you always. Yet it is important to learn positive prayer. When you pray, ask, and then presume that your prayer has been answered. Next, give thanks in advance for the answered prayer. This immediately confirms that you believe your prayer has been answered. Jesus said, "Therefore I say unto you, All things whatsoever ye pray and ask for, believe that ye receive them, and ye shall have them." (Mark11:24) In Mathew 21:21 He says, "Verily I say unto you, If ye have faith, and doubt not, ye shall not only do what is done to the fig tree, but even if ye shall say unto this mountain, Be thou taken up and cast into the sea, it shall be done."

Developing your faith and belief in your prayer develops your power and status as a powerful, spiritual, divine being. The powers of faith and belief take time, care, and attention to nurture into a developed mature thought system.

Criteria for Developing Prayer Power

- Asking in Prayer
- Positive Imagery
- Positive Speech
- Give Thanks in Advance
- Positive Internal Dialogue
- Positive Actions

These areas are in need of the bulk of your attention to promote development. You pray, and then you give thanks in advance, presuming the prayer is answered. You then follow up your prayer and thanks with your imaginings, internal dialogue, speech, and action based on the *assumption* that the prayer has been answered.

It is important that you create the imagery of your prayer being answered. By giving your attention to your internal dialogue, you consciously choose what you say to yourself as based on the answered prayer. It is important to incorporate into your internal dialogue the fact that your prayers are answered. In this way, you begin to associate yourself with the imaginings that your prayers are answered rather than associating with the imaginings of doubt. Always keep in mind that your internal dialogue mirrors your imagery.

What comes out of your mouth reflects your imagery and internal dialogue, so it is equally important to give attention to speak positively. Jesus said, "But the things which proceed out of the mouth come forth out of the heart; and they defile the man." (Matthew 15:18)

Your actions reflect your imagery, internal dialogue, and

speech. Once you realize this compounding sequence, it becomes easy to identify your imagery as the source of negative internal dialogue, speech, and actions. In developing an effective Image Management Plan, to promote change it is important to be able to trace all negativity back to its source.

Doubt undermines your prayer efforts. Giving attention to internal dialogue, speech, and deeds gives you the opportunity to identify your doubts and remove them. The doubt that is within your conscious mind is soon dissolved by giving consistent attention to positive imagery. This occurs whether or not you actually believe the imagery at the present time. The consistent effort and attention reprograms the subconscious mind.

Study

I recommend studying, among others, the works of Neville, Charles Fillmore (co-founder of Unity), Emmet Fox, Catherine Ponder, Stephen Covey, Deepak Chopra, Neale Donald Walsh, Eric Butterworth, Louise Hay, Carl Jung, Daniel Goleman, and the Dalai Lama. New Thought, Buddhism, metaphysics, and psychology are great studies. Psychology books have great value, but typically lack in spirituality. When we learn that there are millions of people who have raised their level of consciousness through the techniques contained within these studies, we feel good about joining up with these elite thinkers. Reading is the supreme chance to hang out with the greatest minds this planet has ever produced.

Affirmations and Denials

An affirmation works with the I AM principle. What we state following I AM becomes true to us. Silent affirmations are good, but when they are spoken the brain gets the feedback of hearing this new truth in your own voice and with your own ears. When we write and speak an affirmation, the affect on the subconscious mind is more profound. This involves more areas of the brain in processing this information and your voice vibrates your intention to the Universe. It may be necessary to affirm something hundreds of times to imprint this truth in your mind. Affirmations set the stage for your new frame of consciousness.

Denials dissolve old beliefs that are untruths. This form of denial is not to be confused with the term denial as it is used in twelve step programs where we are denying that we have a problem. This type of denial is a statement that denies power to the belief in an untruth. Denial statements work to balance affirmations. Affirmations call our attention to a new truth, while denials call our attention to untruths in old beliefs to dissolve them away.

It is recommended that you view any affirmations and denials that I may suggest only as guidelines. You may want to customize them to fit your unique circumstances, and I encourage you to do so.

Relaxation and Meditation Tools and Aids

- **Affirmation Recordings**
- **Nature Sound Recordings**
- **Consciousness Management Recordings**
- **Lecture Recordings**
- **Accelerated Learning Recordings**
- **Self-hypnosis Recordings**
- **Subliminal Recordings**
- **Altered State Recordings**
- **Vitamins and Supplements**
- **Aroma Therapy**
- **Sound & Light Machines**

Affirmation Recordings

Affirmation recordings are wonderful self-help tools. They work best when you are relaxed in a meditative state or even when used as you fall asleep or wake up. You pick the recording that is appropriate to your goal at hand and simply listen and relax. This focus of your attention helps you program your subconscious mind as you give some attention to relaxation—something that too many people do not do enough of. Frequency following effect recordings and sound and light machines greatly enhance the ability of affirmation recordings to reprogram the subconscious mind.

Nature Sound Recordings

These recordings promote peace when used during meditation exercises. There are thousands available. Some are put to soft music; some are just the sounds of nature. Chirping birds and crickets and other animal sounds, running water, waterfalls, white water, ocean waves, wind in trees, and soft thunder are wonderful sounds to relax to. Try a few to see which ones you like. Almost everyone likes the sound of the ocean.

Consciousness Management Recordings

There are literally thousands of recordings available to enhance moods during meditation. These recordings, utilizing the frequency following effect, are designed to enhance the alpha, theta, and delta states through special sounds that induce the appropriate brain waves regarding the goals at hand. They are useful in managing mental states during all hours of the active day. Each state is a window for enhancing abilities. The various recordings to induce these states by audio work well when played in the background during tasks requiring concentration, creativity, or healing thoughts. I have found these to be about fifty percent as efficient as sound and light stimulation during meditation.

Lecture Recordings

There are many wonderful recordings available regarding self-help, New Thought, and spirituality that are great study aids. When used during relaxing meditation, they usually enter your mind through the window of alpha. Used with a sound and light machine, lectures can be fascinating, stimulating information dynamos.

Accelerated Learning Recordings

Accelerated learning is becoming more and more necessary as we grow more involved with the information age. These recordings of today open the mind to learning in speedy ways never before utilized by the average person. The extensive availability of these study recordings has uplifted the learning experience many times over. Now there is even a technique, taught by Paul Scheele and called PhotoReading, that can enhance your ability to cover material at an incredible speed of 25,000 words per minute!

Self-hypnosis Recordings

There is probably more self-hypnosis recordings than any other kind. These recordings induce altered states of mind, taking you into the theta, or delta states through hypnosis where information appropriate to your goals is pumped into your mind to reprogram the subconscious. Hypnosis is helpful to create cues that you respond to during the day. These little cues can help you remember to modify behaviors.

Subliminal Recordings

Subliminal recordings reprogram the subconscious in much the same way as altered state recordings, but you cannot actually hear the information being pumped into your subconscious mind. This lessens the conscious mind's ability to argue or disagree with the information.

Centerpointe Research has taken subliminal technology one step further with it's Holosync®, recordings that use ultra-high-frequency encoded messages that bypass the conscious mind completely after being demodulated by the ear. Your voice is custom-installed on these recordings, providing your subconscious mind with your own commands so that there is the greatest reprogramming efficiency and the least amount of argumentative after thought.

Sound and light machines greatly enhance subliminal recordings by deepening the mental state and creating a more suggestive state for the subconscious mind.

Altered States Recordings

Recordings ranging from classical music to audio frequency following effects are utilized to induce altered mental states. The Monroe Institute utilizes tones in their Hemi-Sync®, recordings that induce alpha, theta, and delta states as appropriate to the goal of the program. There are several companies using the frequency following effect within their programs to induce these states of mind.

Center Pointe's Holosync®, technology is a combination of subliminal and altered states recordings.

Vitamins and Supplements

Science has provided us with hundreds of breakthroughs regarding brain enhancement supplements. These herbs, vitamins, minerals, and supplements are designed to enhance alertness, clarity, and perception. Many are designed to slow the aging clock.

Aromatherapy

Different aromas set off a variety of positive emotional responses. Aromatherapy is the practice of enhancing wellness through the scent of essential oils extracted from many parts of plants. It is believed that the molecules of these extracts have internal affects within the body. Aromatherapy is great for enhancing meditation, setting moods, or just relaxing. Use them also in conjunction with recordings or sound and light sessions.

Sound & Light Machines

Sound and light machines can deepen meditation profoundly. The more experienced the meditator, the slower the brain waves pulsate in hertz per second. The frequency following effect slows the brain waves mechanically so an inexperienced meditator can enjoy the benefits of deep meditation quickly and easily. External audio programs can be included in a session, making any self/help recording much more profound. In my opinion, sound and light machines are the most efficient tool for reprogramming the subconscious mind and for developing deep insights and sagacity.

My favorite model is the Voyager XL, but all of them are quite good clinically. Some have a little better light show. Leading concerns in this field besides Voyager are Orion, Photosonix, David Paradise, and the unique Breathwork Explorer that has a breath sensor at the nose to incorporate breath principles into its sessions.

You see a wonderful light show consisting of geometric patterns twirling and flashing that change into unlimited scenes of imagination. The light show keeps your attention riveted to the session so there is no drifting away. Experiencing the deep states of alpha, theta, and delta are absolutely fascinating and intriguing.

The left and right hemispheres of the brain are actually not in synchronization as registered in hertz per second. They are actually a few hertz different when we are in the beta state. There are theories that teach that much of our misconceptions are a result of this out of synchronization of the hemispheres. As you progress into or toward the delta state, the left and right hemispheres of the brain begin to synchronize their brain waves in hertz per second. Theoretically, this is why insights are experienced in the deeper states of mind.

A great source for all of the above tools is *Tools For Exploration*. You can find them at their website, http://www.ToolsForExploration.com.

Visualization

Meditations where we visualize open the door of opportunity to us. Just as hindsight is 20/20, so we may have this advantage by practicing visualization. We can rewrite the past and prepare for the future. If you respond in an undesirable way, visualizing a similar situation in the future where you respond in a desirable way will prepare your ability to respond the way you prefer. We can rehearse situations where we ideally handle the worse case scenarios. As we do this, we are building response circuitry in the brain, creating neurological furrows to respond ideally. This inhibits being drawn into the disassociated paradigms of our negativity.

Developing compassion with practices such as Tonglen develops our ability to consider different perspectives in our interactions with other sentient beings.

Empathy is an important part of compassion. In order to express compassion, it is necessary to realize, consider, and be aware of the suffering of other sentient beings. This is an extension of our consciousness into the consciousness of others. When we are aware of what is occurring in the minds of others, our ability to interact is increased to the highest level. Doing this is becoming one with the Whole.

Practicing this is not becoming a mind reader as much as it is just being in tune to the emotions of others. We have a built-in emotional radar. Nature provided this to animals so that their survival is enhanced by the ability of emotion to spread throughout the herd quickly. When one bird experiences an emotion, the whole flock quickly experiences it. People are the same way. This is why anger or smiles are contagious. We can begin to read the emotions of others, even when they suppress them. By imagining what may be going on in the minds of others, we are giving this consideration our attention; thus we further develop this ability. What we give our attention to, we get more of.

Desire For Spiritual Ascension

It is necessary to keep the fire burning with a passionate desire for spiritual development. When we reach a level of comfort where we no longer desire spiritual ascension, we may stagnate. We never know enough. We never have enough education. We never develop our spirituality enough to stop the thirst for higher levels. If you do, you have reached a comfort level where you are of the illusion that you know enough or have enough spirituality and, thus, by having enough you close your mind. When everyday is an opportunity to grow in knowledge and spiritually, then everyday is growth itself. An open mind is the key to ascension. Did you ever hear the expression that a mind is like a parachute? It has to be open to work!

Diet, Vitamins, & Supplements

Diet and nutrients are very influential in our imagery creation urges. Chemicals created by a diet lacking in the correct macronutrient ratio necessary to initiate the ideal hormonal response to food will urge many unwanted symptoms within the body. When the micronutrients are not present, the body is lacking the necessary tools it needs to function properly. When the body is short on the supplies it needs to function, it may create chemicals that are less than ideal. This may also lead to undesirable imagery creation urges. We are what we eat and we think like we eat, as well. Keeping a journal of your negative imagery and diet may reveal some intriguing data. You may see a direct correlation between stress levels increasing as you eat less raw whole foods and more refined foods.

Alpha, Theta, and Delta

As the brain waves slow, the two hemispheres of the brain begin to synchronize and the subconscious mind becomes more and more suggestible. Meditation aids that slow the brain waves synthesize the deep meditative states of the masters to initiate insights as well as set the stage for reprogramming the subconscious mind. This becomes very important in creating new schema and subconscious programs for self-improvement. The mind states induced by recordings and sound and light machines are invaluable in your growth and spiritual ascension.

Jose Silva developed an entire technology around the alpha state. The Silva Method is a valuable tool for developing higher levels of consciousness through the alpha state. Silva's developments in prayer ability, healing, positive thinking, and extra sensory perception are profound.

Lee Pulos, Ph.D., has developed a powerful lecture series containing invaluable visualization systems and information.

Alpha (9-13 hertz per second) has been found to enhance our ability to create imagery or visualize when we are involved in meditation. During enhanced imagery and visualization states, we have increased abilities to heal others and ourselves, increased prayer effectiveness, increased athletic ability, and sensual enhancement during activity. During activity, this state is sometimes referred to as *being in the zone.*

When in the theta state (4-8 hertz per second), the mind is in a twilight half-awake, half-asleep state. Problem solving, creativity, and ideas readily emerge from the subconscious mind.

Theta is also an ideal state for reprogramming the subconscious mind with affirmations. The subconscious mind is very suggestive and receives new programming without the conscious mind arguing against the new information. Yet you are aware and in control in the theta state.

The delta state (1-3 hertz per second) is described by Zen and Yoga masters as a state of total peace and tranquility, detachment, bliss, or nirvana. In delta, we recharge, usually in deep sleep. But, with practice, we can learn to remain awake. I see many people begin to fall asleep using sound and light machines when they get too comfortable. Sitting up with no back support helps keep you from relaxing too much and from falling asleep as you approach the delta state.

Examining Common Negative Imaginings and Developing Imagery Management Plans

I have established that we think in images. The image is the primary manifestation in the order of our mental activity. I have also established that we *feel* our imagery in the form of emotion, moods, and states of mind. Additionally, as established, each negative emotion and the imagery it is based on have a particular disassociated paradigm. And, of course, negative imagery and emotions are counter-productive. They are the antis of everything God and we intend in our experiences. I've also shown that our conscious mind is limited to the choices and decisions that the subconscious mind permits. The subconscious mind is the sum total of information in the form of imagery and emotion that we give a great deal of attention to, and of how we perceive our input information. Further, I have established that it is critical to ignore the body's first impulse when it is negative and you are trying to change the way you respond. The object of self-improvement and spiritual ascension is to reprogram the subconscious mind with less and less limitations until we are free. We do this by consistently creating positive imagery. When we create divine positive imagery, we are attaining the highest level of spiritual experience that we are capable of within the moment.

The importance of *avoiding the creation of and of not dwelling in negative imagery* is our immediate goal.

If knowing this is not enough to support the priority of basic Imagination Control Therapy, and you find yourself being drawn into negative imagery and emotion, you can develop an effective Imagery Management Plan. Then, quickly reducing the limitations imposed by the subconscious mind, you can develop the discipline and core beliefs necessary to eliminate the undesirable negative responses.

When you've created or dwelled in negative imagery or entered into negative emotion, it is necessary to *identify the underlying belief* that formed the appearance that this response was logical and justifiable. In other words, identify your limiter. Becoming negative tells us of specific beliefs or limiters that we have within our subconscious mind that need to be worked on. The old beliefs and limitations must be dissolved and replaced with new beliefs based on Spiritual Truth. You do this with a balance of *prayer, affirmations and denials, study, visualization and meditation exercises, diet and nutrition considerations, mind state management* (considering whether to induce alpha, or theta with meditative aids or recordings), and consistently returning your attention to the fact that you are a powerful, spiritual, divine being.

Affirmations and denials change the beliefs and subconscious limitations that lead to justifying negativity. Study teaches us maturity in knowledge that rounds us out and keeps the concept of growth constantly fresh in our minds. Study is always a must for personal development. Visualization and meditation exercises, enhanced with tools and aids, change our conception and mental records of the past and prepare our response in the future by giving us opportunities and insights to cope with situations through knowledge and a preparation that we would not have cultivated otherwise. Mind state management considerations enhance and quicken the attainment of our goals by rendering the subconscious mind more attainable for information input and output. With proper diet and nutrition, we sharpen our wits and clean out junk food thoughts. And, returning our attention constantly to the fact that we are powerful, spiritual, divine beings establishes this extremely important yet seemingly easy to forget information into our core belief system. Returning your attention to this truth embeds it as a never-ending frame of reference in all your choices, decisions, and judgments. You learn to associate these thoughts with your inner-self.

Developing an Effective Imagery Management Plan

• You have attempted basic Imagination Control Therapy and dwelled in or created negative imagery in spite of your attempt to ignore your first impulse. Let it go as soon as possible.

- Question yourself: Did you succumb to your body's organic artificial intelligence program? If the same situation happens again, can you ignore this first impulse?
- Focus the greatest part of your attention of your imaginings, internal dialogue, and emotions. By doing this, you become aware of what is or was going on within your organic artificial intelligence programming.
- Listen and acknowledge what your lower self is or was saying.
- Identify the character your lower self has created. There may be more than one character. Listen and identify them. Identify the justifier that you used to become negative. You now have your limiting belief(s) identified.
- Use the lines of the script and the limiter(s) to develop affirmations and denials.

For example, if your lower self says, *You are too stupid to ever accomplish such a thing,* affirm that I AM intelligent, clever, and insightful. Then say a denial such as *I have no reason to believe that I am anything less than a powerful, spiritual, divine being.* Simply base the affirmations on being basically the opposite of what information the lower self offers you. Then base the denials on dissolving away the belief or limiter that permitted or justified the lower self in stating what it did in the first place. Or, in identifying a limiter, look for what you may have said to yourself. *Who wouldn't want to choke a so and so like that!* These are beliefs surfacing that need work.

- Pray about it. Give thanks in advance that your prayer is answered. When you talk to yourself, reflect that the prayer is answered in you dialogue. Speak as though your prayer is answered. If you can't, don't talk about it. Act as though your prayer is answered. The point is: Don't undermine your prayer with second thoughts, doubting internal dialogue, speech, and actions. Become your answered prayer.
- Always take time to meditate. You can meditate for a few

minutes at any time during the day. You don't need to go
through a ritual every time. Utilize just a few minutes when
you need to. A 2-5 minute break can help a lot. A half-hour per
day minimum is ideal. Sitting in the silence gets you in tune
with God. But aside from silent meditation there is much work
to do. Practice the yoga of bringing the love of God to your
face. This can be done anywhere, anytime.

• Put together a *visualization routine* incorporating goals, relaxation techniques, and other development systems. (I highly
recommend Jose Silva's *The Silva Method* and *The Power of
Visualization,* by Lee Pulos, for developing a visualization routine.) In your daily meditation, take some time to meditate on
any negative experience you may have had that day or earlier
in life, if necessary. Practice one or more of the various visualizations described, or create a new style more unique to you.
You may want to rewrite the past, and then visualize this happening in the future as happening in a spiritual, higher
experience. We always have the option of recreating our past
experiences into a higher quality. When we prepare ourselves
for the future experience by having already experienced it in a
spiritual, high quality way, we then need only to realize the
experience. This is the hindsight is 20/20 principle used in a
rewrite and in advance.

• Use a meditative aid such as recordings or a sound and light
machine with a recording. These aids are very helpful in reprogramming the subconscious mind while inducing the alpha or
theta states for quickening.

• Study! Ninety percent of all knowledge you acquire will
come from reading. In this age of information, there is an
abundance of wonderfully prepared information on every
subject conceivable. Studying New Thought Christianity,
metaphysics, Buddhism principles, yoga, principles of
Hinduism, psychology, philosophy, holistic healing, and
other mental and physical developmental assists will enhance
your growth. Everyone needs to read at least thirty minutes
per day. Be as professional about your studies as you are (or

ideally should be) about your job.
• Review your responsibility in your co-creatorship with God
consistently. Give this a high priority. When you do, expressing
anger, falling into fear, needing to prove a point or control
something—all lose their priorities in your life. This also gets
you so busy creating good imaginations that you don't have
time to fall into creating anything negative. Oh, you little god,
will you not learn to be a good little god? Will you learn to
create only good before you are given more power? Review
your desire for spiritual growth. Review your plan. You may
need to renew your approach.

By incorporating prayer, affirmations, denials, meditation,
visualizations, study, and review into your daily and weekly routines, you walk the path of self-development. Controlling the
imagination through the development of your self-image is the
idea at the heart of these techniques. Work on your beliefs and
the subconscious limitations you may have that are causing you
to slip into creating negative imaginings or becoming negative in
emotion. Don't worry if this sounds like brain washing. It is.
Only I prefer to think of it as *mind cleansing*. Brain washing is
when you wind up believing things you had no intention of
believing through the intentions of another person. In mind
cleansing, *you* have the intention to believe or achieve something,
but through erroneous beliefs you slip away from this intent, so
you take cleansing measures for correction.

If you want to progress, to become illuminated, enlightened, to experience total God realization, it is necessary to
construct new mental pathways that are correlated with the
images that are appropriate. Far too often I hear people speaking as though enlightenment or the mystical experience is an
ideal that they can identify with, yet it is out of reach. The
statement, *We are human*, has been said time and time again to
excuse the worst part of us when it surfaces. *You just have to get
professional about controlling your imagery.* You are more than
human; you are a child of God!

Many psychiatrists will state that we develop control dramas by the time we are four years old. They go on to tell us that there are countless adults still having tantrums, or using these control dramas, portraying the poor me (the victim), the intimidator, the interrogator, or just acting aloof.

It's time to wake up to the fact that we just don't become negative in emotion when things draw us into acting out negative emotion. We are literally having our paradigm drawn to a disassociated personality that sees, hears, feels, and thinks everything from this viewpoint. This is not what we have all believed—until now. Now we know that we are subjecting our experience to an influence with nothing less than a change of viewpoint, paradigm, and personality in a fashion comparable to becoming possessed. Actually it's a possession of attention that causes a temporary disregard for a vast amount of pertinent information.

When you stop and think about it, God couldn't have planned the lessons of our realization experience any better than for our lives and feelings to consistently be a result of our imagery. God granted our awareness; now, we must learn how to create good with our awareness.

Common Negative Imaginations

In the book, *The 10 Dumbest Mistakes Smart People Make and How To Avoid Them,* by Dr. Arthur Freeman and Rose DeWolfe, regular people chose the mistakes listed. These are the erroneous imaginings that lead to more and more erroneous imaginings like a chain reaction in dominos. I have added several such common mistakes to this list. In every case, these are good examples of the imagination running away with itself. Of course, there is the entire spectrum of negative imagery that we may be drawn into, in addition to these common imaginings. The most common of all is the supportive imaginings when the body's emotional system puts forth an impulse. A great deal of supportive imaginings can be found in the following categories. Supportive imaginings can be so intense that Dr. Richard

Carlson has coined the term *analysis paralysis* to describe how the imagination runs away with itself.

• Fear	• Perfectionism
• Hurt Feelings	• Pessimism
• Anger and Hate	• The Should Syndrome
• Insecurity	• Obsessive Comparing
• Assumptions	• Taking things Personal
• Negative Fantasies	• Believing Criticism
• Worry	• Believing Flattery
• Exaggerating Circumstances	• Control
• Mind Reading	• Needing to be right

Fear

Although the common denominator of all the above negative modes is fear, an understanding of basic fear and its initiation through imaginings of threats is important in gaining the insights needed for entraining the mind to avoid these modes of imagery. Fear leads us into negative imagery and is the root of all negativity. It initiates The Fight or Flight Response and its array of chemicals within the body. From a subtle imagined threat to serious life threatening situations, The Fight or Flight Response is constantly at work dumping its chemicals in the body and causing stress and illness. Invariably, the threats are imagined or exaggerated.

For example, a supervisor at work intimidates you. You feel scared or uneasy when he or she reprimands you. Since you've been reprimanded, you feel uneasy and intimidated when around this person. To handle this situation, you process it through the guidelines for Imagery Management, always keeping in mind to eat correctly, take proper supplements, and meditate daily. The following example is a good Imagery Management process for this situation. Each situation has its own idiosyncrasies that may need to be customized in the Imagery Management process, so bear this in mind.

Antidote for Fear

- **Identify:** The problem is intimidation when being repri-manded, which has extended into uneasiness or intimidation when in the presence of the supervisor. What is it within the belief system that permits this intimidation? For the sake of this example we will say that it is a timid nature and job inse-curity. What was the internal dialogue? What justified you becoming negative?
- **Pray about it.**
- **Affirmations:** I AM a powerful, spiritual, divine being. I AM secure in my job and in my life. I AM a worthy and fearless. I AM improving in my job performance more and more, every day in every way.
- **Denial:** There is nothing to fear. All is well. No one has the power to intimidate me.
- **Meditate about it.**
- **Consider a meditative aid and the appropriate mental state (alpha or theta).**
- **Visualization:** Meditate on visualizing the person who intimidates you as being kind and loving. See a kind and loving interaction with him or her. Hold an imaginary con-versation where you both praise each other and arrive at an intelligent understanding. See yourself as invincible to intimidation. Visualize a new ending to the last intimidation where you respond in a kind and loving way as you would respond to a two-year-old child who said the same things to you.
- **Study:** Good topics to study would be The Fight or Flight Response, psychology articles on intimidation, New Thought metaphysics.
- **Diet and nutrition:** How much refined and processed foods were involved this day? How many raw fruits and vegetables

were eaten this day? Is there a possibility that there is a mineral or vitamin deficiency?

Hurt Feelings

Hurt feelings are one of the most common modes of negative thought that we justify. Probably more negative images have been formed because of hurt feeling than from any other mode of error. The imagined retaliation from hurt feelings is usually much worse than the negativity or perceived negativity that induced the hurt feelings. Yet you have to be delusional to *choose* to have your feelings hurt in the first place.

For example, someone yells at you and your feelings become hurt. First of all, in order to respond to yelling by choosing hurt feelings, you must imagine that the other person's behavior caused your hurt feelings. This is the first delusion. You have chosen to respond to the behavior of this person with hurt feelings. In order for you to believe the person's behavior caused your hurt feelings, you have to fail to consider a few important facts. One fact is that you are a powerful, spiritual, divine being. Another fact is that being in constant unity with God, there is nothing to hurt about. We hurt when we are connected to our past pain rather than God. Remember that the greatest part of our suffering is caused by our beliefs. When our beingness is grounded in God, the behavior of another has nothing to do with the way we feel.

Most likely the yelling and behavior of this person has *reminded you* of inadequacies, limitations, and images of lack that you have about yourself. This self-image of limitation may be conscious or subconscious, but it is there nonetheless. If it were not, you most likely would not have hurt feelings.

When people are reactive in their responses, they usually respond to hurt feelings with scornful imagery. Pause for a moment to contemplate some of the terrible, scornful imaginings you may have had after choosing to experience hurt feelings.

A vast amount of hurt feelings stemming from a limited self-image is a matter of perspective. I once asked a woman who was tying to work through a complex that consistently led to hurt feelings to change her perspective. She was a Cherokee Indian by nationality. I looked her straight in the eye and said, "You are a black woman." She replied that this was ridiculous, that anyone could see that she was obviously not a black woman. I pointed out that when we completely know something to be true, we have the same conviction as she had exhibited about who she is in regard to her nationality. The difference is that she could easily get countless people to agree with her regarding her nationality. But whether or not others agree with the truth has no bearing on truth itself. When you possess the complete conviction that you are a powerful, spiritual, divine being you will make all of your choices and decisions from this reference point.

Being vulnerable to hurt feelings is an important problem to solve. I have witnessed countless people turn very nasty and mean after having their feelings hurt. I once described this tendency as being a *sensitive alligator.* Isn't it intriguing how sensitivity can be a motivation for extreme hateful or angry behavior?

Hurt feelings may be caused by other factors, such as embarrassment. Embarrassment is nothing more than bringing our limited self-image to the attention of others or ourself. If our child acts up in public, we may feel that this behavior results from some inadequacy as a parent, and then reflect this limitation as being symbolic of our worth as a being. Our boss may make a degrading remark to us in front of others and we feel that he sees our inadequacy and has made it known to others. Even if we are limited at a particular field of knowledge, such as a job aspect, this does not reflect on our essence as a being. We are lacking only in knowledge about our job, not worthiness as a being. The only true lack or limitation we possess is a lack of knowledge or experience. This has nothing to do with our value as a being, as a person, as a child of God. Again, returning your attention to the fact that you are a powerful, spiritual, divine being trains your mental habit to except this and use it for a frame of reference. As you deepen this belief, the very notion of others hurting your feelings dissolves away.

Antidote for Hurt Feelings

• **Identify:** What was it that justified your choice of hurt feelings?
• **Pray about it.**
• **Affirmations:** I AM a powerful, spiritual, divine being. I AM secure in my self-image and my worthiness as a person. I AM able to respond with love and kindness in all situations. I AM a good, wonderful, compassionate, kind, caring person. I AM experiencing the Christ potential within me.
• **Denials:** Any limitation that I may have is not a limitation as a person or a spiritual being. Within my unity with God, there is no reason to have hurt feelings. The behavior of others has nothing to do with my value as a person.
• **Meditate about it.**
• **Consider a meditative aid and the appropriate mental state (alpha or theta).**
• **Visualizations:** Take a moment to visualize yourself as a beautiful angel or some idea of a powerful, spiritual, divine being. Now, visualize another you as the way you become when you are experiencing hurt feelings. Have the powerful, spiritual, divine *you* speak to the *you* with hurt feelings. As these two facets of your mind converse, observe the different points of view each of these disassociated paradigms possess. Have a nice talk.

Visualize the hurt *you* fading and becoming absorbed into the powerful, spiritual, divine *you*. Visualize someone behaving in ways that would normally hurt your feelings. See yourself as a powerful, spiritual, divine being who is grounded in unity with God. See yourself as an understanding soul and create a beam of light filled with love surrounding this person. Bless this person. Visualize this person as a powerful, spiritual, being that is being drawn to God's light.

Affirm that you will always respond to a situation such as this in this positive way and reject the idea that you will ever respond with hurt feelings again.

This is a new cue of how you act in this Play of Life. Your old cue had you become hurt. When a person behaves in a way that normally would have hurt you, you now have a wonderful opportunity to exercise your powers as a divine being by casting a love beam and visualizing this person as uplifted.

- **Study:** The metaphysics of our core belief system and self-image.
- **Diet and nutrition:** How much refined and processed foods involved this day? How many raw fruits and vegetables were eaten this day? Is there a possibility that there is a mineral or vitamin deficiency?

Anger and Hate

Becoming angry and hateful are serious problems to solve. We are really tapping into primitive areas of the brain when we activate this behavior response. His Holiness, the Dalai Lama, has stated many times that the antidote for anger and hate is patience and tolerance—a state of mind developed through compassion. This is very true, but we need to examine what beliefs we harbor that justify the anger and hate in the first place. When we approach anger and hate by dissolving the beliefs that justify their existence, our development of compassion has a more profound affect.

Subconsciously, many people believe that it is OK to get angry, so they go right ahead with the urge. It is rarely OK to get angry, and it is not OK at any time to act out with angry behavior. Once in a while, anger can be channeled into something productive if it is kept in perspective and The Fight or Flight Response is avoided. It's one thing to know injustice and take umbrage to the point of motivation while not actually feeling angry in the physical sense. Intellectual and ethical anger can be a powerful motivator. If you get physically angry, consider reprogramming it out of your mind.

General Antidote for Anger and Hate

- **Identify the belief that justifies it.**
- **Pray about it.**
- **Affirmation:** I AM a tolerant, patient, compassionate, powerful, spiritual, divine being.
- **Denial:** Through my connection with God, there is no situation that can influence me to choose an angry or hateful response. I release all my anger.
- **Meditate about it.**
- **Consider a meditative aid and the appropriate mental state (alpha or theta).**
- **Visualizations:** Visualize yourself in a situation that has made you very angry or hateful in the past. Now, visualize yourself as the powerful, spiritual, divine being that you really are. Imagine these two facets of yourself speaking to each other. Observe the disassociated perspectives that each one possesses. Have a nice talk and learn.

  Visualize any person that you blame your anger or hate on and cast a beam of love light upon them. Bless them. See them as coming to God's light and realizing the powerful, spiritual, divine being they really are. At the first sign of anger or hate, this is your cue to your new response.

  Visualize yourself in a situation that would normally make you angry or hateful. Handle the situation the way the powerful, spiritual, divine being that you are would handle it. This develops the ability to respond in this way if and when a real situation develops.
- **Study:** The metaphysics of our core belief systems, self-image, and The Fight or Flight Response in humans. Do a concordance search on anger and hate in the Bible.
- **Consider your diet and nutrition.**

Insecurity

Being insecure is like walking on thin ice. You are always

anticipating falling through the ice and being swallowed up. Insecurity is a lack of self-esteem manifesting in various ways. To dissolve insecurity, it is necessary to build a confident self-image and release the conscious mind from these unconfident, insecure subconscious limitations. Affirming that you are a powerful, spiritual, divine being is the foundation of self-confidence.

Have you ever wanted to ask your boss for a raise, but didn't have the confidence? Or have you missed out on a ski trip or other fun because you didn't have the confidence to try? Have you ever wanted to ask someone out on a date, but just couldn't? These are all examples of a lack of confidence. One reason many people don't do something is because they fear failure. Thus, *failure is guaranteed*, but without the failing. It's OK to fail. Let go of the urge to be right all the time. It's OK to be wrong. Just take off the pressure. Try your best and then let go of the results. Whether or not you do well has nothing to do with the fact that you are a powerful, spiritual, divine being. It has nothing to do with your worthiness as a being.

You can do most anything that you put your mind to. It is only the fear of being inadequate that holds you back. Try it. Put forth a professional attempt and you may surprise yourself. Study what it is you may want to try. Learn about it. Make friends with someone who is already proficient in the subject. Join a club that deals with it.

Project yourself as confident. When you project yourself as shy and insecure, everyone in contact with you picks up on it. Being rejected is not a disaster. Actually, it's great practice for building your character. The more you interact, the more you develop your ability to interact. If you specifically study the science of interacting, you gain more success. People can't read your mind but they can read your vocal tones, facial expressions, and body language. Each of these projects your underlying imagery.

When someone is insecure in a relationship, they have a constant need to see a demonstration of caring attention. Sometimes, even negative attention is better than no attention.

Children are prone to this type of reasoning, although it is common in adults.

You have the constant attention of the indwelling God within you. Keep connected to God and you will have no need to create the imaginings of insecurity.

Antidote for Insecurity

- **Identify the belief that causes the insecurity.** Consider the lines of your internal dialogue. What are you saying to yourself about your lack of confidence? What are you speaking in regard to your insecurity? How are you projecting yourself?
- **Pray about it.**
- **Affirmation:** I AM confident and secure in my abilities and worth as a being.
- **Denials:** I have no fear of rejection or failure. No one is better or worthier than I am.
- **Meditate about it.**
- **Consider a meditative aid and the appropriate mental state (alpha or theta).**
- **Visualizations:** Visualize yourself as a confident, secure person. See yourself doing the things you would do as a confident, secure person. If you find yourself becoming afraid during this exercise, affirm over and over that you are confident and secure.
- **Study:** Review the Fight or Flight Response. Find some articles in psychology about confidence and security. Read something in New Thought about the subject.
- **Consider your diet and nutrition.**

Assumptions

What you assume to be true is true for you. So be careful what you assume. Positive prayer is an assumption. When you pray and assume that your prayer has been answered, you give thanks in advance. Many assumptions are based on a lack of confidence and insecurity. Many are based on a lack of the facts. Many times, we will assume that a person will behave in a previous manor and urge this same behavior by the way we treat them due to our assumption.

Persist in leading your mind to assume the best. Visualize the best. Expect the best. All the imagery of anything less works against you. We urge the truth to come forth when we create the imagery that sees the truth. Judge not by appearances. Create an image of goodness.

Many times we get caught up in assuming negative things regarding circumstances and the behaviors of children and adults. Yet, through negative assumptions, we urge the negative circumstances and behaviors. A negative assumption is pretty much forming a prayer image of what you do not desire to happen.

No matter how you look at it, when you assume something, you are *dreaming it up* within your mind. It's an educated guess at best. As you are working on your ability to assume the best, don't put a lot of stock in your assumptions if they are less than the best or appear to be "realistic." Just let them ride and pass through your mind. They may be completely wrong. That's why it is necessary to focus on the creation of positive imagery despite all appearances.

Antidote for Negative Assumptions

- **Identify the justifier and the script.** How are you visualizing the situation or behaviors of the people involved? Are you judging by appearances? If you could change things merely by creating a visualization of the situation in the preferred outcome, how would you visualize it? Is there an opportunity that the situation has manifested? What are you saying to yourself about it?
- **Pray about it.**
- **Affirmations:** I AM willing and capable of assuming the best in all situations and behaviors of people. I see the Good in everything.

- **Denial:** The appearance of that which is less than Good does not attract my attention.
- **Meditate about it.**
- **Consider a meditative aid and the appropriate mental state (alpha or theta).**
- **Visualization:** Visualize yourself as an angel. See yourself as creating Good positive scenes in reality through the power of your mind.
- **Study:** Read *The Power of Awareness* by Neville to learn about the Law of Assumption.
- **Consider your diet and nutrition.**

Negative Fantasies

When we become angry or frustrated, we may create skits in the mind where we are vindicated. Choking the boss, ramming other cars on the road, beating up people, or playing dirty tricks on people are all examples of negative fantasies people create to rectify situations they cannot accept. When the mind cannot accept something, the skit may continue to repeat itself over and over. This is the *negative emotional response loop* as termed by Dr. Frank Young.

Although most of the time these fantasies may seem harmless, they are dumping toxic chemicals within the body in response to these images. These same images may later become schemata for future references. When imagery and emotion intensifies, people begin to act on their negative fantasies. For example, after visualizing choking the boss for a period of time, the boss may pick up on the vibration and act his role with more intensity. You may get so spun into the ongoing situation that you argue or even attack the boss. Negative fantasies on the road turn into road rage. Fantasies of hurting people lead to violence. Fantasies of being the prankster lead to further harm. Sexual fantasies may lead to base imagery. It is hard to ascend spiritually when you spend considerable time each day visualizing sexual fantasies with everyone whom you are attracted to.

When you consider that the negative natural instincts of an

animal are to kill, dominate, repel, and avoid, you can gain insight into why you may have some of the imaginings that run through your mind. Considering the natural instincts of sexuality that we possess as a mammal also gives you insight into our sexual fantasies. But it is also necessary to consider whether your animal nature or your true spiritual nature is making your choices and decisions regarding the imagery you create.

Antidote for Negative Fantasies

- **Identify the belief that justifies the negative fantasy.** Is the fantasy projecting from your higher nature or from your animal nature? What visualizations would you create if you were an angel?
- **Pray about it.**
- **Affirmations:** I AM a powerful, spiritual, divine being. My imaginings are consistent with my status as a powerful, spiritual, divine being. I AM Spirit. I AM a co-creator with God in the Universe.
- **Denials:** I have risen above my animal nature. I have no desire to create imaginings of killing, dominating, repelling, or avoiding other beings. Sex is a precious celebration of life.
- **Meditate about it.**
- **Consider a meditative aid and the appropriate mental state (alpha or theta).**
- **Visualizations:** Create a vision of yourself as an angel or deity. As this angelic being, visualize your past situations and how they may have been changed by rewriting them through the mind of this angel or deity.
- **Study:** The Buddhist Eight Fold Path. New Thought metaphysics.
- **Consider your diet and nutrition.**

Worry

Many people have convinced themselves that they demonstrate

how much they care about others by the degree of worry they project. If we had the power, we could put our seal of guaranteed safety on everyone we care about, but we can't. We *can* create imagery of their safety. And this imagery will go a long way toward urging their safety compared to creating the imagery of their disaster. You only need to consider negative possibilities once to be aware of them. From the second you begin to *dwell* on the negative possibilities, you are worrying.

Worry is negative prayer. If all worries were converted into positive prayer, there would be an immense flood of positive imagery into the Universe. In addition to this flood of positive imagery there would be an immense reduction of negative imagery. When you consider that images held in mind eventually manifest, this alone should be enough to deter worry. It is quite possible to quickly scan the possible negative results of decisions without dwelling in this imagery long enough to initiate The Fight or Flight Response or for the imagery to be urged into manifestation.

When you worry, you are demonstrating your lack of faith and trust in God. Staying connected with God promotes your faith and trust and projects it into your imagery. Striving to be one with God aligns your imagery with Gods intent. You are co-creating with God. A protector in the Universe holds imagery of beings as protected within their mind.

Antidote for Worry

- **Identify the belief that justifies the worrying.** Do you have faith and trust that God will protect and care for the person or people you're worrying about? Do you believe that God can bring about a desirable situation? Can you look at the situation through the view of a bigger picture? What are you saying to yourself about it?
- **Pray about it.**
- **Affirmations:** I AM completely confident in my faith and trust in God. I AM confident that all things happen for my greatest Good.

- **Denials:** I release all my will to control things. I accept all situations with the help of God.
- **Meditate about it.**
- **Consider a meditative aid and the appropriate mental state (alpha or theta).**
- **Visualizations:** Visualize yourself as a protector through the use of imagery. Create images of protection for everyone you care about. Visualize situations occurring as you desire. Hold the images. Take care to align your internal dialogue, speech, and actions with the imagery.
- **Study:** The Bible, The Bhagavad Gita, New Thought metaphysics, Buddhism, psychology articles on worry.
- **Consider your diet and nutrition.**

Exaggerating Circumstances

How many times do people make mountains out of molehills? Yet, an enlightened mind makes molehills out of mountains. Exaggerating the size or the seriousness of a situation only puts the mind in a position where it is overwhelmed or creates a perception that we are much less powerful or able. When you exaggerate a situation, you are really exhibiting your sense of smallness, your feeling of neediness, and your beliefs in your inadequacies. When you put your faith in God, you become much larger in the perception of yourself.

As the size and seriousness of a situation appears to grow, it may represent the size and seriousness of your need to gain the control of the situation that you feel you have lost. The more control that you feel you have lost and need, the greater the size and seriousness of a situation appears. Practicing acceptance and surrender dissolves the size and seriousness of a situation. It's all a matter of perception. Through striving for a unity with God, you literally grow in might in proportion to your degree of connectedness. *If God is for us, who is against us?* (Romans 8:31)

Antidote for Exaggerating Circumstances

- **Identify the belief that makes the circumstance seem big.**
  What is it that you are saying to yourself in your internal dialogue? What are you speaking? What are you doing? Compare
  how you are responding to how you would respond if you
  were an angel.
- **Pray about it.**
- **Affirmations:** I AM a powerful, spiritual, divine being. I AM
  calm and intelligent in all situations. I AM one with God and I
  AM powerful through Him. I Am accepting of all circumstances.
- **Denials:** As God is for me, no one can be against me. I do not
  sweat the small stuff. Everything is small stuff.
- **Meditate about it.**
- **Consider a meditative aid and the appropriate mental state
  (alpha or theta).**
- **Visualizations:** Visualize yourself as a spiritual giant who can
  handle all situations. Rewrite some of your past situations
  where you felt the situation was too big or too serious for you
  to handle. Change the script to seeing yourself as powerful and
  handling everything with ease. Move to the future. Visualize
  yourself as this spiritual giant, in unity and supported by God,
  accepting situations and handling everything with ease.
- **Study:** The human mind; articles on the amygdala, frontal
  lobes, and limbic system.
- **Consider your vitamins and nutrition.**

Mind Reading

Mind reading is a very common assumption. Many people
presume that those in contact with them regularly (especially
mates) are naturally inclined to be able to read their minds.
Others assume that they can read the minds of their mates or
people in close contact with them. Sometimes we can estimate or
put forth an educated guess regarding what people are thinking,

but to involve these guesses in our responses and the decisions and choices we make often leads to trouble. Mind reading can lead to some very wrong assumptions and responses. It gives the illusion that communication may be lessened or eliminated completely. But this is a fallacy. Communication is essential in any relationship.

Mind reading is not to be confused with showing empathy. Empathy is very important in developing emotional intelligence. Identifying intellectually with the feelings, thoughts, or attitudes of another person opens the door to the illusion of mind reading, so be careful. A big part of practicing and developing empathy is *asking* how another person feels.

If you do find yourself mind reading or assuming that someone should be able to read your mind, it's not so bad if you give him or her the leeway to make mistakes. If it's OK to be wrong, you won't respond negatively to the error. But if it's not OK to make a mistake, communication is important. And *you are responsible* to make sure there is no failure to communicate.

Antidote for Mind Reading

- **Identify:** What was it that you failed to communicate? Is it really important that a mistake not be made? What can you do to assure communication? Do you know each other as well as you thought? What reason is there that holds you back from asking?
- **Pray about it.**
- **Affirmations:** I AM able and willing to communicate smoothly and easily. I AM responsible for communicating in my interactions with others.
- **Denials:** I cannot read other people's minds, nor can they read my mind. If it is important there be no error, I take responsibility to communicate this importance.
- **Meditate about it.**
- **Consider a meditative aid and the appropriate mental state (alpha or theta).**

- **Visualizations:** See yourself as a great communicator. Visualize yourself communicating everything others need to interact well with you. Visualize others communicating everything you need to interact well with them. Leave nothing to chance that is too important for error.
- **Study:** *The 10 Dumbest Mistakes Smart People Make and How To Avoid Them* by Dr. Arthur Freeman and Rose DeWolf.
- **Consider your vitamins and nutrition.**

Perfectionism

Many of us fall into the perfectionism prison. Perfection is OK until it is taken to extremes. Then it is nothing but a problem. The need for perfection is often exaggerated. Many things just don't need to be so perfect. And nobody is perfect. Some people are closer to perfect than others are, but no one is perfect.

The eyes and ears of the layman naturally seek perfection. When a layman looks at art, usually their eyes see the perfection first. When listening to music, the layman's ears usually hear perfection first. On the other hand, an artist or musician usually sees and hears the imperfections first, especially regarding one's own work. And this is natural for an artist or musician. After all, an artist and musician devote a great deal of attention to imperfections in order to perfect their work. But the layman has never done this. He or she is an observer or listener. The attention here is geared toward finding the perfection in order to marvel.

I've seen parents get irate with children who have done chores a little sloppily. These same parents will fuss for longer than it takes to touch up the mistakes. And supervisors sometimes do the same thing to employees. Why complain for ten minutes because someone didn't do five minutes worth of work? Sometimes a perfectionist becomes nothing but a perfect nag.

Everyone has standards, but are these standards realistic? Are these standards realistic for the particular situation? A professional baseball player coaching a little league team has to reset his standards. You can't expect more out of people than they have to give. Perfection is not an all or nothing proposition. Everyone needs to do the best he or she can, and this *best* is either sufficient or it isn't. So, we can't put someone at a higher level than that person can perform. And we can't expect a higher level of performance than is necessary. There's a balance.

Antidote for Excessive Perfectionism

- **Identify:** What level of expertise is actually necessary to achieve the goal at hand? Are the people and the situations (yourself included) compatible in expertise levels and importance of perfection or lack of error? What harm will an error cause?
- **Pray about it.**
- **Affirmations:** I AM balanced between perfectionism and realism. I AM willing and able to consider all situations and appropriately judge within the balance between the level of perfection necessary for the goal at hand and the level of skill of the people involved.
- **Denials:** I shall not become drawn into seeing a need for a higher level of perfection than is necessary for the situation at hand. It's OK to make mistakes on occasions where it is not critical to be precise.
- **Meditate about it.**
- **Consider a meditative aid and the appropriate mental state (alpha or theta).**
- **Visualizations:** Visualize yourself as having the proper judgment in all situations regarding perfectionism. Return to a situation where you may have been too fussy or overbearing with perfectionism. Rewrite a new ending to the situation where you are patient and realistic. Visualize how you see something you know nothing about. Now, visualize something you know a great deal about. Take notice of the difference in how your attention is drawn to the perfection in the subject you know nothing about and compare it to how your attention is drawn to the imperfections regarding the subject you know quite a bit about.

- **Study:** Read some psychology articles on perfectionism. Read some New Thought metaphysics.
- **Consider your vitamins and nutrition.**

Pessimism

We have all heard Murphy's Law: *Anything that can possibly go wrong—will—at the worst possible moment.* This is true pessimism at its highest level. Although most of us have experienced this affect, it is not the law of all situations. A pessimist can appear quite adept in drawing many people's attention to the negative aspects of every facet in a situation. Research shows that pessimists simply don't perform as well as optimists, even when the optimism is unrealistic. The pessimist devotes too much attention to the problem and not enough to solving the problem. On the other hand, the optimist acknowledges the problem, then devotes a great deal of attention to solving it. It is quite possible to acknowledge all of the possible negative consequences of decisions and choices in situations without dwelling on them until The Fight or Flight Response initiates. But this is what happens to the pessimist. He or she gets drawn into a condition of fight or flight, the mind's filter kicks in and everything positive becomes insignificant. Here only that which is negative is important—this is where the threats are.

Antidote for Pessimism

- **Identify:** What belief is it that causes you to dwell on the negative aspects and to neglect the positive? What will happen if you focus on the positive aspects of the situation? What justifies a negative outlook? Is there anyone who has experienced this before and benefited from an optimistic attitude? Can you model this experience after them? What are you saying to yourself about it?
- **Pray about it.**
- **Affirmations:** I AM willing and able to find the silver lining in

every cloud. I AM willing and able to focus my attention on the positive aspects in every situation. I AM mighty through God.

- **Denials:** I merely acknowledge negative aspects and possible negative consequences long enough to make an intelligent decision or choice. I then let go. Negative aspects of a situation have no power over me.
- **Meditate about it.**
- **Consider a meditative aid and the appropriate mental state (alpha or theta).**
- **Visualizations:** Visualize yourself as a master at finding the good in all situations. See yourself as quickly scanning the negative aspects of a situation, acknowledging them, then quickly finding the good and focusing your attention on it. Visualize yourself as an optimist in a few situations.
- **Study:** Read some psychology articles on pessimism and optimism.
- **Consider your vitamins and nutrition.**

The Should Syndrome

Comparing how a situation *should* be to how things appear to be is very misleading. How it should be and how it is—is a matter of perspective. How it is—is a matter of perspective.

You can get so caught up in imagining how it should be that you lose focus on the present and all of its wonderful aspects. The gap between how it should be and how it is can be very wide and frustrating. This constant comparing uses up attention on the comparison that can be utilized on creating necessary changes or acceptance. It's another matter of wasting attention focusing on the problem rather than the solution.

When you accept how the present is at this moment, you have considerable attention left to devote toward the creation of positive things. Each moment presents an opportunity for you to discover who you are and what you are all about. As you discover that you are a powerful, spiritual, divine being you transform each moment into an experience that should be just the way it is.

Raising the quality of your experience moment-by-moment removes the illusion that things should be different than they are.

When the idea of a *should* makes a situation negative, let it go. Ideals are fine, but they don't have to get in the way of anything positive. Guilt, shame, obligations, unworthiness, and resentment are only a few consequences of comparing how things should be or how someone should behave. Accept things as they are, and then look for the good that the situation can lead to.

Your shoulds that conflict with the shoulds of others are another problem. One person thinks something should be a certain way and another thinks it should be another way. You can bend or you can protest. Bending is easier, but many times it is less than desirable. Calculate the consequences. Ask yourself if they are worth the effort. The battle of the shoulds is not fun. Again, acceptance is the path of least resistance. But occasionally we must stand up for what appears to be right.

Antidote for the Should Syndrome

- **Identify:** Identify the difference between how it is and how you think it should be. Why not accept things as they are? What is it that you cannot accept? What is it that you believe justifies your not accepting the situation or behavior? Can you bless it and let it go? Are you looking for the good in the situation?
- **Pray about it.**
- **Affirmations:** I AM willing and able to accept things as they are. Every situation is an opportunity to find good.
- **Denials:** *Shoulds* are only opinions and ideals; they have no power over me. I calculate the consequences of decisions and choices. I practice the Serenity Prayer. *Lord, please give me the strength to bring change where it is needed, the patience to stop trying to change what I cannot, and the wisdom to know the difference.*
- **Meditate about it.**
- **Consider a meditative aid and the appropriate mental state (alpha or theta).**

- **Visualizations:** Visualize yourself as being willing and able to accept the situations of life. See yourself as a rock that stands for good, but practices the concepts of the Serenity Prayer. Go back to a few situations where you would prefer a different outcome. Rewrite the ending. Go into the future. Visualize a few predictable situations where you may need to alter your behavior or feelings to a more acceptable state. See yourself as being accepting, understanding, and patient.
- **Study:** Read chapter 10 of *The 10 Dumbest Mistakes.* Read a few articles in psychology on the subject.
- **Consider your vitamins and nutrition.**

Negative Comparisons

Comparing yourself to others can leave you feeling very small. There is always someone bigger, better, stronger, faster, smarter, more efficient, wittier, more proficient, or better at whatever comparison you care to make. Comparing is good for a frame of reference that can be utilized to make good choices. But, you have to be careful that you don't use the comparison as a standard that will negate good, solid efforts that may fall short of the standard.

The guideline for healthy comparing is whether it becomes a source for justifying the dwelling in or creating of negative imagery or furthering your positive spectrum of imagery. Keeping up with the Jones, feeling inferior, feeling as though goals become out of reach, or feeling inadequate are a few examples of comparing that lead to negative imagery.

When you compare, you must keep your perspectives regarding the issues, yourself, and others. A comparison that leads to anything less than positive imagery is misleading and may be considered a cue to change perspective to something more positive. Always remember: Anytime you *feel* negative emotion beginning, this is the Universe's way of letting you know that you are creating or dwelling in negative imagery. So, if comparing perpetuates your good feelings, you are on the right track.

Antidote for Negative Comparisons

- **Identify:** What belief is it that you feel justifies becoming negative after making comparisons? How do you feel? What are you saying to yourself about it?
- **Pray about it.**
- **Affirmations:** I AM willing and able to compare myself and my situations while remaining a powerful, spiritual, divine being. I AM a unique being who is wonderful, intelligent, and worthy.
- **Denials:** Nothing can make me feel inadequate, inferior, or unworthy. No comparisons have any power to render me in a negative state of mind.
- **Meditate about it.**
- **Consider a meditative aid and the appropriate mental state (alpha or theta).**
- **Visualizations:** Return to a time where comparing something left you feeling negative. Rewrite the ending where you change your perspective to a new viewpoint that leaves you feeling positive. Go to the future. Visualize a predictable comparison situation where you would normally feel negative. See yourself as remaining strong, calm, and positive.
- **Study:** Read chapter eight, Comparisonitis, in *The 10 Dumbest Mistakes*. Read a few psychology articles on comparing yourself to others.
- **Consider your vitamins and nutrition.**

Taking Things Personally

Taking things personally can lead to feelings of hurt, frustration, anxiety, inferiority, inadequacy, resentment, and more. When you respond to the behavior of others by taking things personally, you are most likely rationalizing what it would take to influence you to behave in this way. This analysis will most likely be rational only to *you* or to others who take the same perspective as you. Yet we cannot rationalize irrational behavior. The whole reason irrational behavior is irrational is that the behavior is not based on anything rational.

When people act out their irrationalities, they are not necessarily directing them at you; they are merely acting out their irrationalities—their fears. On occasion a behavior may appear to be directed at you, but you still have the option of not taking it personally. You may merely be available at the time the person felt they required someone to direct their irrational behavior toward. And always remember: When someone treats you negatively, they are acting out of fear or pain. It's nothing personal, even if it seems personal.

My mother used to constantly tell me as a child, "It's not what you say; it's how you say it." How someone speaks to you usually influences the perspective we assign to their intent behind what they say. We can be criticized, scolded, and even ridiculed, but as long as it is done lovingly, sweetly, with kindness, we don't mind. We may even like it. As long as we still feel loved and liked, people can say almost anything to us.

So, taking things personally usually renders us feeling as though we are no longer liked or loved. And this hurts. But, if you use the fact that you are a powerful, spiritual, divine being as your frame of reference, you aren't going to take things personally, you aren't going to become hurt, you aren't going to feel inadequate. If a two-year-old child says something negative to you, you aren't going to take it personally. You will most likely smile and feel very tolerant. You can be big about the whole thing. Well, we are all children; we just got big.

Antidote for Taking Things Personally

- **Identify:** What belief is it that seems to justify taking things personally? What are you saying to yourself about it? Have feelings of inadequacy emerged? What frame of reference are you using to judge from?
- **Pray about it.**
- **Affirmations:** I AM a powerful, spiritual, divine being. I AM confident that I AM worthy and adequate as a being.

- **Denials:** The behavior of others has no power over me. The behavior of others does not reflect my worthiness or wholeness as a being.
- **Meditate about it.**
- **Consider a meditative aid and the appropriate mental state (alpha or theta).**
- **Visualizations:** Return to a time where you took something personally and felt hurt or inadequate. Rewrite the ending to where you did not take the situation personally and felt strong and powerful. Move to a predictable future encounter where you may be involved in a situation where you take something personally. Handle the situation as a powerful, spiritual, divine being. Demonstrate loving kindness.
- **Study:** Read some Bible scripture, a few psychology articles on taking things personally, chapter four of *The 10 Dumbest Mistakes*. Read chapter three of *The Four Agreements*, by Don Miguel Ruiz.
- **Consider your vitamins and nutrition.**

Believing Criticism

We are all going to have critics suggesting things, trying to change things about us, complaining about our work or behaviors, trying to help us, or trying to straighten us out some way. Some criticism is wonderful and very beneficial while other criticism is much less so. We have to live with it nonetheless. We can change our perspective regarding criticism to where we look forward to it as a form of valuable feedback. And feedback is important. If one hundred people tell you that you are doing something wrong, and you know for certain that you are doing it right, you will at least know that these people all do things differently and perhaps wrong. The idea is to not get upset by criticism. When you do, you are surfacing some idea of inadequacy in yourself that you need to work on.

Criticism is only an opinion. That's why we have different opinions about movies and songs. One critic says the movie is great with wonderful acting, another says the movie was terrible and so was the acting. Criticism is valuable as feedback and not much more. It's a general forecast and has nothing to do with your value as a being. Probably the most highly criticized people have been inventors. Yet, everything that we have today that is progressive, we owe to the inventors.

Antidote for Believing Critics

- **Identify:** What feelings did your critic surface in you? What are you saying to yourself about it? What beliefs are limiting you from cultivating a blissful state of mind?
- **Pray about it.**
- **Affirmation:** I AM confident and secure in my worthiness and wholeness as a being. I AM willing and able to accept criticism as a valuable feedback and nothing more.
- **Denials:** The criticisms of others have no power over me. I do not take criticism personally nor do I take it too seriously.
- **Meditate about it.**
- **Consider a meditative aid.**
- **Visualizations:** Return to a time where you were upset by criticism. Rewrite the ending where you were thankful for the information and remained strong and confident. See yourself as a powerful, spiritual, divine being handling the situation lovingly. Move to the future. Visualize a situation where you may be criticized. Handle the situation with love and kindness.
- **Study:** Read a few psychology articles on criticism. Read some scriptures. Read some metaphysics.
- **Consider your vitamins and nutrition.**

Believing Flattery

Every con knows how people fall for flattery. Some people seem to appreciate flattery even when it is evident that it is superficial, such as "sucking up" to a boss, co-worker or client. Many boys and girls grow up and discover that they are not as

William Marts

handsome or pretty as their mother told them they were. Guys learn to sweet talk girls in an attempt to manipulate them. Kids flatter parents in an attempt to manipulate them. We learn at a tender age to flatter someone before we ask for something.

The more you need flattery, the more vulnerable you are to flattery and the more you want to believe flattery. This is all fine up to a point. Then flattery becomes a tool for manipulation. If you crave flattery to the point that you can be manipulated, you have a problem that needs consideration. Flattery that crosses the line of politeness is usually born of an ulterior motive. People don't "butter you up" for nothing.

In a world where praise comes few and far between, you can get lost in the ulterior motives of others. By coming to terms with the reality that you are a powerful, spiritual, divine being you will not have a subconscious need for flattery and you will be able to distinguish between praise and manipulative flattery.

Antidote for Believing Flattery

- **Identify:** What are you saying to yourself about the flattery? Is the praise too much like being "buttered up"? Does flattery leave you feeling better? Is it possible that the person flattering you has an ulterior motive?
- **Pray about it.**
- **Affirmations:** I AM a powerful, spiritual, divine being. I AM confident in all that I do. I accept praise graciously and humbly.
- **Denial:** The flattery of others has no power over me.
- **Meditate about it.**
- **Consider a meditative aid and the appropriate mental state (alpha or theta).**
- **Visualizations:** Visualize yourself as a powerful, spiritual, divine being. See yourself as confident and strong and able, while handling the situation with love and kindness, to quickly identify possible ulterior motives of others.
- **Study:** Metaphysics, psychology articles on flattery.
- **Consider your vitamins and nutrition.**

Control

Perhaps one of the biggest obstacles to be overcome in our quest for enlightenment or inner peace is our basic need to control. This urge to control is one of the first urges we develop in our life. As babies we learn we can control our mother by crying.

Control is nothing more than our mind forming an image as to the way we prefer things to be concerning our needs, wants, desires, and considerations. We form an image of how it should be or how we would like it to be. And there is nothing wrong with attempting to control our environments, our relationships, our disciplines, our beliefs, our experiences, and the experiences of others. Yet a great portion of our troubles in life stem from attempting to control these things.

Responsibilities demand that we control many things. As we mature in life we are entrusted with controlling the intricacies of maintaining life and expected to do it well. Great pressure can be put on us to fulfill these high expectations of control. Our ability to control, thus, needs to grow to meet these demands in responsibilities. There is a world to run and each of us is expected to do our share in running our part in proportion to the responsibility delegated to us.

We are rewarded in many cases when we become better controllers and relieve responsibility from others who are, perhaps, over-taxed. Better control means more efficiency. The fate of civilization itself relies on our individual responsibility to implement controls in regard to rules, laws, procedures, and organizing.

Ideally, we are molded, shaped, motivated, and rewarded by control and expected to implement good controls. So, where does it all go wrong?

Excessive Control

Perhaps the most abused aspect of control is excessive control. The Nazis, many dictators, communist parties, and even the US government in many regards are all guilty of excessive controls. Too many controls cause too much unnecessary work, expense, or aggravation in our lives or business concerns.

Patterns of excessive controls forming are usually observable. In government they may be hard to stop, but within ourselves they are not. When we see people we are attempting to control consistently rebelling against us, ignoring us, or plotting against us, we had better reexamine our control initiatives.

It is quite true that occasionally we get involved with situations that are out of control for reasons such as deteriorated disciplines or attitudes within groups, and it may be our job to change the situation. So, the importance of the control needed is a judgmental decision in factoring the level of control that is implemented. But to change a group, we need authority to be behind our efforts. Without the authority of a larger group or higher office, we may be merely forcing our opinion of the change needed on a group. This can be true in a one-on-one situation such as single parenting. The single parent may need the authority of the law to effectively deal with a teenage son or daughter.

As we implement our controls, we surely must observe that improvements or maintenance are actually happening. If a large part of our efforts are not yielding any results, we are spinning our wheels. If our *effort to results ratio* is low, we need to examine if we are getting the attention of others. Is anyone listening? Does anyone even want to listen? Are we becoming a pain in the neck? Do we indeed have the authority to initiate the controls we are attempting? Are we quoting rules to people who have no intention of following them or even think they are wrong?

Does it matter if you are right or wrong? Haven't we all heard the expression, "I may not be right, but I'm still the boss"? We all love to be right and we all do not like being wrong. This is an area that we have to watch carefully.

As we implement our controls we begin to assume a definite role. We may be a boss, a parent, a supervisor, a lead person, or an assistant. Or we might be in charge of particular duties. As we portray our role, are we adding or subtracting attributes from the accepted behavior? Are we called the dumb boss, the grouchy parent, the supervisor with an attitude, or the brown-nosing assistant? What image are we projecting?

Many people try very hard to control things that just don't matter. It may matter to the one attempting to control, but it may not matter at all—so it is just an opinion. What is accepted as normal control efforts should always be considered. Even this consideration sometimes may be outweighed by an important need. It all boils down to good judgment.

Is our control interfering with another's development of responsibility? Parents need to clip their apron strings from children. Parents who try to run their children's lives, even when the finest intentions are the motivation, usually deprive the children of necessary developments in responsibility.

Compulsive Control Dysfunction

Haven't we all been involved with someone who seems to be a control freak? Yet, we probably don't notice when we are portraying a control freak once in a while. While it may be true that some people have a deep need to control to the point of dysfunction, we all overdo it once in a while. It can be very easy when we deeply believe in a change that appears to be desperately needed. We may be trying to protect someone. But there are those among us who, the biggest part of the time, simply must have their own way—right or wrong. If we are often experiencing mis-emotion trying to implement our controls, we are most likely becoming compulsive. Someone who is consistently mis-emotional in his or her attempt to control most likely has a compulsive control dysfunction. And there are those who are in positions of authority where they may not be mis-emotional often, but they are cruel, even deadly in their decisions. Some control freaks don't get upset—they just have you beaten or killed.

A deep need to control stems from our animal nature to dominate. Most animals have a dominant member of their community. Our planet is in a power struggle of people who want to rule the world or a good size portion of it. They want power. We can give consideration to whether we are trying to control for dominance or to actually *serve* the group or humanity. Questioning our own motives as to whether we are controlling for our personal benefit or for the benefit of the many is a good guideline to our decision-making.

If you find yourself suffering for control, ask yourself, "Can the world go on without me?" The answer is yes, it can and it will.

What Happens When You Let God Be in Control?

Controlling *with* God is the way to a peaceful control system. We just do our best and then let God take it from there. We don't have the big picture from which to adequately judge what to do so we are usually making an educated guess in our judgment. We can pray for good judgment, give thanks to God in advance that we have received good judgment, affirm "I AM of good judgment," and focus more attention on judging well; but, the most important thing to consider about our efforts to control, as in all our efforts, is *not to be addicted to the results*. This is where we can truly draw the line in our efforts. It is the need to see the results of our efforts that leads us down the path of erroneous thinking. Do your best and let go, let God take it from there. You stay peaceful and clear minded and are of more value to yourself and others as a clear-minded thinker.

Control is a matter of imagination. However you imagine it, you control it in this way. Control is an entire realm of imagery itself. And it's easy to spend too much attention on unnecessary needs to control. It's an area that requires a great deal of consideration to balance.

Antidote for Excessive Control

• **Identify:** What are you saying to yourself about needing to control? What do you believe that justifies your control attempts? What will happen if you do not try to control things? Are the potential losses so great that you can't let the people involved make their own mistakes?

• **Pray about it.**
• **Affirmations:** I AM a powerful, spiritual, divine being. I accept that other people need to make their own mistakes. I do my best and I AM not addicted to the results.
• **Denial:** The mistakes of others have no power over my state of mind.
• **Meditate about it.**
• **Consider a meditative aid and the appropriate mental state (alpha or theta).**
• **Visualizations:** Visualize yourself as a powerful, spiritual, divine being. See yourself as confident and strong in a past situation where you implemented controls and no one listened. Change the way you reacted by handling the situation with love and kindness. Move to a predictable situation in the future where this may happen again. Quickly identify possible mistakes that others may make by not listening to you while handling the situation with love and kindness.
• **Study:** Metaphysics, psychology articles on control.
• **Consider your vitamins and nutrition.**

Needing to Be Right

The average person suffers from an exaggerated need to be right. After all, when we arrive at our conclusions, we obviously imagine that we have concluded rightly or we would have concluded otherwise. There is probably nothing more harmless than expressing an opinion that you think someone is wrong, but it is generally received as a threat. The Fight or Flight Response usually initiates when the average person is told they are wrong. I have witnessed blood pressure rise to the point of an aneurysm simply by saying, *You are wrong.* We all like to be right. Learning that it is OK to be wrong is the tough part. But it is OK to be wrong! People get so caught up in being right that they will continue to argue when they know darn well they have been proven wrong. It's the subconscious program, *I AM always right.*

The more open we are to the possibility that we may be wrong, the more open our mind becomes to improvement, better ideas, help, advice, or critique. We can see the value of the input of others. We have the opportunity to melt into the synergy of the whole.

You're going to be wrong often in your life—get used to it, accept it, and surrender. Being wrong is usually harmless. It's OK. Avoiding the initiation of The Fight or Flight Response when you appear to be *threatened* with being wrong is a great step toward peace of mind. You then have nothing to defend and nothing to control.

Antidote for Needing to Be Right

- **Identify:** What are you saying to yourself about needing to be right? What do you believe that justifies needing to be right? What will happen if you are wrong?
- **Pray about it.**
- **Affirmations:** I AM a powerful, spiritual, divine being. I accept that I might be wrong. It is OK to be wrong. I do my best and I AM not addicted to the results.
- **Denial:** Being wrong does not affect me and has no power over my state of mind.
- **Meditate about it.**
- **Consider a meditative aid and the appropriate mental state (alpha or theta).**
- **Visualizations:** Visualize yourself as a powerful, spiritual, divine being. See yourself back at a time where you discovered that you were wrong about something and acted negatively. Change the way you reacted by handling the situation with love and kindness, feeling that it is OK to be wrong. Move to a predictable situation in the future where this may happen again. Visualize yourself discovering you are wrong and seeing the merit in the other person's ideas while

handling the situation with love and kindness.
• **Study:** Psychology articles on needing to be right.
• **Consider your vitamins and nutrition.**

As you can see, an effective Imagery Management Plan takes a sincere effort to implement, but the product is well worth the effort. It is not a difficult thing to do and it has the benefit of peace of mind and finding your place as a co-creator with God.

When you devote this much attention to all of these considerations, higher levels of thought come naturally, lovingly, and easily as your day-to-day experiences and responses reprogram a freedom from the limitations set forth by your subconscious mind. It's simply a matter of staying nice within your imagination despite appearances or first impulses. Suppressing emotion for the sake of good behavior is frustrating and spiritually ineffective. The time has come to learn to clean up the imagination, as well as behavior, with *Imagintelligence.* When the conscious mind is cleansed of the first impulse to become negative as suggested by the organic artificial intelligence programs, it reflects that the subconscious mind is reprogrammed with *Imagintelligence.* Thus you are programmed for a total love response.

Routine Imaginings

Most of us have routines that get us through the day. Routines consist of *devoting attention* to things and may involve action. From the time we get up in the morning to the time we fall asleep, we are engaged in some sort of routine. Some routines are positive and some routines are negative. Most of us try to set forth work, chore, and hygiene routines that promote benefits. The good routines we develop support us while the erroneous routines hold us back, such as routinely neglecting things.

Some people get up in the morning and start the day with prayer, thanks, and appreciation; others begin the day cursing the day they were born. Most people are somewhere in between. Some people have worry routines; others have nagging routines. There are those who begin the day with dread: dread for work, dread for traffic, or dread for whom they are waking up beside. Some students dread going to school; some teachers dread teaching. People in chronic pain may dread facing another day of pain. The list of morning routines goes on and on.

As the day goes on, people experience depression, anxiety, hopelessness, anger, upset, impatience, and a wide variety of other negative imaginings and emotions that seem to be part of everyday life interaction. You can get used to these everyday negative routine imaginings as they become part of your life. It's so easy to believe that everything is happening *to* you. And, much of life can be very difficult to accept.

When you can't accept things as they are, the mind begins imaginings where everything is corrected; you handle the people suppressing you; you give them a piece of your mind—or worse. The mind dreams the dream of *how it should be,* how you would prefer things to be. And after the mind runs the *how it should be* script, you again "see" things as they "really are" and the mind loathes as it stands on the sea of yearning in the gulf between the *wish it were world* and the *how it is* world. STOP!

What You're Up Against

I have renamed the body's emotional system *organic artificial intelligence* because that is what it really is. As noted, your life experiences and responses have been distilled into a suggested response by the body to save you the trouble of contemplation. You don't have to consciously think about how to react, there is already a program. In order to change the way you respond, especially if you want to change your regular negative responses to positive, it is necessary to ignore this first impulse. Ignoring your body's first urge to react may seem quite difficult, but it is necessary if you desire to change. It is necessary if you desire to learn and imbed *Imagintelligence* into your organic artificial intelligence programs.

Since it is necessary to learn and develop your prefrontal lobe override of the emotional system, it is also necessary to know that a left prefrontal lobe domination urges more optimism as opposed to a dominant right prefrontal lobe that urges more pessimism. Studies have shown that pessimists who have had right prefrontal lobe damage become much more optimistic and cheery. And their spouses have testified to this.

A great exercise to develop the left prefrontal lobe is to relax and visualize a beam of love light making figure eights in the left prefrontal lobe area. Visualize the light going back and forth, and to and fro in the figure eight pattern. Also, focus your attention on this area when you are rethinking a negative situation. This will stimulate your neural connections within the left prefrontal lobe and the body's emotional system.

Developing Positive Routine Imaginings

Every routine is the result of priorities. You are a co-creator with God. This is the top priority. The second priority is realizing that you are a powerful, spiritual, divine being. When these priorities become the reference point that you use in all of your decision-making and imaginings, you naturally begin to challenge any imaginings to the contrary.

We all desire inner peace. Inner peace comes hand-in-hand with taking responsibility as a co-creator with God and being aware that you are a powerful, spiritual, divine being. So, it is necessary to begin new positive imaginings to replace the old negative imaginings. In order to stop imagining negative scripts, you must begin to write positive scripts.

When you open your eyes in the morning, begin creating wonderful imagery. Pray and give thanks; cultivate the feeling of gratitude and appreciation for life—then get up. Once you are up, forget about appearances; create imaginings of good, wonderful, uplifting scenes in your mind. You are about to undo everything negative you have manifested in the past. This is a new life, a renewal of the mind. Don't let anything "trick" you into dwelling in or creating negative imaginings. As negative images pop into your mind, quickly **bless them and let them go** and begin the creation of good. To change your response as an organism, you must override your feelings and emotional urges. They are incorrect. They have not been designed based on love. They are primitive. Tap into God and override negative imaginings at their first appearance.

Again, there are two of you occupying your body—you and God. You have the option of letting go of your imaginings and letting God do the thinking. After all, God is sharing your experiences with you, so God can help you create the highest quality within your experiences. **Constantly create new positive imaginings.** This is the renewing of the mind. You can't have the old imaginings and be renewed. Create imaginings as though you are an angel. **Challenge every thought that comes into your mind if it is negative.**

Start beaming everyone in contact with you with a beam of uplifting and healing light. Be nice in all situations. You can say this in two ways—be nice in all situations, or be God in all situations. It's the same thing. You can even learn to express your outrage for grave injustice and still be nice. Although it may appear illogical to create positive uplifting, healing imaginings in all situations, within the big picture—God's picture—it is logical.

When in doubt or if you are at a loss as to what to imagine in a situation, visualize Jesus or a deity sitting or standing beside you. Or visualize a tiny angel circling your head sprinkling love dust on you. The point is to distract your mind away from dwelling in or creating negative imaginations. **Distraction is a key technique in interrupting a flow of preconditioned imaginations.**

Pretend that you are an angel with weak powers. Angels use the power of their minds—their imaginations—to influence situations. So can you. Your powers may be weak but that's because you haven't devoted time to developing them. On the other hand, you have devoted time to developing your power of negativity. Now you are becoming who you really are by developing your God-like powers.

You must no longer judge people harshly. Judge with uplifting, healing images. Never judge a person; if you must judge, judge behaviors. Constantly keep in mind that behaviors are not a representation of a person's essence. And conclude each judgment with an uplifting image.

Don't take anything personally. Anything negative directed at you is not about you; it is originating out of the fear within the other person. *Just be nice.*

Think before you act. *If you don't, your emotions of the past will create what they think you should do, and you will do it.* Give God a chance to flow through you. God can't flow through you if you're on automatic pilot. Your animal nature will probably be your first urge until you develop a connectedness with God that overrides negative urges. Biologically, this is developing a left prefrontal lobe override in the brain circuitry.

Develop a plan on how you are going to handle conflicts or disagreements. You can't react the way you have in the past if you are going to stay connected to God and desire spiritual growth. Practice now handling predictable future situations in the correct way within your imagination. You know how you have reacted in the past. You know the results. Change everything and base your response on love.

Challenge your pessimistic imaginings that are associated with negative situations. Stop and let God flow through you.

When you walk down the street or at a mall, practice beaming people with uplifting, healing love. When you look at people, see them as divine beings. Let go of other imaginations of anything less.

Pretend that everyone you meet is an enlightened being with a message for you. This will develop humility and teach you to listen.

As Stephen Covey says, **seek first to understand, then to be understood.** This habit teaches you like tapping into the sage within.

Create happy imaginings. Look for the good in all situations. No matter how bad the appearance, there is good to be found through imagination mastery.

You are reeducating your emotional response. This is developing emotional intelligence. But beyond emotional intelligence is imaginational intelligence—or what I call *Imagintelligence*. Imagintelligence is simply basing all your imaginings on love, values, ethics, empathy, compassion, altruism, and character. Routine *Imagintelligence* is a direct path to loving God with all your heart, all your soul, all your mind, and all your strength. AND THOU SHALT LOVE THE LORD THY GOD WITH ALL THY HEART, AND WITH ALL THY SOUL, AND WITH ALL THY MIND, AND WITH ALL THY STRENGTH; this is the first commandment. And the second is like, namely this, THOU SHALT LOVE THY NEIGHBOR AS THYSELF. **There is none other commandment greater than these** (Matthew 12:30-31).

Writing Exercise

- Write down the responses, feeling, and emotions that you want to change. What's bugging you? What's eating at you? What's wearing you out? What's frustrating you? What's hurting you? This is the first step in giving attention—acknowledgement.
- Write down how you can reframe situations to give you a new way of looking at things. Challenge every negative imagining you have been creating. View the situation through the eyes of an angel. Note the difference. Think of as many loving, kind, empathic, nonviolent solutions as possible.
- Write down the benefits of changing your responses, feelings, and emotions in situations.
- Write down the consequences if you do not change your responses, feelings, and emotions.
- If you are beyond your threshold of tolerance, consider a time out from the situation.

Imagintelligence is an awareness of *what not to imagine* combined with *what to imagine*. The bottom line: You can't imagine the same old things and feel differently. If you don't like the way your feel, change your imagination!

The Prefrontal Lobe Override Exercise

Attempting to practice new beliefs may be difficult when the emotional system puts forth its mode of feelings and imaginings. We have the ability to override our emotional suggestions, but we might fail to remember to do so or we might find the emotional suggestion overwhelming. Many situations seldom arise to practice our new plan of response. It's difficult to deal with stimulations when they pop up seldom and unexpected. To speed things up for the sake of practice, find a partner to help do the following Prefrontal Lobe Override Exercise. Perfect practice makes perfect.

- Sit in a chair with your feet comfortably on the floor, your back straight, and compose yourself in meditation with your eyes open.
- Your partner starts to intimidate you by saying things that *hit home.* You attempt to retain your composure by practicing the Prefrontal Lobe Override. When you begin to show signs of responding negatively, the partner says, *Stop.*
- Take a moment to recompose yourself and begin again. The partner says and does the exact same thing until you either respond negatively or until it is evident that you can retain your composure throughout this particular type of needling.
- The partner then pursues another type of needling that *hits home* and might cause you to respond negatively.

By doing this exercise, you create stimulus over and over in a short period of time that will desensitize you through consistent prefrontal lobe override practice. Practicing this tells your emotional system that this is how you will respond from now on and transforms the hardwiring of your neuron connections quickly.

You also develop an imagery plan to handle this type of situation. Mentally beaming the person needling you with love light or a forgiveness ray will promote a connectedness with God and retain your composure. You feel like the stuff you run through your head even while you are being needled.

Image Streaming

In his book, *The Einstein Factor,* Win Wenger has developed a technique he calls Image Streaming for mind development. I highly recommend this book and the extensive techniques outlined in it.

Preliminary tests have demonstrated an increase of one IQ point for every 80 minutes of Image Streaming practice. Apparently, we use many parts of our brain not normally utilized when Image Streaming is practiced. The development of these brain areas increases brain function.

Find a friend to listen or start a tape recorder. Begin Image Streaming by verbally describing the imagery you see in your mind. You can start by describing a corner of your room or anything you choose. The description needs to be elaborate, and contain as much sensual information of all senses as possible. Describe tastes, smells, what you are feeling internally and externally, what you hear and see. Keep up the description for ten to fifteen minutes. Practice each day.

For more information, contact Project Renaissance, P.O. Box 332, Gaithersburg, MD 20877 with a SASE with 64 cents postage, or call (301) 948-1122 or (800) 649-3800.

16

Parallel Teachings

Matthew 6:34: *Take therefore no thought for the morrow; for the morrow shall take thought for the things of itself. Sufficient unto the day is the evil thereof.*

Since The Parable of the Coin was revealed to me, I have stumbled upon quite similar teachings, not only in the Bible but also in some other very interesting books. One of these is *The Aquarian Gospel of Jesus The Christ,* by Levi, published first in 1907. Tears came to my eyes as I read this wonderful literary marvel. Chapter eight, especially, moved me because of the parallel to the concept of imagination control resulting in a heavenly state of mind.

1. Again Elihu met his pupils in the sacred grove and said,
2. No man lives unto himself; for every living thing is bound by cords to every other living thing.
3. Blest is the pure in heart; for they will love and not demand love in return.
4. They will not do to other men what they would not have other men do unto them.
5. There are two selfs; the higher self and the lower self.

We can compare these two selves as the higher self being the positive mind, and the lower self as the negative mind.

6. The higher self is the human spirit clothed with the soul, made in the form of God.
7. The lower self, the carnal self, is a reflection of the higher self,

distorted by the murky ethers of the flesh.

8. *The lower self is an illusion, and will pass away; the higher self is God in man, and will not pass away.*
9. *The higher self is the embodiment of truth; the lower self is truth reversed, and so is falsehood manifest.*

I find it amazing that Levi also explained the negative mind or lower self as truth reversed. This is what I have termed *anti*. The negative mind is truth reversed.

10. *The higher self is justice, mercy, love and right; the lower self is what the higher self is not.*
11. *The lower self breeds hatred, slander, lewdness, murders, theft, and everything that harms; the higher self is mother of the virtues and the harmonies of life.*
12. *The lower self is rich in promises, but poor in blessedness and peace; it offers pleasure, joy and satisfying gains; but gives unrest and misery and death.*
13. *It gives men apples that are lovely to the eye and pleasant to the smell; their cores are full of bitterness and gall.*
14. *If you would ask me what to study I would say, yourselfs; and when you well had studied them, and then would ask me what to study next, I would reply, yourselfs.*
15. *He who knows well his lower self, knows the illusions of the world, knows of the things that pass away; and he who knows his higher self, knows God; knows well the things that cannot pass away.*
16. *Thrice blessed is the man who has made purity and love his very own; he has been ransomed from the perils of the lower self and is himself his higher self.*
17. *Men seek salvation from an evil that they deem a living monster of the nether world; and they have gods that are but demons in disguise; all powerful, yet full of jealousy and hate and lust;*
18. *Whose favors must be bought with costly sacrifice of fruits, and of the lives of birds, and animals, and human kind.*

19. And yet these gods possess no ears to hear, no eyes to see, no heart to sympathize, no power to save.

20. This evil is a myth; these gods are made of air, and clothed with shadows of a thought.

21. The only devil from which men must be redeemed is self, the lower self. If man would find his devil he must look within; his name is self.

22. If man would find his savior he must look within; and when the demon self has been dethroned the savior, Love, will be exalted to the throne of power.

23. The David of the light is Purity, who slays the strong Goliath of the dark, and seats the savior, Love, upon the throne.

The higher self and the lower self are good ways of describing the positive and negative mind, emotion, and imagination. Positive imagination and emotion can be well likened to the higher self because it contains all the feelings, emotions, and imaginings of the higher self. This is the consciousness that will unite us with God's consciousness. The lower self can be likened to our negative imagination and emotion because it contains the lower, animal urges of the flesh, the carnal self.

Another wonderful excerpt from this book that parallels the concept of The Parable of the Coin can be found in chapter thirty-three where Jesus speaks of Heaven.

1. In silent meditation Jesus sat beside a flowing spring. It was a holy day, and many people of the servant caste were near the place.

2. And Jesus saw the hard drawn lines of toil on every brow, in every hand. There was no look of joy in any face. Not one of all the group could think of anything but toil.

3. And Jesus spoke to one and said, Why are you all so sad? Have you no happiness in life?

4. The man replied, We scarcely know the meaning of that word. We toil to live, and hope for nothing else but toil, and bless the day when we can cease our toil and lay us down to rest in Buddha's city of the dead.

5. And Jesus' heart was stirred with pity and with love for these poor toilers, and he said,

6. Toil should not make a person sad; men should be happiest when they toil. When hope and love are back of toil, than all of life is filled with joy and peace, and this is Heaven. Do you not know that such a Heaven is for you?

7. The man replied, Of Heaven we have heard; but then it is so far away, and we must live so many lives before we reach that place!

8. And Jesus said, My brother, man, your thoughts are wrong; your Heaven is not far away; and it is not a place of metes and bounds, is not a country to be reached; **it is a state of mind.**

9. God never made a Heaven for man; he never made a hell; we are creators and we make our own.

10. Now, cease to seek for Heaven in the sky; just open up the windows of your hearts, and, like a flood of light, a Heaven will come and bring a boundless joy; then toil will be no cruel task.

11. The people were amazed, and gathered close to hear this strange young master speak,

12. Imploring him to tell them more about the Father-God; about the Heaven that men can make on Earth; about the boundless joy.

13. And Jesus spoke a parable; he said, A certain man possessed a field; the soil was hard and poor.

14. By constant toil he scarcely could provide enough of food to keep his family from want.

15. One day a miner who could see beneath the soil, in passing on his way, saw this poor man and his unfruitful field.

16. He called the weary toiler and he said, My brother, know you not that just below the surface of your barren field rich treasures lie concealed?

17. You plough and sow and reap in scanty way, and day by day you tread upon a mine of gold and precious stones.

18. This wealth lies not upon the surface of the ground; but if you will but dig away the rocky soil, and delve down deep into the Earth, you need no longer till the soil for naught.

19. The man believed. The miner surely knows, he said; and I will find the treasures hidden in my field.

20. And then he dug away the rocky soil, and deep down in the Earth he found a mine of gold.

21. And Jesus said, The sons of men are toiling hard on desert plains, and burning sands and rocky soils; are doing what their fathers did, not dreaming they can do aught else.

22. Behold, a master comes, and tells them of a hidden wealth; that underneath the rocky soil of carnal things are treasures that no man can count;

23. That in the heart the richest gems abound; that he who wills may open up the door and find them all.

24. And then the people said, Make known to us the way that we may find the wealth that lies within the heart.

25. And Jesus opened up the way; the toilers saw another side of life,

26. And toil became a joy.[1]

Heaven is a state of mind. This is a huge statement said in six words. Six words describe what man has tried to figure out for millenniums. Zen tells us that life is exactly what we believe it to be. When we take responsibility for our co-creatorship in the Universe with God by consistently creating positive imagery, we find that positive imaginings and emotion contain all the answers to the sought after questions about life. Heaven is a state of mind and a positive state of mind is heavenly.

The Bhagavad Gita also has some close parallels. In chapter sixteen, The Division of Divine and Demoniac Treasures, there is a beautiful rendition of life's treasures and the qualities of the carnal self.

1. The Lord said: Fearlessness, purity of heart, steadfastness in knowledge and yoga; charity, self-control, and sacrifice; study of the scriptures, austerity, and uprightness;

2. Non-violence, truth, and freedom from anger; renunciation, tranquility, and aversion to slander; compassion to beings and freedom from covetousness; gentleness, modesty, and absence of fickleness;

3. *Courage, forgiveness, and fortitude; purity, and freedom from malice and overweening pride—these belong to him who is born with divine treasures.*

4. *Ostentation, arrogance, and self-conceit; anger, rudeness, and ignorance—these belong to him who is born to the heritage of the demons.*

5. *The divine treasures are said to be for the purpose of liberation, and the heritage of the demons, for bondage. Grieve not, O Pandava; you are born with divine treasures.*

6. *There are two types of beings created in this world: the divine and the demoniac. The divine have been described at length. Hear now from Me, O Partha, concerning the demoniac.*

7. *Men of demoniac nature know not what to do and what to refrain from doing. Purity is not in them, nor good conduct, nor truth.*

8. *They say: "The world is devoid of truth, without a moral basis, and without a God. It is brought about by the union of male and female, and lust alone is its cause: what else?"*

9. *Holding such a view, these lost souls of little understanding and fierce deeds rise as the enemies of the world for its destruction.*

10. *Giving themselves up to insatiable desires, full of hypocrisy, pride, and arrogance, they hold false views through delusion and act with impure resolve.*

11. *Beset with innumerable cares, which will end only with their death, looking on the gratification of desire as their highest goal, and feeling sure that this is all;*

12. *Bound by a hundred ties of hope, given up wholly to lust and wrath, they strive, by unjust means, to amass wealth for the satisfaction of their passions.*

13. *"This I have gained today, and that longing I will fulfill. This wealth is mine, and that also shall be mine in future;*

14. *"That enemy I have slain, and others, too, I will slay. I am the lord of all; I enjoy; I am prosperous, mighty, and happy;*

15. *"I am rich; I am of high birth. Who else is equal to me? I will*

*offer sacrifice, I will give, I will rejoice," Thus deluded by igno-
rance,*

16. *Bewildered by many fancies, entangled in the meshes of delusion, addicted to the gratification of lust, they fall into a
loathsome hell.*

17. *Self-honored, haughty, filled with the pride and the intoxica-
tion of wealth, they ostentatiously perform sacrifices, which are
so only in name, in utter disregard of precepts.*

18. *Possessed of egotism, power, and pride and also of lust and
wrath, these people, envious by nature, hate Me in the bodies of
others and in their own.*

19. *These cruel haters, these evil-doers, these vilest of men, I hurl
always into the wombs of the demons in the cycle of births and
deaths.*

20. *Having fallen into the wombs of the demons and being
deluded from birth to birth, they never attain Me, O son of
Kunti, but go farther down to the lowest state.*

21. *Three are the gateways of this hell leading to the ruin of the
self—lust, wrath, and greed. Therefore let man renounce these
three.*

22. *The man who has escaped these three gates of darkness, O son
of Kunti, practices what is good for himself and thus attains the
Supreme Goal.*

23. *He who discards the injunctions of the scriptures and acts
upon the impulse of desire attains neither perfection nor happiness nor the Supreme Goal.*

24. *Therefore let the scriptures be your authority in determining what
ought to be done and what ought not to be done. Having learnt the
injunctions of the scriptures, you should do your work in the world.*[2]

Here, The King James Version of the Bible is quoted, showing
the teachings that parallel The Parable of the Coin concept.

• Matthew 6:33-34: *But seek ye first The Kingdom of God, and his
righteousness; and all these things shall be added unto you. 34.
Take therefore no thought for the morrow: for the morrow shall*

take thought for the things of itself. Sufficient unto the day is the evil thereof.

• Matthew 12:28: *But if I cast out devils by the Spirit of God, then The Kingdom of God is come unto you.*

• Matthew 15:17-20: *Do not ye yet understand, that whatsoever entereth in at the mouth goeth into the belly, and is cast out into the draught? 18. But those things which proceed out of the mouth come forth from the heart; and they defile the man. 19. For out of the heart proceed evil thoughts, murders, adulteries, fornications, thefts, false witness, blasphemies: 20. These are the things which defile a man: but to eat with unwashen hands defileth not a man.*

• Mark 7:18-23: And he saith unto them, *Are ye so without understanding also? Do ye not perceive, that whatsoever thing from without entereth into the man, it cannot defile him; 19. Because it entereth not into his heart, but into the belly, and goeth out into the draught, purging all meats?* 20. And he said, *That which cometh out of the man, that defileth the man. 21. For from within, out of the heart of men, proceed evil thoughts, adulteries, fornications, murders, 22. Thefts, covetousness, wickedness, deceit, lasciviousness, an evil eye, blasphemy, pride, foolishness: 23. All these evil things come from within, and defile the man.*

• Galatians 5:14-26: *For all the law is fulfilled in one word, even in this; Thou shalt love thy neighbour as thyself. 15. But if ye bite and devour one another, take heed that ye be not consumed one of another. 16. This I say then, Walk in the Spirit, and ye shall not fulfill the lust of the flesh. 17. For the flesh lusteth against the Spirit, and the Spirit against the flesh: and these are contrary the one to the other: so that ye cannot do the things that ye would. 18. But if ye be led of the Spirit, ye are not under the law. 19. Now the works of the flesh are manifest, which are these; Adultery, fornication, uncleanness, lasciviousness, 20. Idolatry, witchcraft, hatred, variance, emulations, wrath, strife, seditions, heresies, 21. Envyings, murders, drunkenness, revellings, and such like: of the which I tell you before, as I have also told you in time past, that they which do such things shall not inherit The Kingdom of God. 22. But the fruit*

of the Spirit is love, joy, peace, longsuffering, gentleness, good-
ness, faith, 23. Meekness, temperance: against such there is no
law. 24. And they that are Christ's have crucified the flesh with
the affections and lusts. 25. If we live in the Spirit, let us also
walk in the Spirit. 26. Let us not be desirous of vain glory, pro-
voking one another, envying one another.

• Philippians 3:8: *Finally, brethren, whatsoever things are true,*
whatsoever things are honest, whatsoever things are just, whatso-
ever things are pure, whatsoever things are lovely, whatsoever
things are of good report; if there be any virtue, and if there be
any praise, think on these things.

Heaven starts as a state of mind. If we seek first, The
Kingdom of God or Heaven and the righteousness of the Lord,
we will be in the right state of mind for Him to provide our
needs. Rebuking the urge to create negative imagery today will
bring about a tomorrow that will take thought for the things of
itself. It is that which starts within and then comes out of a
person that defiles the person.

The *Tao Te Ching*, written by Lao-tzu about five centuries
before Jesus, is one of the world wonders of philosophy and
wisdom. Though the *Tao* is more of a guideline for a positive
mind to attain perfection, which is beyond positive, it contains a
few hints that parallel the concept of the need to be rid of the
negative self. I wholeheartedly recommend everyone read The
Tao to experience its insight

Chapter 1

Free from desire, you realize the mystery.
Caught in desire, you see only the manifestations.

Chapter 10

Embracing the Way, you become embraced;

Breathing gently, you become newborn;
Clearing your mind, you become clear;
Nurturing your children, you become impartial;
Opening your heart, you become accepted;
Accepting the world, you embrace the Way.
Bearing and nurturing,
Creating but not owning,
Giving without demanding,
This is harmony.

Chapter 15

Wait quietly while the mud settles
Remain still until the moment of action
Seek not fulfillment
Desire not change
Welcome all things

Chapter 46

There is no greater illusion than fear,
no greater wrong than preparing to defend yourself,
no greater misfortune than having an enemy.
Whoever can see through all fear
will always be safe.

Chapter 52

If you close your mind in judgments
and traffic with desires,
your heart will be troubled.
If you keep your mind from judging
and aren't led by the senses,
your heart will find peace.
Seeing into darkness is clarity.
Knowing how to yield is strength.

Use your own light
and return to the source of light.
This is called practicing eternity.

Chapter 56

Those who know the natural way
Have no need of boasting,
Whilst those who know but little,
May be heard most frequently;
Thus, the sage says little,
If anything at all.

Not demanding stimuli,
He tempers his sharpness well,
Reduces the complex to simplicity,
Hiding his brilliance, seemingly dull;
He settles the dust,
Whilst in union with all natural things.

He who has attained enlightenment
(Without contriving so to do)
Is not concerned with making friends,
Nor with making enemies;
With good or harm, with praise or blame.
Such detachment is the highest state of man.

Chapter 67

I have three treasures.
Guard them and keep them safe!
The first is love,
The second is moderation,
The third is humility.

From love one gains courage,

From moderation one gains ability,
From humility one achieves greatness.

To forsake love and courage,
To forsake moderation and ability,
To forsake humility and rush to the forefront,
Is death to all hope.
With love battles can be won,
With love defense proves invulnerable,
With love heaven arms those it would protect.

[1]Reprinted from The Aquarian Gospel Of Jesus The Christ, by Levi, Chapter 8, Page 22, 23., Chapter 33, Page 54,55., DeVorss Publications. Used by permission of DeVorss & Company, Marina del Ray, CA.
[2]From THE BHAGAVAD GITA, as translated into English by Swami Nikhilananda; Published by the Ramakrishna-Vivekananda Center of New York; Copyright 1994 by Swami Nikhilananda.

The Physiology of Light

Matthew 6:22: *The light of the body is the eye: if therefore thine eye be single, thy whole body shall be full of light.*

Light is a fascinating, mysterious, marvelous wonder. It is the ingredient that gives us the illusion that there are so many different substances in the Universe. The bold physicist would admit to such a thing.

Dr. Clinton J. Davisson and Dr. Lester H. Germer of the Bell Telephone Laboratories in New York City discovered the principle of the electron microscope in 1929. Dr. Davisson received the Nobel Prize in physics for his discovery of the dual nature of the electron, having both the characteristics of a particle and a wave. Dr. Davisson observed that electrons revolving around atoms, when viewed from a certain aspect, take on the characteristics of particles of matter; but from another context, they seem to take on the characteristics of light waves. More recently experiments have been done with other subatomic particles such as protons, photons and mesons that also demonstrate the dual nature of these particles.

Quantum physicists now find that viewing particles seems to be affected by the thoughts of the person involved in the experiment. The expectations of the viewer actually affect the view. Most physicists want to believe that subatomic particles are particles of matter. If they would admit that these particles are light waves, they would be forced to admit that the whole Universe is merely an illusion. This has been a subject of debate among the philosophies of physics since we have viewed the atom and its electrons.

I wonder if most people can accept the fact that this whole Universe is an illusion, that all of this is a product of the mind stuff of God? Is it the presence of light in an atom that makes the elements all appear to be different substances? Is light what creates an atom and a molecule? What a miracle it must be that each living cell is made up of substances that may not really be here as "true matter" but only as a series of force fields made up of light in various forms.

It is as though matter is made up of tiny force fields creating protons and neutrons held together by a nuclear force in the form of pions. Protons and neutrons are made up of quarks held together by gluons. Quantum physics now demonstrates that all these particles have light wave characteristics. It is a difficult concept to comprehend that everything is a force field conglomeration of light.

Many people describe God as pure light. Some say He is pure Love. I don't know if these are a complete enough description. I would say that God is everything that I could possibly conceive, and then so much more that all my conceptions are just a tiny speck of what God is. God is light. At least a part of Him manifests as light on this plane of existence—matter, energy, time and space.

Some believe that God is thought, that light is thought slowed down, and that matter is thought slowed down to a point of coagulation. This means that atoms are God's thought slowed to coagulation. Some unified field theories suggest that God is the image that is held by the Universe.

God causes many things on the Earth to happen by the use of light. Most of life would die without light. Plants need light for photosynthesis. In this process, light actually is part of a chemical action or reaction. Light is part of the formula. Humans need light to keep their eyes alive. Without light stimulation, the eyes cease to function. We need sunlight for various reasons. We get vitamin D from sunlight. The lack of sunlight in many people causes depression. Sunlight is also healing in many ways.

God's light, in the form of waves, is within and revolving

around all atoms. God's light is the light in every star. It is in the light in the Moon. Most especially, He is the light of our lives. The Bible says many times that the Word of God is light to us.

Matthew 6-22-23: "The light of the body is the eye: if therefore thine eye be single, thy whole body shall be full of light. But, if thine eye be evil, thy whole body shall be full of darkness."

Our bodies are electrochemical organisms. Our neuron brain cells convert electricity into chemicals and then recreate the electricity from the chemicals within the intercellular communication network. Electricity is a flow of electrons. Electrons are particles of light. There is a tremendous possibility that the light which makes up matter is encoded with intelligence like a computer chip made of light waves.

As a living organism, we have the ability to draw in God's light in the form of electrons and other sub-nuclear particles, then convert it into organic chemicals, and then recreate His light again from flesh to light or electrons in the form of electricity. Our brain cells are the most wonderful examples of the electrochemical process. Each brain cell takes in electricity (waves of light) and converts it into chemicals. These chemicals are the chemicals of the body or flesh. The electricity is then recreated when the brain cell's neuron fires. This electricity then travels down an axon stimulating the release of neurotransmitter molecules from the synaptic knob into the synaptic gap, causing intelligence to be passed onto the receptor cell. The intelligence within this electron and neuropeptide flow eventually finds its way to the pituitary gland via other neuropeptides.

The pituitary gland is the king of all glands. The light (or intelligence) that fires upon the pituitary regulates this gland in the way it sends its messages to the pineal and hypothalamus glands. The intelligence of light unfolds into the human organism awakening our divine energy centers or depositing information in the form of negative imagery.

Something happens when we convert God's light to flesh and then recreate it back into light. When God's light is converted into chemicals of the flesh, our state of mind has everything to do with the quality of the conversion process. When we are in a negative state of mind, God's light is converted into a flesh that greatly affects the quality of the reconversion. The original light wave becomes encoded with our own intelligence (or unintelligence, I should say). Our own projections, perceptions, and emotions that are added to the intelligence encoded in God's light, depending upon the degree of negativity verses the positive state of mind, is then transported throughout the body where it is deposited within cellular tissue.

The quality of light information that fires upon the pituitary affects the pituitary functions. Pure light in pure form, the way it enters the body, uncontaminated by the imaginings of the mind causes the pituitary to regulate the pineal and hypothalamus glands in an extraordinary way. It signals them to regulate the glands and organs in the most healthful ways the body can create for its self, which is more than a state of homeostasis. Negative encoded light, in turn, has the pituitary, hypothalamus, and pineal glands regulate the body in a way that is less than that of optimum health. Further, it has been demonstrated that cells also produce neuropeptides within the communication network. Thus, mind and body have a two way communication established. Doctors and scientists are beginning to understand just how much negative imagery affects the body.

There is a great possibility that all disease, other than genetic, is a by-product of negative imagery that sets up neuropeptide disturbances and a disturbance of hormonal balance urged by chemicals produced by negative emotions and improper nutrition. Divine, positive imagery, on the other hand, has the opposite effect. This we see when miracle healings occur. A mother that is negative in her imagery and or deficient in nutrition can influence a child's health in the womb and after birth. The holistic healer should consider that illness lies somewhere between our first bite of food in the morning and the last thought we have at night. Positive imagery and proper nutrition can even greatly enhance the body's ability to combat genetic illness, which may have been caused by the negative imagery of our ancestors.

We all know that any negative emotion taken to extremes can cause havoc on the physiology of the body. Immediate reactions include rapid heart, elevated blood pressure, shortness of breath, anxiety, nausea, and dizziness. Strokes and even heart failure are not unheard of reactions. These effects do not stop here. The negative imaginings of our mind induce the pituitary to cause the pineal and hypothalamus to regulate the glands and organs in a way that is a set up for disease and illness to occur more easily. Recent research suggests that the same neuropeptides produced by the pituitary and other glands are also produced by organs, the immune system, and cells. This opens the door to the possibility that the body is virtually a brain holograph the way it communicates with the mind.

Our negative imaginings cause the body to produce a setting for illness and then illness causes the brain and body to be deficient in vitamins, minerals, enzymes, and chemicals. These are needed in our array of electrolytes within the electrochemical processes throughout the body, of which deficiencies urge us to have more negative imaginings. The imaginations of the thoughts of the negative human emotional spectrum are culprits that do real havoc to the body and the mind.

As noted, there has been much research done on the effects of the placebo. We know that the mind can bring about great changes in the body when it is convinced that a medicine has been ingested that will supposedly cure a particular ailment.

Shamans and witch doctors create a faith that healing will occur and it does. We know that the mind can cause the body to produce healing chemicals when a placebo effect is initiated.

Inasmuch as fasting, eating right, taking herbs and the like, can purify the body which will purify the mind, the imaginings of the mind can set forth a purification of the body if the mind remains pure in all the imagery it creates or dwells within. The more pure imaginings that the mind experiences, the more the pituitary, pineal and hypothalamus glands stage a better chemical scenario for the body to achieve health. A healthy body can contribute greatly to a healthy mind, just as positive imaginings contribute greatly to a healthy body.

When we become completely positive in our imaginings and interweave the many facets of the positive spectrum until all positive emotion is a product of love, we will be, in fact, filling our bodies with God's light. And this light of God will have little or none of God's encoded Spirit information filtered out or degraded by our negative imaginings. This is pure Holy Spirit energy.

Matthew 17:1-2 states: "And after six days Jesus taketh Peter, bringeth them up into an high mountain apart, And was transfigured before them: and his face did shine as the sun, and his raiment was white as the light." This is the ultimate example of the body being filled with light. Jesus was trying to teach that we also can be filled with light until we are transfigured. Have you ever known anyone pure at heart that had a glow about his or her essence? I have seen many people who have this glow and I am never surprised to discover that they are highly spiritual people. Pure imaginings cause the body to attain the most optimum health it can, and more. Many pregnant women experience times when they appear to have a glow about them when they are in tune with the miracle of life within them. Many saints have achieved a state considered incorruptible that has rendered their bodies preserved with a sweet odor after death. Some are on display in glass cases.

The Polish Saint Andrew Bobola was killed in 1657. Forty years later his body was exhumed and found to be intact. His body has been examined many times by doctors throughout the years and in 1917 his well-preserved body was put on display for the public. Joan Cruz, author of the book, *The Incorruptibles,* cites 102 cases of Catholic saints whose bodies defied decay.

Hatha Yoga is a perfect example of the purification concept. There are up to eighty-five yoga positions and different meditation techniques used, designed to stimulate the body's glands and organs so that the ultimate mental stimulation can occur that releases the body's energy for a scientific God-realization process. A person can scientifically become filled with God's light by these practices.

Yoga stimulates the body, which in turn stimulates the mind. Positive imagery, on the other hand, stimulates the mind, which in turn stimulates the body. One thing is certain. We need physical and mental stimulation to spiritually ascend.

In order to experience enlightenment, one needs to stimulate the neuron cells in the brain. With proper stimulation, we can reach higher levels of neurotransmission within the thought processes. The use of a variety of drugs can cause a temporary surge of higher-level neurotransmission. The American Indian uses the organic drug peyote for vision quests in religious practices. These higher levels of neurotransmission need not be induced artificially. These levels can be achieved naturally when the proper mind stimulation takes place. This is a natural physiological process that causes thought levels to increase to an extent that enlightenment can be achieved. In other words, divinity has a physical effect on a being.

According to Barbara Marciniak, author of *Bringers of the Dawn,* the Pleidians, whom she channels, tell us that there are twelve helix in our DNA of which we use only two. We will at some point evolve our DNA and begin to employ all twelve helix, thereby being more receptive to light. Light, say the Pleidians, contains encoded filament. Also, the human cells contain light-encoded filament explained as fine gossamer threads of energy that carry information, working together like a fiber optic cable to form the helix of our DNA. When in tune to light and sound, our DNA should begin its evolution, opening the door to vast knowledge. If this is true, humanity is about to take a giant spiritual leap. I feel that assuming our responsibility in the Universe with God as a co-creator through consistent positive imagery is a great part of this process. As humanity improves the quality of its collective imaginations through *Imagintelligence,* the light within will open us to a greater level of existence.

18

Conceptual Transfers

II Samuel 23:2: The Spirit of the Lord spake by me, and his word was in my tongue.

The imagination is
The primary manifestation of
Mental activity.

From an abundance
Of imaginings
We choose
Our thoughts.

The positive spectrum of imagery
Is the gateway
To divinity
Of the mind
And the entrance
Into The Kingdom of Heaven.

In The Kingdom of Heaven,
God is our Father/Mother;
We are her sons and daughters.
Within The Kingdom
Are the love and the brotherhood
Of all mankind.

Serve mankind and you serve God.
This is the Intention of God
Moving through us.

This is The Kingdom that must be
Preached and renewed
Throughout the world.
The negative spectrum of imaginings
Is demonic in quality,
The beast,
The desires of the flesh,
Our animal nature,
The realm of illogic,
The anti-life,
Darkness,
Hell.

Within
The teachings of Jesus
Is relief from
The imaginations
Of the thoughts
Of our evil hearts.

When Jesus poured Himself
Into all flesh
After His resurrection,
He was giving us
The Spirit of Truth
To live in our hearts.

This truth will
Help you find
The proud imaginations
Of your heart,
The positive spectrum
Of imagination.

If we keep our minds positive
We will be like angels.

To eat from
The Tree of the Knowledge
Of Good and Evil
Is to know judgment
And to experience
Our negative imaginings
As we separate from Love
And feel separate from God.

The imaginations
Of our negative thoughts
Work directly against
The imaginations
Of our positive thoughts.
We create,
With our imaginations,
The world we live in
As a people.
The world is the result of
All mankind's imaginings combined
That manifest onto this Earth.

As God created mankind,
Mankind created the appearance
Of an evil force
Through the power
Of the evil imaginations
Of our hearts.

When mankind saw the darkness
It had created
It saw the need
To create God.
And so
We have created
Concepts of God.
But we were fearful
And created
A fearful God.

Jesus gave us
The Image of
The loving and merciful
Father.

Prayer is the most divine imagination.
We must believe
Our positive imaginations
With total faith
In order for them
To become powerful
And manifest.

As more people create
The same imagery,
The more powerful it becomes.

The mind is the avenue of our spirit,
Capable of the free will
To choose between
Positive or negative imaginings.

After we choose,
Our will is then influenced
By the Intention of God (love)
Or darkness (fear).

To lose one's imaginings
In the positive
Is to lose one's thoughts
In God's will.

When all desires
Of the carnal mind
Are lost,
Our ego or
Negative self dies.

This is the casting out
Of the beast
From the heart.

Cast the beast
From the heart
And this is the death
Of your own will,
Your will now being
That of God's will.

That which is left is
The Kingdom of Heaven.

When we have the urge
To receive the fruits
Of our own efforts
We are separated from God.

To serve mankind
And the needs of the Earth

With no urge
To bear the fruits of our own efforts
Is the will of God
Moving through us.
This is putting up
Our treasures in Heaven.

Execute the will of God
With no ego
And the fruits of life
Will flow freely
Into our lives.

Our spirit is
The Holy Breath of God.

It is a drop
Of the ocean
Of the body of God.

God is the origin
Of our positive imaginings.
The spirit embraces these images.
The mind can choose this imagery.

When we choose this imagery,
We are a vehicle
For the Intention of God
To move through us.

The flesh is the origin
Of our negative imaginings,
Born of our delusion of
Being separate from God.

We can liken
The beast in us
To the beasts in nature.

When we create negative imagery,
We are as the beasts of nature.
As our beastly emotions grow
They become demonic.

Nature is what we
Were put here
To rise above.

Jesus came into this world
As a man
With no advantages over man.

He is an example
Of what we can become
On Earth;
As He was on Earth.
This is our potential.

Continually creating positive imagery
Is only the beginning of perfection.

Perfection is the lacing together
Of all the positive spectrum
Of feelings,
Emotions,
Imaginations,
With love
Until all is love.

The imaginations and emotions
Of the spectrum
Of positive imagery
Are the attributes of love.
Separate them not from
Love itself.

We are not to concern ourselves
With the mysteries of God,
The Word of God,
God's law,
Life, or love
To the extent
That it interferes with or distorts
The spirit of these things.

If we stay positive in our imagery,
All we need to know
Will be revealed to us
Through the indwelling
Holy Spirit.
We can now choose
To eliminate
The evil imaginations
From our hearts

Through the Christ within us.

This resurrection
Of humanity's collective consciousness
Is marking
The Age of Aquarius,
The oncoming millennium,
The Second Coming of the Christ.

We no longer need
The negative spectrum of thought.
It is primitive.

God has permitted darkness
Only to teach us,
To give us experience,;
To show us the difference
Between light and darkness,
Right and wrong.

For it is important
To know why
We should be righteous.
Resurrected minds
Are the souls
Who are
The fruits of the Earth.
They are God's
Children of the Light.

The resurrection
Of humanity's minds
Will change
The Heavens and Earth.

The concepts of
Jesus' teachings
Were the original
Concepts of God
That Jesus came
To reestablish.

These concepts
Were of God's intentions
For All
Holy Scriptures.

All other additions
Were from man's nature
To complicate,
And an inability to comprehend
Past the traditions, superstitions,
Concepts, fears,
And viewpoints
Of the era.

Goodness,
Is simple in Spirit.

It is not important
To prove weather
The scriptures
Are true or legends.
What is important
Is to learn
The concepts of the lessons.

It has taken
Until this century
To develop the concept
Of positive and negative
Imagination and emotion,
Thereby giving
A more distinct separation
Between light and darkness.

Our negative imaginings
Are a veil of ignorance.
Remove it and knowledge will come
From the unity of thought
With God.
This is enlightenment.

The more our imaginings
Are in unison with God,
The more faith
Is transformed
Into reality.
Every negative imagining we embrace
In our hearts and minds
Diminishes our capacity
To love and see
The intangible things
Of God's Kingdom.

The fear that we embrace
In our hearts and minds
Is the key
To the door
Of the negative spectrum of imagination.

Total forgiveness transforms
This key to fit
To the door of
God's Divine plan.

We can cry
Tears of forgiveness and love
Instead of tears
Of hate or anger.

Reincarnation exists.
Only God
Works his miracles
And knows of these things.
There is no set pattern.

God loves us enough
To teach us our lessons
Until our veil of ignorance
Is lifted.
Time is insignificant.

We then remember who
We really are.

To those of you
Whose feelings become hurt
And carry a great hurt
In your hearts;
You must learn
That you choose
These emotions or feelings
When you choose to return to them.

If you have faith
And trust in God
And forgive those
Who trespass against you,
There is no reason
To have hurt feelings.
Faith and trust
Build confidence.

The church must begin
To speak to the people
About
Their negative imaginations
And emotions
In order to rid its flock
Of the evil one
Who steals the Word
From their hearts—
Our negative self.

The time has come
To slay the beast.

Work is love
Manifested into deeds.

A humble good deed
Is greater than
The most noble intention.

An eccentric positive thought
Will manifest more good
Into life
Than any negative thought.

No greater character
Can be developed
Than a character
Born of positive divine imaginings.

This is the beginning
Of the Second Coming of the Christ.

These things I pray are conveyed as the Lord intended. I believe this to be the Word of God moving through me. May the fruits of these words be my witness. This I pray in Jesus' name, Amen.

19

Thoughts

Our greatest wisdom merely saves us from total igno-rance being our guide and father.

—William Marts

Learning

Each day must
Be a lesson
Lest it be
Time wasted.

As the road
To enlightenment
Is long and hard
And takes much thought.

In our constant thinking
We search ourselves
And all things
For answers.

And our answers
Raise many questions.
And our thirst
For enlightenment
Is found in the need
To find answers
In the questions
That our answers reveal.

And in that thirst
We spin a web
Of question and answer
Unto the depths of all things.

And the more we think
The deeper question and answer,
Unto the infinity of all things,
Will take us.
For depth is infinite.
And so must be our thoughts
If we are to be
Not superficial.

And we must know
There is much to think about.
So we must learn
To be thinkers.

There is a discipline
To be learned by thinkers
In their constant search,
And need to look
So they may see.

For all that is taken for granted
Has its story and signs and lessons,
No matter how seemingly insignificant
On this road to enlightenment.

As we know and realize
That all of which we see now
Is merely a tiny fraction
Of what there is
In the depths of all things,
We then perceive
On what little thought
We base our decisions,
As they affect ourselves
And all that is around us,
And our ability to Love.

Know then that it is not
Our greatest wisdom
That guides us through life,
But our ignorance.

And our greatest wisdom
Merely saves us
From total ignorance
Being our guide and father.

Weakness

A friend spoke of a
Problem of weakness.
And I asked,
"What is strength?"

He asked,
"Is it enlightenment?"
I said that enlightenment
Is a product of strength,
Forgiveness, compassion, and
Mercy through God's will.

And I asked,
"What is weakness?"
I heard a story of
Pain and misfortune
Because of outside forces.

Are these forces
Real or imagined?
More are imagined, I know.
For out of our fears
Comes the imagined.
And we cannot see
What we turn our heads toward
After turning them away
When we are afraid.

With our every imagining
We create
Our own Reality.

Learning to face
Our fears
Is to know
Confront.

And through confrontation
We will find strength.
And through strength
We will find
A way to remain
Pure in our imaginings.

And through positive imaginings
We will find
The path to enlightenment.

And with the wisdom
Found in enlightenment
We will look with more depth
Unto all things.

So we may truly
See reality
And look into life
And know Love.

For what Love
Can be found through weakness?
As it is our seduction
Unto all that is wrong.
For, is not weakness
Merely fear?

Love
And Love of life
Are the guides
For our purpose.

Would such a wonder
As Love
Guide us
The wrong way?

Behold, a Love
Tormented by fear
Seduces us into
The errors of life.

We must be guided
By the Love
Of what is right
In our hearts.

And let our strength
Be found
In the obligation
To the duties
Of our purpose.
For all our pain and suffering
Is meant to prove to us
That we must overcome,
So we may know why
Not to be afraid.
And we will learn the suffering
Of an unforgiving heart.
And can compare it to
The joys of forgiveness.

Though we may suffer
And wish to join the dead
For comfort,
We must realize
Our stay here is brief.

And when we do
Pass this life
Those still here will rejoice
If they can say
You have Loved life and
Have left behind
Your good deeds
And Love.

Confrontation

Confrontation is
The most difficult.
It is facing head on
The things we fear.

And so, we must
Know our fears.
And we will see them
By what turns
Our heads away.

And if we are
Like the ostrich,
With our head
In the sand,
We shall then
Not see,
But pretend
And lose reality
To dark imaginings.

Then our decisions
Are based not on fact,
But fears from
The imagination.

The world sees
The head in the sand
But what is, is,
Just the same.

And evil, even as a whisper,
And danger, threatening,
Though unrealized,
Are there
Just the same.

How can we face
What we fear
When we tremble
At its sight?

How can we face
Our deepest pain
When the very thought
Is a knife to our heart?

Through inner strengths
We gain,
With Faith and Wisdom,
The ability to see reality
With careful consideration
Through a desire to look.

And, though I am weak
I am mighty in God,
With God,
As a vessel for God.

A head in the sand pretends.
But the wise one
Cares to see into the depths
Of deeds, of life
Of intentions, of affects.
And we will see our fears
Crumble as rubble
As we make battle
With the dark side
As a warrior
For the Light.
For there is great power
In what is right.
And what is right
Will give us strength
In our confrontations.

And one must know well
Right from wrong
To be a warrior
And stand for
What is good and right.

And one must pay
Close attention
To the depth of all things
And everyone
To see what is good and right
And what is wrong,
What is born of darkness
And what is born of the light.

And one must care
About life
And give Love to life
To find wisdom.

And care enough
Not to blunder through life.
And care enough
To make certain
We do not make
Countless mistakes
That hurt others
Or ourselves.

And care enough
To give guidance
With grace to youth
And respect to elders.

What may look right,
May in depth be wrong.
And what may look wrong,
May in depth be right.

We must care enough
To look
And know the effects
Of our powers.

And as I have found
Some to have a big heart
With a large capacity
And ability to Love,
So do I find many
Who have not these virtues.

And a warrior
May feel alone
Giving Love to life
And spreading Light.
A warrior may feel
Compassion for all
Who cannot show Love
And live to help others.

Love
And give Love
To all
Who will accept it.

And if no one soul
Will accept Love,
Be joyous to
Give Love to all.

Watch others to know,
Through their deeds,
Their capacity to Love
And to accept Love,
And to be kind and fair
In their hearts.

In dealing with others
Insist they be honest
And speak their heart
So you can know
With whom you are dealing.

This way
You will not hurt others
Because they have
Kept you in the dark.

And desire
Not to close
Any soul who opens
To you or the world.

For to Love
Any at all,
To be of real value
It must be virtuous.

The depths of Love
And passion
Must have foundation
And not be pointless
Or mere pleasure.
For our depths contain
Our goals and needs
And must have meaning.

Anything less
Is dangerous
To all that is sensitive
In your heart.

It Is Love

Chase it
And it
Runs away.

Try to
Possess it
And it
Eludes you.

Demand it
And it
Closes its ears.

Long for it
And it
Becomes distant.

Need it
And it
Becomes only
Food for the need.

Hurt for it
And it
Becomes Pain.

Be empty
Without it
And it becomes
The object of emptiness.

To find it
You must
Look within.

To receive it
You must
Give it
Without expectations
Like the flower
Gives its scent
Asking for
Nothing in return.

20

God's Special Angel

Psalm 8:4-5: *What is man, that thou art mindful of him? and the son of man, that thou visitest him? For thou hast made him a little lower than the angels, and hast crowned him with glory and honour.*

The Lord God had a very special angel in Heaven. God desired that this angel know the depths of light and darkness through experience. The Lord then sent this beloved angel to Earth to educate her so that she would know and experience not only His righteousness and Goodness, but also experience what darkness is. And so, the angel was born into a world where there was both light and darkness. A veil of ignorance was given this angel to cause her to forget who she really was so that The Lord God could begin to teach her the lessons of light and darkness.

And so, this angel of God began life on Earth as a human child with human parents. The angel began to experience life and all the trials, tribulations, and pain it brings through darkness and separation from God. Many trials befell the angel and it was not long before this angel learned to become part of the darkness in many ways. She learned to fight with other children, to sometimes be greedy with others, and to do mischief with the other children.

When the angel became an adult, she had learned many lessons in a world of hate, greed, lust, fear, worry, anger, and other negative imaginings. Some of these ways of thinking rubbed off on her and she became confused over whether to be a child of light or to continue to be seduced by the darkness. So it was that she became a little of both. She learned to become prejudiced to other races of people, to steal, but only a little, and to use violence, but not always. As the angel committed her evil deeds, she learned many lessons. She saw that she hurt others unnecessarily.

One day, God's angel was filled with hurt and pain as a result of the pain she had caused others. With her heart filled with sorrow and grief, she remembered the religious teachings of her youth. The angel began to read the Bible and her heart was comforted by the teachings of Jesus. She paid close attention to Jesus' teachings of The Kingdom of Heaven. She read that The Kingdom of God is within you. She also read that we must humble ourselves as little children to enter into The Kingdom of Heaven, that we must seek first The Kingdom of God and the Father will provide for our every desire, and to give no thought for tomorrow, but only of the evil of today and tomorrow will take its course.

These teachings began to lift the veil of ignorance from the angel's mind as she practiced them. Soon, the angel began to see that her life was a projection of her own imaginings. The more she acted within the intention of God, the more her veil of ignorance was lifted. The angel quickly discovered that her imagination was very powerful. She learned that it was her negative imaginings that kept the veil of ignorance overshadowing her true self. She also learned that her good or positive imaginations were parallel with God's intentions. As she practiced God's intention with her imaginings and deeds, a great change came upon her. She noticed that many coincidences occurred in her life to guide her to the Father and to provide her with the abundance the Father wanted her to have.

As time passed, the angel began to realize that she was God's special angel and that she was sent to Earth to learn and remember who she really is. She realized that she must always keep her imagination within The Kingdom of God to project God's intentions to the world. And the angel became God's tool to manifest His works upon the face of the Earth. She could see that all of God's sons and daughters were also angels. No longer did she see mere people. She saw angels with a veil of ignorance inhibiting their self-realization. And she could now see the true beauty of all God's angels on Earth.

This special angel of God is you.

Resource Bibliography

- *ABC's of the Human Mind,* Reader's Digest Association, Inc., Pleasantville, New York, 1988.
- *A Course In Miracles, Foundation For Inner Peace,* published by the Penguin Group, New York, New York, 1996.
- *An Easy Guide To Ayurveda: The Natural Way To Wholeness,* by Roy Eugene Davis. CSA Press, Publishers Center For Spiritual Awareness, Lakemont, Georgia, 1996.
- *A Twelve-Power Meditation Exercise,* by Charles Roth. Unity Books, Unity Village, Missouri, 1989.
- *Autobiography Of A Yogi,* by Paramahansa Yogananda. Self-Realization Fellowship, Los Angeles, 12th Edition, 1993.
- *Awakened Imagination,* by Neville. DeVorss & Company, Marina del Ray, California, 3rd printing, 1998.
- *Bringers of the Dawn,* by Barbara Marciniak. Bear & Company Publishing, Santa Fe, New Mexico, 1992.
- *Chakras,* by Harish Johari. Destiny books, Rochester, Vermont, 1987.
- *Christian Healing,* by Charles Fillmore. Unity School of Christianity, Unity Village, Missouri.
- *Conversation with God: An Uncommon Dialogue, Book 1,* by Neale Donald Walsh. G. P. Putnam's Sons, New York, New York, 1996. Originally published by Hampton Roads Publishing, Inc., 1995.
- *Dianetics: The Modern Science Of Mental Health,* by Ron Hubbard. Bridge Publications, Inc., Los Angeles, California, 1992.
- *Emotional Intelligence,* by Daniel Goleman. Bantam Books, New York, New York, 1995.
- *Energizing The 12 Powers of Your Mind,* by Howard E. Hill. Parker Publishing Company, Inc., West Nyack, New York, 1966.
- *Enter The Zone,* by Barry Sears, Ph.D. with Bill Lawren. Regan Books, HarperCollins, New York, New York, 1995.

- *Enzymes, The Fountain of Life,* by D. A. Lopez, M.D., R.M. Williams, M.D., Ph.D., And K. Miehlke, M.D. The Neville Press, Inc., 1994.
- *God Alone Is,* by Shankar Das. Sadhana Ashram, Sevierville, Tennessee, 1989.
- *God & The New Physics,* by Paul Davies. Simon & Schuster, New York, New York, 1984.
- *Handbook Of Positive Prayer,* by Hypatia Hasbrouck. Unity Books, Unity Village, Missouri, revised edition, 1995.
- *Heal Your Body,* by Louise L. Hay. Hay House, Inc., Carlsbad, California. Expanded/Revised Edition, 1998.
- *Inner Knowing,* edited by Helen Palmer. Jeremy P. Tarcher/Putnam, a member of Penguin Putnam Inc., New York, New York, 1998.
- *Jesus and Buddha: The Parallel Sayings,* Editor, Marcus Borg, Introduction Jack Kornfield, Co-editor, Ray Riegert. Ulysses Press, Berkeley, California, 1997.
- *Lessons In Truth,* by H. Emily Cady, Unity Classic Library, Unity Village, Missouri fiftieth printing, 1995.
- *Life After Life,* by Raymond A. Moody, Jr. Mockingbird Books, Atlanta, Georgia, 1975.
- *Life Beyond Death: Quest for the Unknown,* The Reader's Digest Association, Inc., Pleasantville, New York, 1992.
- *Love Without Conditions, Reflections of the Christ Mind,* by Paul Ferrini. Heartways Press, South Deerfield, Massachusetts, 1994.
- *Molecules of Emotion,* by Candace B. Pert, Ph.D. A Touchstone Book Published by Simon & Schuster, New York, New York, 1999.
- *Mysteries Of The Bible,* The Readers Digest Association, Pleasantville, New York, 1988.
- *New Thought: A Practical American Spirituality,* by C. Alan Anderson and Deborah G. Whitehouse. The Crossroad Publishing Company, New York, New York, 1995.
- *Prosperity,* by Charles Fillmore. Unity Books, Unity Village, Missouri, 1995.
- *Psycho-Cybernetics and Self-Fulfillment,* by Maxwell Maltz,

M.D. Bantam Books, 14 printings by April, 1985.

- *Quantum Healing,* by Deepak Chopra. Bantam Books, New York, New York, 1990.
- *Radical Healing,* by Rudolph Ballentine, M.D. Harmony Books, New York, New York, 1999.
- *Reinventing Medicine,* By Dr. Larry Dossey. Harper San Francisco, 1999.
- *Resurrection,* by Neville. DeVorss Publications, Marina del Ray, California. 12th printing 1998.
- *Seedtime and Harvest,* by Neville. DeVorss Publications, Marina del Ray, California. 3rd printing, 1993.
- *Spontaneous Healing,* by Andrew Weil, M.D. Fawcett Columbine, The Ballintine Publishing Group, New York, New York, 1996.
- *Stranger By The River,* by Paul Twitchell. IWP Publishing, Menlo Park, California, 1970.
- *Sugar Busters,* by H. Leighton Steward, Morrison C. Bethea, M.D., Sam S. Andrews, M.D., and Luis A. Balart, M.D. Ballantine Books, New York, New York, 1998.
- *Tao Te Ching: A New English Version,* by Stephen Mitchell. HarperPernnial, a Division of HarperCollins Publishers, 1991.
- *The Ages Of Gaia,* by James Lovelock. W. W. Norton & Company, Inc., New York, New York, 1995.
- *The Anti-Aging Zone,* by Barry Sears, Ph.D. Regan Books, HarperCollins, New York, New York, 1999.
- *The Aquarian Gospel of Jesus The Christ,* by Levi. DeVorss & Company, Marina del Ray, California, 15th printing, 1995.
- *The Art Of Happiness,* by His Holiness, The Dalai Lama and Howard C. Cutler, M.D. Riverhead Books, a member of Penguin Putnam Inc., New York, New York, 1998.
- *The Celestine Prophecy,* by James Redfield. Warner Books, Inc., New York, New York, 1993.
- *The Einstein Factor,* by Win Wenger, Ph.D., and Richard Poe. Prima Publishing, Rocklin, California, 1996.
- *The Four Agreements,* by Don Miguel Ruiz. Amber-Allen Publishing, San Rafael, California, 1997.

- *The Golden Age of Zen,* by John C. H. Wu. Image Books, Doubleday, 1996.
- *The Higher Self,* by Deepak Chopra, M.D. A six-cassette production by Nightingale-Conant, Niles, Illinois, 1997.
- *The Holotropic Mind,* by Stanislav Grof, M.D. with Hal Zina Bennett. HarperSanFransisco, HarperCollins, 1993.
- *The Light Beyond,* by Raymond A. Moody, Jr., M.D. Bantam Books, 1988.
- *The Law and the Promise,* by Neville. DeVorss Publications, Marina del Ray, California. 5th printing, 1995.
- *The Melatonin Miracle,* by Walter Pierpaoli, M.D., Ph.D., and William Regelson, M.D., with Carol Colman. Simon & Schuster, New York, New York, 1995.
- *The Messengers,* by Julia Ingram and G. W. Hardin. Pocket Books, a division of Simon & Schuster, New York, New York, 1996.
- *The Modern New Testament From the Aramaic,* by George M. Lamsa, B.A., F.R.S.A. DeVorss Publications, Marina del Ray, California, first DeVorss edition 1998.
- *The Path to Love,* by Deepak Chopra. Three Rivers Press, New York, New York, 1997.
- *The Power of Awareness,* by Neville. DeVorss Publications, Marina del Ray, California. Revised edition, 1992.
- *The Power of Positive Thinking,* by Norman Vincent Peale. Prentice-Hall, 1952.
- *The Power of Visualization,* by Lee Pulos, Ph.D. A six-cassette production by Nightengale-Conant, Niles, Illinois, 1998.
- *The 7 Habits Of Highly Effective People: Powerful Lessons in Personal Change,* by Stephen R. Covey. A Fireside Book Published by Simon & Schuster, New York, New York, 1990.
- *The Silva Method,* by Jose Silva. A six-cassette production by Nightingale-Conant, Niles, Illinois, 1996.
- *The Soul's Code: In Search of Character and Calling,* by James Hillman. Random House, New York, New York, 1996.
- *The Super-Hormone Promise,* by William Regelson, M.D., & Carol Colman. Simon & Schuster, New York, New York, 1996.

- *The Urantia Book,* The Urantia Foundation, Chicago, Illinois. 11th printing, 1993.
- *The 10 Dumbest Mistakes Smart People Make and How To Avoid Them,* by Dr. Arthur Freeman and Rose DeWolf. Harper-Collins, New York, New York, 1992.
- *The Tibetan Book of the Living and the Dying,* by Sogyal Rinpoche. Harper, San Francisco, 1992.
- *The Twelve Powers of Man,* by Charles Fillmore. Unity Books, Unity Village, Missouri.
- *The Way Of The Wizard: Twenty Spiritual Lessons for Creating the Life You Want,* by Deepak Chopra. Harmony Books, New York, New York, 1995.
- *The World of Tibetan Buddhism,* by Tenzin Gyatso. The Fourteenth Dalai Lama. Wisdom Publications, Boston, 1995.
- *Unlimited Power,* by Anthony Robins. Fawcett Columbine, New York, New York, 1986.
- *Virus Of The Mind,* by Richard Brodie. Integral Press, Seattle, Washington, 1996.
- *Working With Emotional Intelligence,* by Daniel Goleman. Bantam Books, 1998.
- *You Can Heal Your Life,* by Louise L. Hay. Hay House Inc., Carlsbad, California, 1987.
- *You Can't Afford The Luxury Of A Negative Thought,* by Peter McWilliams. Prelude Press, Inc., Los Angeles, California, 1995.
- *Your Faith Is Your Fortune,* by Neville. DeVorss Publications, Marina del Ray, California. 18th printing, 1997.
- *Your God-Given Potential,* by Winifred Hausmann. Unity Books, Unity Village, Missouri, 1978.

Internet

- CASEL (Collaboration for Social and Emotional Learning)
  http://www.casel.org
- Health Journeys, The Guided Imagery Resource Center
  http://www.healthjourneys.com
- Semiomorph
  http://www.pulsar.org/springwebb/eco/semi.html
- Kid's Source On Line
  http://www.kidsource.com/kidsource/content/news/headaches.
  5.27.html
- Daniel Kortenkamp, Ph.D.
  http://www.uwsp.edu/acad/psych/dk/danielpg.htm
- ConsciousNet
  http://www.consciousnet.com/index.html
- Imagination, Mental Imagery, Consciousness, and Cognition:
  Scientific, Philosophical and Historical Approaches, By Nigel
  J.T. Thomas Ph.D.
  http://web.calstatela.edu/faculty/nthomas/index.htm
- The Gersten Institute For Higher Medicine,
  http://www.imagerynet.com/index.html
- Mental Healing: Studies
  http://www.libraries.wayne.edu/shiffman/altmed/therapy/
  stu_mental.html
- Mental Therapy: Alternative Medicine,
  http://www.libraries.wayne.edu:80/shiffman/altmed/therapy/
  mental.html
- The Hay House
  http://www.hayhouse.com by Louise Hay.
- Academy For Guided Imagery by Martin L. Rossman, M.D.
  http://www.healthy.net/univ/profess/schools/edu/imagery/
  index_netscape.html
- The Enchanted Mind, http://enchantedmind.com/imagine.htm
- Using Mind Power For Healing, by Marcia Middel, Ph.D.
  http://www.physsportsmed.com/issues/jul_96/middel.htm

- The World Institute Of Healing Technologies
  http://www.healer.ch/
  Founded by Sir Martin Brofman, Ph.D.
- The Hartley Film Foundation
  http://www.fcinet.com/hartleyfilms/index.html
- Institute Of Alternative Healing
  http://www.ronmann.com/iah/index.htm
- Ronald L. Mann, Ph.D.
  http://www.ronmann.com
- The Manifesting Web Site, by Todd Varnum
  and Fred Fengler Ph.D.
  http://www.uvm.edu/~afengler/
- The Life Sciences Institute
  http://www.cjnetworks.com/~lifesci/index.html#NW
- Use Of Complementary Therapies in Cancer Patients Receiving
  Chemotherapy, by Susan M. Bauer, RN, MS, DNSc Candidate
  http://www.meniscus.com/dscc/Art3_1-1.html
- Simonton Cancer Center
  http://www2.lainet.com/~simonton/index.html
- Guided Imagery, by Patricia Norris, Ph.D.
  http://www.healthy.net/library/articles/norris/therapy.htm
- Harvard Medical School, articles
  http://www.med.harvard.edu/publications/Focus/complete_tex
  ts/Mar1_1996_complete.html FOCUS March 1, 1996 Off the
  Quad: The Healing Powers of the Mind
- Spirituality and Positive Affirmations Heal the Soul,
  http://www.mjbovo.com/Healing.htm,
- Tony Birch, Ph.D., http://www.gis.net/~tbirch/
- Psyche
  http://psyche.cs.monash.edu.au/
- David Chalmer's Home Page,
  http://www.u.arizona.edu/~chalmers/
- Consciousness And The Brain, by Ralph D. Ellis, Ph.D., Clark
  Atlanta University
  http://home.earthlink.net/~dravita/index.html

Index

Imagintelligence:
Beyond Emotional Intelligence

Send check or money order for $19.95 plus $4.00 Shipping & Handling to:

The Imagination Institute
236 Bonnacroft Dr.
Hermitage, TN 37076
Or:
Mastercard and Visa accepted at:
http://www.imagintelligence.com

Checks, MasterCard, and Visa accepted by e-mail, fax, or phone.

E-mail: imagedoc@bellsouth.net
Fax: (810) 958-0877 (Fax This Form) Phone: (615) 902-9697

Name:_____

Address:_____

Check Account Number:_____

☐ MasterCard ☐ Visa Card #:_____

Name on card:_____Exp. Date:_____

Recordings

☐ The Parable of the Coin — $12.00
☐ Imagintelligence — $12.00

For more information on current available recordings send SASE
Sales Tax: Please add 8.25% for products shipped in Tennessee.

Shipping & Handling: $4.00 first item and $2.00 each additional item.

Total Payment:_____

Shipping Address:_____
_____
_____

Shipping Address _____
For Gifts:_____
_____